NATALIE

A young mother brutally murdered

The Search for her Killer
A True Story

Former Detective Superintendent

Paul Davison

If Roses grow in Heaven
Lord, please pick a bunch for me.
Place them in my Mother's arms
and tell her they're from me.

Tell her that I love her and miss her,
and when she turns to smile,
place a kiss upon her cheek
and hold her for awhile.

Because remembering her is easy,
I do it every day,
But there's an ache within my heart
that will never go away.

We Love You, Mum - your three children xxx

Through the wild cathedral evening the rain unraveled tales

For the disrobed faceless forms of no position

Tolling for the tongues with no place to bring their thoughts

All down in taken-for-granted situations

Tolling for the deaf an' blind, tolling for the mute

Tolling for the mistreated, mateless mother,

the mistitled prostitute

For the misdemeanor outlaw, chased an' cheated by pursuit

An' we gazed upon the chimes of freedom flashing.

Chimes of Freedom

Bob Dylan

Acknowledgements

I wish to thank:

David Hilditch, Stephen Hodgson, John Goddard, and Sam, Jack and Cal Davison, for reading my early drafts and giving me the courage to publish NATALIE.

Tony Burke for his friendship and support, and for being an outstanding deputy SIO.

My investigation team for their extraordinary dedication every day of the investigation, which ultimately led to justice for Natalie. They know who they are. There are too many to name individually. I could not have done it without them.

The Underwater Search team, Dog and Horse teams, Forensic officers and staff. Their contributions were outstanding.

HOLMES team for their forensic attention to detail and for providing the investigation with a clear direction.

Gary Shaw for his wit and for providing professional expertise during the interviewing of suspects.

Lisa Hodson for her sensitivity and compassion, and unwavering commitment to keeping Natalie in the public eye.

Dean at G T Graphics, Pocklington for the inspired and creative book cover art work.

Jack and Cal Davison for their invaluable help in formatting the book content.

Finally, my family - Fiona, Sam, Jack and Cal - for their love and unwavering support during some difficult times.

Abbreviations

SIO: Senior Investigating Officer
DI: Detective Inspector
DCI: Detective Chief Inspector
DS: Detective Sergeant
DC: Detective Constable
HOLMES: Home Office Large Major Inquiry System
FLO: Family Liaison Officer
POLSA: Police Search Advisor
DCS: Detective Chief Superintendent
SOCO: Scenes of Crime Officer
DCC: Deputy Chief Constable
ACC: Assistant Chief Constable
PDF: Personal Descriptive Form
FIB: Force Intelligence Bureau
RCS: Regional Crime Squad
TWOC: Taken Without the Owners Consent
TIE: Trace, Interview and Eliminate
ONB: Officer Note Book
FSG: Force Support Group
PACE: Police and Criminal Evidence Act 1984

CONTENTS

Title Page
Dedication
Epigraph
Acknowledgements
Abbreviations

PART 1: THE EARLY DAYS

1: 'The word CHAOS was tattooed across the forearm, scrawled in faded blue ink'
2: 'She's been dead for about three months'
3: 'We've found some more body parts'
4: 'Nobody said a word as Russell began to gently remove the first bin liner'
5: 'What's the best chance of us detecting this?'
6: 'The smell would be familiar to any police officer'
7: 'A slim figure walked towards me out of the shadows'
8: 'You could always get a second opinion, if you're not happy'
9: 'All progress depends on the unreasonable person'
10: 'Natalie loved to be loved'
11: 'He moved as if in slow motion, eyes black and vacant'

PART 2: THE GATHERING MOMENTUM

12: 'DC Long designated the discovery as exhibit TML/4'
13: 'She opened her legs wide and pointed to an open wound'
14: 'How's the car Archie? Still going strong?'

15 'What colour is that red bike?'
16: 'I was pretty sure they weren't destined for greatness'
17: 'They were both trembling, beads of sweat glistened on their foreheads'
18: 'Sunman must have wondered whether he was having a bad dream'
19: 'It wasn't what I signed up for'
20: 'ITV's got Lynda La Plante. We've got Natalie'
21: 'Time to make my own luck'
22: 'Brilliant, there was no other word to describe it'
23: 'Look, I know I'm no Leonardo Da Vinci'
24: 'It was as if he was dead inside'
25: 'I've served her up. We was temaze'd up with some Russian shit'
26: 'So be it heart; bid farewell without end'
27: 'Everything passes, everything changes just do what you think you should do'
28: 'As I listened, tears of relief streamed down my face'
29: 'News of the almighty cock-up, would travel across the force like lightning'

PART 3: THE FIGHT FOR JUSTICE

30: 'Cruel and unforgiving world of prostitution'
31: 'I couldn't help thinking that everything was going too well'
32: 'But everyone tells lies, don't they?'
33: 'I couldn't blame him after the brutal attack on his honesty'
34: 'Stitch up by them coppers'

35: 'The voice of negativity raised its ugly head again'
36: 'Criminals are just as capable of telling the truth'
37: 'Deep in thought, I nearly fell off my chair when the phone rang'
38: 'The wounds we inflict on our soul when we look the other way'
39: 'We can find no evidence of police corruption'
Epilogue
About the Author
Copyright

PART 1

THE EARLY DAYS

ONE

'The word CHAOS was tattooed across the forearm, scrawled in faded blue ink'

It was 7.30 in the morning, Thursday, 30 July 1998. I was at home getting ready for work when the telephone rang. As a Detective Chief Inspector, I was used to being called out to deal with serious crimes. It was one of the reasons why I loved being a police officer. But as I answered the call, I wasn't expecting to hear the booming voice of the Assistant Chief Constable.

"Paul, a dismembered arm's been found at a pumping station on Bransholme. I want you to be the SIO. You'll need to speak to Detective Chief Superintendent Jordan."

Bloody hell. I sat down at the kitchen table and told my wife about the call as she got the boys ready for school. My heart was pounding. My mind raced with questions. Why me? Sure, I'd some experience and success as a SIO working in my own Division solving local serious crimes: a baby starved to death by his own mother, and the anal rape of a 92-year-old lady, both sprang to mind. Thinking about those cases gave me a fleeting surge of confidence that passed all too quickly. But this was something else. This was force level on a much bigger stage. I knew that the other SIOs were all busy investigating a recent spate of prostitute murders. Is that why I'd been assigned to this case, I wondered?

As I drove to the scene in my dark blue Audi 80, I tried to imagine how on earth I'd cope with the challenge of leading a full-blown murder inquiry. I presumed the person who was missing an arm had been murdered. It sounded a daft question when I thought about it, but if there was one thing I'd learned as a SIO, it was never to assume anything. My stomach churned as a mental picture formed in my mind of what needed to be done. This was really happening to me, and I already had the feeling that my future career as a SIO would be inextricably linked to the outcome of this case.

I made my way through Bransholme famous for being the biggest housing estate in Europe. I saw people going about their daily lives. There was a man jogging and parents walking their kids to school. I almost wished that I was out jogging or taking the kids to school, or doing anything ordinary for that matter, rather than being about to face a challenge that might well be beyond me.

Driving through the depressing landscape of never-ending roads lined with houses built to resemble giant rabbit hutches, brought back memories of when I used to patrol the area as a uniform sergeant. The two blocks of high-rise flats provided residents with the perfect elevated position from which to launch missiles at marked police cars, including TVs, microwaves and pretty much any object that had the potential to injure or cause damage. On one occasion, it was about two in the morning and I was responding to a reported burglary. As I got out of my car, a fridge came crashing down from above narrowly missing my head by inches. The sight of a copper very nearly meeting an untimely death was met with a round of applause from the residents, who no doubt judged the fact that my police car was a complete write off to be a victory worth celebrating. 'Fucking bullseye copper. Shame it missed your fucking head. Grey-haired twat'. Not surprisingly, the levels of crime were amongst the highest in the country, and I couldn't help thinking that the creation of such a monster estate wasn't the city of Hull's finest hour.

The bleakness of my surroundings offered little hope that the day would get any better. I was way out of my comfort zone and I tried to remember what all those self-help books I'd read would suggest in such circumstances. A book called 'Feel the Fear and Do it Anyway' was my trusted friend, and its overall message was that if you knew you could deal with anything in life, there'd be nothing to fear. You couldn't argue with those words of wisdom but it was much easier said than done. Nevertheless, it'd helped me in the past deal with my debilitating shyness, which isn't a particular strength for a police officer, never mind a SIO.

I approached the pumping station via a desolate dirt track road that seemed to go on forever. I braced myself with a sharp intake of breath because the culture of the police was brutal and unforgiving. As a SIO, you were there to be judged by everyone to see if you found the killer or killers and secured a conviction. Those who failed to do so, suffered with their reputations destroyed. Accordingly, I knew that I couldn't afford to show any lack of confidence or indecision. I wondered at that moment why I'd wanted to be a SIO in the first place. Although it was July, I felt cold and very lonely.

When I arrived, I was pleased to see a friendly face. It was DI Chris Chambers, head of SOCO. He'd been there for some time and organised a cordon surrounding what he considered to be the scene marked with blue and white police tape. A tall thin man with a huge moustache and a shock of black hair, he had a quiet way about him that made you feel as though he'd seen everything there was to see at a crime scene. He radiated a sense of calm that you could almost touch, and I could feel my nerves begin to settle as he shook my hand with a firm grip. I hadn't worked with Chris before but as the head of SOCO, he'd vast experience to call upon. I hoped that he'd give me some good advice. I was going to need it.

Chris briefed me as I put on a white protective suit and overshoes.

"The arm's badly decomposed. It's missing some fingers. Looks like rats or something have had a go. It's going to be difficult to determine when this was done or who the arm belongs to although we've an idea already from the tattoo."

I followed Chris as he walked over stepping plates to where the arm was laid on some long grass. It was a right arm severed at the shoulder and the word CHAOS was tattooed across the forearm, scrawled in faded blue ink. It didn't look like it'd been done professionally.

"Looks like the arm could belong to Natalie Clubb. She's a missing working prostitute. Been missing for some time apparently. That's all we've got at the moment."

"Who found the arm?"

"A man called Snowden. He works for the Environment Agency as a river operative and lives nearby. It looks as though those giant pumps you can see keep the water in the drains moving. My theory is the arm was in the water and was dredged up by that small crane and put onto that rubbish heap."

He pointed towards a mound of mud and debris about six feet high bordered by a fence.

"Snowden says that the crane's used to clear crap from the water every week which can't get through those gigantic turbines. The rubbish heaps then burnt."

We sat down for a coffee inside the mobile police caravan and he asked me if I was OK. Although I was the senior officer as the DCI, I sensed that he was really asking whether I knew what I was doing. I would've done. After all, he'd know that this was my first big case, and maybe it was his way of diplomatically offering his help and advice. And, before I could reply, he launched into a detailed update on what action he'd already taken and what he thought our approach should be. Thank God.

Accordingly, the Home Office Pathologist, Russell Walker, was already on his way, together with a forensic entomologist, Hugh Blunt and a POLSA, Sergeant Bob Downs. Bob arrived as we finished our coffee. He was a likeable, stocky figure blessed with an impressive encyclopedic knowledge of just about everything, which earned him a reputation for being someone that you could never impress. Although I felt confident that whatever evidence was present at the pumping station would be recovered, I knew that I couldn't afford to miss anything, and that got me thinking about my old DI, Gary Scaife. As a young DC, he'd given me some advice about how to properly and thoroughly investigate a crime, and it was an approach I'd adopted ever since.

"Look Paul, be brave enough to call out whatever resources you need to make sure that you don't miss anything. Dogs, horses, helicopter, SOCO, forensic scientists, supervision, and anybody else you can think of. You can always bring things down a level, but you can't do the opposite. Evidence lost or overlooked is gone forever. You might get away with people not knowing that you messed up but YOU'LL know. Don't worry about what people might say."

I'd witnessed him do the same thing time and again at the scene of a crime. Gary would leave no stone unturned in his relentless pursuit of villains. He liked to call it good old-fashioned problem solving, and his approach would be to treat this as just another problem to solve, a bloody big one, admittedly, but as I gazed over my grim surroundings, I didn't know what else to do. I'd never come across anything like this before, and I was pretty sure nobody else had either.

The arrival of Russell Walker and Hugh Blunt brought me back from reminiscing about my old DI. I knew Russell from other cases I'd worked on, and I found him to be approachable and not at all prickly as some pathologists could be. A tall, thin figure with mousey-coloured hair, he kept his head bent slightly forward in a shy kind of way, and his gold metal-framed glasses suited his bookish appearance. I'd not met Hugh before. There was a nervous edge to his mannerisms that suggested he wasn't entirely comfortable meeting people. That was something I could understand. They both studied the badly decomposed arm, and as Chris and I waited for their reaction, my mind went into overdrive thinking about what needed to be done. A post-mortem on the arm and any other body parts recovered. Form a major incident investigation team. Set up a HOLMES incident room. Put out press releases…

It was time to move things on and I held a meeting in the caravan to decide how best to conduct a forensic search of the scene. DC Tim Long arrived to act as the SOCO supervisor and sat in on the meeting. Whenever I'd worked with him in the past, he'd impressed me with his meticulous attention to detail when investigating a crime scene. He also possessed boundless enthusiasm for his work, and it didn't surprise me to learn that he'd been away out of force studying the latest techniques in the SOCO world. I sensed some tension though between Tim and his boss, Chris, that's all I needed right now, I thought, and so I chose to ignore it.

I looked around the table, and I knew that I'd have to trust each and every one of them to do their job. But I also knew that it wouldn't be long before I'd probably offend some of them. I'd already written in my notebook, 'don't forget Gary Scaife's advice'. It was a reminder for me, as the SIO, to keep an open mind, not to miss anything, and to treat everyone with the same - 'I'm not going to believe what you tell me unless it can be corroborated' - approach. The problem was that by doing so, I'd gained a reputation for being hard to please, someone who questioned every detail and someone who didn't trust anyone to do their job. I was now about to adopt the same approach again with individuals who possessed far more expertise than I in their chosen field.

I gave Russell centre stage to begin with. He told us that in order for him to give an opinion on where and when the deceased was killed and the cause of death, we'd need the remaining body parts. But all we had was the arm and, although it was badly decomposed, I wanted to know whether Hugh would be able to estimate the likely time of death. Hugh clearly loved his job and saw me as a willing audience ready to be lectured on his favourite subject.

"After the initial decay, and the body begins to smell, different types of insects are attracted to the body. The insects that usually arrive first come from the order of Diptera, such as Calliphoridae, known as blow flies and Sarcophagidae, known as flesh flies."

Whilst this was really interesting, I politely interrupted him in full flow and asked him to get to the point.

"In a nutshell, the theory behind estimating time of death or rather the post-mortem interval, with the help of insects, is very simple. Since insects arrive on the body soon after death, estimating the age of the insects will also lead to an estimation of the time of death. But and it is a big but, there are many factors that can influence the speed of decay such as temperature, whether the body's been buried, whether the body's been wrapped up in something. I'll do my best but this isn't an exact science."

Finally, it was agreed that under the watchful presence of Russell and Hugh, a team of search-trained officers under Bob's command would meticulously sift through the rubbish heap in layers from the top to bottom. Tim would be on hand to video, photograph and preserve any evidence recovered. Although I was happy with the plan, for a moment, I felt sorry for Russell and Hugh. I'd given them the third degree, asking question after question. They must have both wondered why they'd agreed to come in the first place. It wasn't my intention to make them feel uncomfortable, but I'd learned a valuable lesson as a young an inexperienced DI - everyone makes mistakes.

It was the tragic case of a dead baby called George Lofty, who was left abandoned on a doorstep weighing only three pounds. I was baffled because the baby measured about twenty inches in length and was emaciated beyond recognition. At the post-mortem, the pathologist concluded that the baby had been born prematurely at about twenty-eight weeks and lived for only a matter of hours. He told me that I should be looking for the mother who would probably require medical attention. Back then, I didn't have the confidence to tell him that I didn't agree with him: in my opinion, the baby was too long to be premature. A consultation with a paediatrician, however, confirmed that the baby boy had lived and been gradually starved to death. I called the pathologist and asked him to examine the baby's lungs. He admitted that he was wrong. The baby hadn't been born prematurely and apologised for his mistake. I launched a full-scale murder investigation. The mother was, eventually, convicted of manslaughter. I remember thinking at the time that although it was a valuable lesson to learn, there would be other similar battles to be fought in the future.

I wanted to get a picture in my head of the location of the pumping station and so Bob and I flew over the area in the force helicopter. On the north side of the pumping station, the drain travelled in an almost straight line to Wawne

Common before turning westward at almost ninety degrees towards Tickton. It crossed the Beverley to Tickton road, at which point you could see a small booster pumping station. Between this station and the scene there were two tributaries: the Forsedyke Stream (west) running for about a mile to Perronet Thompson School, and Forsdyke Stream (north east) linking White Cross and onwards. The scene was remote surrounded by nothing but open fields. There was only one road in and the same road out. I looked for any signs of life but there were no houses to speak of, in any direction, which meant that there'd be little or no chance of finding any witnesses.

As the helicopter landed, Chris motioned for us to come over to the rubbish heap. They'd found a human head concealed within three black polythene bin bags, each one was knotted separately. Two were heat damaged and fused together. It was badly decomposed with the skull emerging from what was left of the skin, and there were strands of mousey-coloured long hair that appeared to have been dyed. The bin bag was swarming with maggots as they fed off the rotting flesh. We all thought that it was the head of a female but it was hard to tell. If the head was female, was it Natalie Clubb's? Did the arm and head come from the same body? DNA would eventually give me the answer. Tim photographed the head in situ and Russell, Hugh and Chris spent the next few hours taking every sample possible. I'd seen much in my career to shock me but seeing a severed head somehow, for a moment, made time stand still as we all tried to make sense of what the discovery meant.

I knew only too well that the next twenty-four to forty-eight hours would shape the investigation, and I hoped and prayed that the force would assemble a team of experienced officers for me that could hit the ground running. In reality, some poor officer in charge of duties, probably a police constable, would be scrambling around pleading with much more elevated ranks across the force to release staff on my behalf. The force didn't have detectives on standby waiting to swing into action the minute a murder was committed, and I was worried because there were already three other protracted murder investigations on the go, each headed by a Detective Superintendent. Who'd be left for my investigation, I wondered. Who'd be my deputy, HOLMES office manager, FLO's? I stopped myself going any further. It wouldn't make any difference, no matter how many times I thought about it. I'd know soon enough. And then my mobile rang and it was the unmistakable thick scouse accent of Inspector Tony Burke.

"Boss, it's Tony Burke. I'm going to be your deputy."

"How come?"

"Sorry, but there's nobody left. All the DI's are either on incidents or can't be released from Division. You sound disappointed."

For a moment my heart sank. I hadn't worked with Tony before. He was ex-crime squad with a wide-boy image and, apparently, hard to handle. How would we get on? Could I trust him?

"No, it's fine. I just wasn't expecting it to be you. I know you're in uniform at the moment and this is likely to run for some time."

"I just fancied a change that's all. Enjoying being back in

uniform but I jumped at the chance. Don't worry, I'll do you a good job."

"It's good to have you. I don't know how much you know but we've found an arm and head. Can you get Lisa, the press officer, to put only brief details out to the media. It could be Natalie Clubb but we're not sure yet. Arrange for a briefing at six. Do we have an incident room?"

My conversation with Tony was cut short with the discovery of three more bin bags, each one inside the other and knotted separately, containing five fingernails. It seemed likely that the arm had been inside the bags. I spent the rest of the afternoon watching as the meticulous search of the rubbish heap continued. Nothing else was found. Eventually the search team called it a day. I thanked everyone at the scene for their help, and then I left to go to the briefing that was due to be held in the large conference room at headquarters in the centre of Hull.

It was about twenty minutes from the pumping station, and I was grateful for this time so I could collect my thoughts. This was the bit I hated, an audience waiting for me to deliver a performance in front of a team of individuals who'd been summoned to the briefing at short notice. Some would want to be there, others wouldn't. I started to panic. I was angry with myself for allowing this debilitating state of perpetual lack of confidence and shyness to invade every aspect of my life. I knew that as I walked into the conference room that all eyes would be fixed on me, a six-foot three tall upright figure with a shock of silver-grey hair. You couldn't miss me if you tried. The police culture was always far too quick to judge individuals, and I'd often been told that people saw me as arrogant, aloof, overbearing and someone defined by an overblown ego. The great irony was that they were all about as far away from the truth as they could possibly be - it was all just an act on my part to cope with the shyness.

I put on some Dylan in the hope that the sound of his voice would make me feel more self-assured. His music was like an old friend that never let you down as if a hand reached out from the speaker offering a warm, comforting embrace to make you feel that you are never alone. It had, I think, something to do with growing up steeped in the majesty of his songs. They brought back fond memories of when I was a kid, when life was much simpler and the world seemed to be a far better place. By now, I was only a few minutes away from HQ and I was going to be late. I hated being late for anything, never mind probably one of the most important briefings of my career.

I was met by an anxious looking Tony Burke.

"Boss, good to see you again. They're all waiting for you. The room's packed."

I told Tony to go in and that I'd follow shortly. There was a buzz in the air. I could hear the room alive with people talking, waiting for me to come in and brief them on progress at the scene. They'd be looking to me to lead them and give clear direction on just about every aspect of the investigation. This was it. It was time for me to deliver a performance and provide the team with a strong leader whom they would want to follow. Easier said than done, I thought, as I entered the room filled with apprehension. I wasn't expecting to see the ACC, DCS Mike Jordan, head of

CID, and the city's Divisional Commander, also a Chief Superintendent, sat at a long table at the other side of the room. There was a seat left for me in the middle. This was unusual to have anyone of rank at a major incident briefing. I wondered why.

I walked nervously across the room. The ACC nodded and DCS Jordan smiled in my direction. I sat down and looked around me to see if there were any familiar faces. Although I was used to keeping an open mind, I hardly recognised anyone. Many were in uniform, which meant that they'd been told to attend the briefing by their own Division at short notice. The force had a formula they used to calculate how many officers to assign to a major incident that depended on the category of murder. It also depended very much on how many other incidents were on the go at the same time. Unfortunately, this was a busy time for the force. Hayley Morgan was a prostitute found dead, dumped on waste ground last October with a rag stuffed in her mouth and a bag over her head, and Samantha Class was brutally murdered in May of this year and her body washed up on the banks of the River Humber. The force was stretched and I knew there was talk of linking the murders. That would explain the presence of senior ranks; they must have got wind that the deceased could be another prostitute.

I introduced myself but then disaster. My mind went blank, mouth dry, heart-racing, panic set in. I'd allowed the occasion to get to me, and at that moment, I'd have given my right arm to be anywhere else but sat here letting myself down looking like a bloody bumbling idiot. I took a sip of water but it didn't help. I looked around the room, everyone looked uncomfortable. This wasn't what they were used to. And then I remembered seeing a celebrity on the television talking about how the loss of his father had changed his outlook on life. In an emotional response, with a trembling voice, he'd said that he'd nothing to fear in life now that his Dad had passed away. What could possibly be worse? Of course, he was absolutely right and I knew exactly what he meant. I'd lost my father too. By comparison, there was nothing to fear in life, certainly not giving a briefing. It made me angry with myself for being so inadequate but, thankfully, it gave me some much-needed perspective. Panic over, at least for now. The audience of about thirty or so must have been relieved that their SIO had recovered his composure and so was I.

Talking about the detail settled my nerves and I became less self-conscious as I gave clear instructions about what needed to be done for the rest of the day. I'd enough experience to know that decisions made early in an investigation needed to stand the test of time. They'd all be my decisions, my responsibility if things went wrong, and they'd be open to scrutiny by anyone and everyone: the judge, jury, prosecution, defence, senior officers, deceased's family and media, to name a few.

I asked for a show of hands from those who'd worked on a major incident before. In the circumstances, a good result would be maybe half. I counted three. There was Shaun Weir, a DC from the city, Lisa Hodson, press officer, and Acting DI Steve Holding, HOLMES office manager. I tried not to show disappointment but this case already looked as though it would be a runner. I needed experienced detectives who could hit the ground running. DCS Jordan intervened by announcing that he'd set the staffing levels at one DI, three DSs and twelve DCs. I knew, and everybody else knew, that twelve DCs didn't mean twelve DCs. It meant twelve constables and could be anybody who happened to be on duty at the time, whether they had detective skills or not. I tried to remain positive but I'd be at a significant disadvantage if the majority of officers had little or no experience of working on complex and protracted investigations. Looking back, SIOs used to handpick their own teams to work on murder inquiries and you had to be an experienced detective to stand a chance of being selected. But those days had long gone and, although this would be a massive learning curve for many of them, I wondered if they knew just how lucky they were to be given this unique opportunity and whether they'd rise to the challenge. Only time would tell.

I left Tony to finish the briefing because I was due at the mortuary at seven-thirty for a post-mortem on the arm and head. I motioned for Lisa to follow me outside. She was bright and intelligent, and we'd worked well together in the past because she knew that I was always very careful about what I released to the public.

"Don't worry, I know how you operate. Cooperate with the press but on our terms. Run everything by you first and restrict interviews to just you and me."

TWO

'She's been dead for about three months'

The late July evening sunshine brightened the gloomy mortuary that hadn't changed over the years. It brought back memories of my first visit as a young constable still in my probation. I'd been sent by control to an old run-down house on the Avenues on the outskirts of the city together with my colleague, PC Dick Graham, a unique individual well known for his huge stature and pronounced stammer. When I'd first met him, I thought that he was taking the piss. He wasn't. It meant that any conversation with him had the potential to be a long one, including interviews with suspects, but he couldn't care less what other people thought. I admired him for the way he coped with his speech impediment, given the unforgiving nature of the police culture.

Our task was to gain entry to the house because an elderly lady who lived there hadn't been seen for some time. I couldn't get any reply and so we shoulder charged the front door. Whilst it looked easy on the television, it was the opposite in real life. The Avenues were a series of streets noteworthy for their four to five-story Victorian houses and this one was no different. There was furniture crammed into every inch of the five floors: chairs, tables, sideboards, beds etc. Together, we searched high and low for the elderly lady with no luck. We searched again. Still we couldn't find her. I sensed that I was being set up. Every probationer received a so-called initiation of some kind and mine was still to come. But to my great relief, I eventually found the poor lady slumped forward seated in a chair with a high back. If we hadn't, the piss-taking would have been relentless and brutal.

It was nearly midnight. Her local GP came and issued a death certificate. PC Graham stammered an instruction to the effect that I was to accompany the undertakers to the mortuary for continuity. I was met by Mike, the mortuary technician, a tall thin man with a pointed nose and a huge moustache that was far too long for his narrow face. It completely covered his top lip and most of his chin. I wondered why anyone would want to work in a mortuary. The place was bloody freezing with rows of dead bodies for company.

"You're new. I haven't seen you before. I can show you round if you like. I always do with the new ones."

"Thanks, but I'm already late off."

But he insisted and before I knew it, he'd opened one of the fridges and slid a body out to show me.

"This poor girl's been here for three years. Only twenty-nine when she died. Parents are separated and her father's disputing how she died and so the coroner can't release the body."

"I didn't know that a body could be kept for so long."

With that, he turned to a row of body bags all zipped tightly closed.

"These are just from today. Must be something in the air. This one's yours."

I glanced at the body bag and it started twitching, followed by a muffled groaning sound. To say that I panicked would be an understatement. I flew out of my chair. She must be dead, she must be, the doctor certified death.

"Open the bag. Quick."

He unzipped the bag and he started to chuckle. Sure enough, there was a living member of my shift inside, PC Helen Watson. Bastards. This was my initiation, or so I thought, and I had to hand it to them, it was well planned and humorously executed. But there was more to come. When I eventually left the mortuary, it was almost pitch dark and then, from nowhere, came the crashing sound of what I thought was gunfire. I ran for cover towards my car and crouched down low. Suddenly, the lights came on and I was met with a huge round of laughter from my shift colleagues perched high above me on the mortuary roof. It wasn't gunfire - they were firecrackers. The mortuary technician had been in on the plan to lure me into thinking that the initiation was Helen Watson, when all along it was to try and frighten me to death. It worked. I did think I was being shot at and someone with a weak heart would probably have died of shock.

The familiar smell hit me as I entered through the rear doors of mortuary. It was the smell of death that lingered on your clothes long afterwards. I never got used to it, despite the amount of time I'd spent here through the years. I was met by the familiar sight of Mike, the mortuary technician, who was busy making cups of tea. Russell Walker, DI Chambers and DC Long were already there, together with two SOCO fingerprint experts I hadn't met before, Rob Doak and Nick Longman. I pulled out my notebook and a bottle of aftershave from my briefcase. I learned through experience to smother my wrists in aftershave to mask the sickly smell of a large intestine being sliced open by a pathologist's scalpel.

I started to write down everything Russell said. It seemed to unnerve him and put him off his train of thought. I'd already given him the third degree at the scene. He didn't look comfortable then and he didn't look comfortable now. Maybe he wasn't used to a SIO treating him like everyone else, but after the experience with baby George, I couldn't afford to stand on ceremony anymore with so-called experts. I think Russell knew that he was in for a tough time, when I asked if it was OK for me to go into the operating room with him to observe the post-mortem on the arm and head. Some SIOs didn't attend post-mortems, some attended but stood outside and observed through a glass window, others would go inside and be present on the shoulder of the pathologist. I always went inside because the duration of the post-mortem was a crucial part of the investigation and this meant listening to every word uttered by the pathologist, who was the only person qualified to give an opinion on the likely cause of death. It also gave me the opportunity to ask question after question as the post-mortem progressed, questions that I anticipated would be posed by my investigation team at the morning briefing. Russell started with the arm.

"I'd say it was dismembered about three months ago at the shoulder with something heavy and sharp. Axe maybe but can't be sure. Humerus bone's been fractured at an angle with a blunt instrument and then snapped."

Without a hint of irony, he continued with,

"I'm afraid whoever this is will not be identified from fingerprints because there are no fingers left."

I shot a frustrating glance towards DI Chambers. He knew, we all knew, that a proper means of identification was needed. The tattoo, CHAOS, on the lower arm suggested that it might well be Natalie Clubb but it wasn't enough. Chris and his team got to work on what little remained of the palm. The only possibility would be to use the palm print for identification assuming that the person had a criminal record in the first place. If it was Natalie Clubb and a working prostitute, she might well have been arrested in the past. There was a glimmer of hope. I watched nervously as Rob and Nick meticulously and delicately lifted tapings from the rotting flesh.

"What do you think?"

"We've got what looks like a partial print. Rob and Nick are going back to the bureau to do a check against the database."

After Russell finished his examination of the arm and head, we all sat down in the briefing room to discuss his preliminary findings. He said that in his opinion, both the arm and head were dismembered after death. The head was female severed at the sixth cervical, possibly by a thin bladed saw, and there were no injuries or fractures to the skull.

"I've taken hair samples. It looks as though it's been

dyed. I've taken body tapings for fingerprints and fibres. I'd say she's been dead for about three months but it's hard to tell."

"What about toxicology. Will you be able to get anything after so long?" I asked.

"I'll do my best. But it'll take some time for the results to come back."

Russell was reserved in what he was prepared to say at this early stage. All pathologists were and I understood why. It didn't stop me from being frustrated though, I needed answers to so many questions but there was nothing more we could do tonight. By now it was gone eleven. It'd been a long day and Russell had to get back to Sheffield.

The drive home was a lonely one. I lived about twenty miles away in a small village called Hutton Cranswick, where they still played cricket on the village green. It gave me time to think. This morning I was expecting a fairly routine day at work dealing with local crimes such as burglaries, rapes, serious assaults, and now I was the SIO on this case. I was out of my depth. Would I be able to cope? What if I made a complete mess of the investigation? What if they had to bring in another SIO to take over? I screeched to a halt and I screamed out loud, 'For fuck's sake Davo, get a fucking grip'. If all those who judged me to be arrogant and aloof could see me now, they'd be laughing, I thought. Giving myself a much-needed kick up the arse gave me some perspective. I'd no option but to trust in my ability to lead the investigation based on what had worked in the past on, admittedly, more routine cases. After all, I was an engineer before joining the police, and my mind had been taught to solve problems in a methodical and logical way. I hoped that this approach would be good enough now, I hoped that I'd be good enough, but I sensed that I was going to need a great deal more than logic to unravel this mystery.

I carried on driving through the darkness. I loved the country but at times you could go for miles and not see another soul. I felt better now that I'd given myself a good telling off. At least I'd a plan of action based on trusting myself; it didn't seem like much of a plan though, as I turned into the village. Although it was gone midnight, I guessed the Black Swan would still be open. They made more money after eleven than before. I could see the lights were on through the half-closed curtains. I knew that it was a bad idea to go in but I went in anyway. The briefing at eight in the morning seemed a long way off. I walked in to some nervous looks from the landlord and his regulars because they all knew that I was a policeman, but I put their minds at rest by sinking several pints.

It was gone two when I left. I got into bed with my head spinning from too many pints and before long, the phone rang. It was DI Chambers.

"Good news. We got an ID from the palm. It's Natalie Clubb. No doubt. Rob and Nick did a fantastic job."

"That's brilliant. Where are you?"

"I'm at the bureau with Rob and Nick."

"Can you thank them from me. I'll thank them personally when I see them. The briefings at HQ at eight. Will you be there?"

"I was going to go to the scene to carry on with the search if that's OK."

THREE

'We've found some more body parts'

I woke early around five, tired and anxious. I recognised the feeling - the rush of adrenalin coursing through my veins would be my friend in the weeks to come and give me the energy to work long hours demanded of SIOs. But I also knew that I'd be a pain to live with and my family life would suffer as a consequence. Before I left, I kissed Fi and my boys, Sam, Jack and Cal lightly so as not to wake them.

I was at HQ for seven. I wanted time to plan the briefing and start my policy book. When I arrived, Tony was already in the makeshift incident room that had been set up in the Gold Command Suite. He explained there was no alternative but to run the investigation from here because all the other available incident rooms were busy. Tony was what was affectionately known in police circles as a character. He wasn't afraid to be controversial, which meant that you would often hear about what he'd been up to and the trouble he was in. His thick, scouse accent made him instantly recognisable. You could be sitting on the opposite side of the canteen and you would know he was there without looking. Self-confident with a bold attitude, he wore black-framed glasses and had curly black hair that looked suspiciously lacking in any grey, given his age.

"I need a word in private."

He looked at me in a way that was all too familiar in the police. When someone of a higher rank did this, it always meant that you were in for a bollocking of some kind, or to be given words of advice. It was never to say thank you for a job well done and it'd happened to me many times. I'd never run an inquiry from here before and Tony had already designated the biggest office for me. The glass walls gave a good view of the incident room. He closed the door.

"What's up boss?"

"Look Tony, I don't know why you're in uniform given your CID background. Is there anything I need to know?"

"No, there's nothing you need to know other than you'll have no problems with me. I'll prove it to you. Just let us have a go."

"We've never worked together so please don't take this the wrong way. I'm only going to say this once. You'll only get one chance with me. If you let me down in any way, you'll be off the case without a moment's hesitation."

Tony looked surprised and hurt by my comments, but I didn't care. However Natalie Clubb died, I was determined to carry out the most thorough investigation that I could, and to have any chance of succeeding, I'd need a deputy I could work closely with and who'd be loyal. I'm not sure my direct approach with Tony would meet with the approval of the Police College at Bramshill. The police service had undergone a touchy-feely transformation in recent years: it was all about considering the feelings of others and, true to form, our force had embraced the concept with open arms. Consequently, people spent most of their time at work worrying whether or not they'd upset a colleague over some ridiculously minor issue.

I recalled a recent case were a constable put in a complaint against a sergeant for allegedly failing to say good morning as they passed in the corridor. But what made matters worse was that the force took the complaint seriously and investigated the poor sergeant. I imagined trying to explain the new touchy-feely approach to ordinary members of the public. I'm pretty sure they'd think that it was April Fool's Day. I had a feeling that I'd be the perfect target for such a policy; it would just be a matter of time. But not today. Tony was old school, he came from an entirely different era were complaining about a colleague was unthinkable and totally unacceptable.

"Look boss, I'll support you all the way and do the best that I can. Don't expect me to be a yes man. If I don't agree with you, I'll tell you. You're the boss at the end of the day though and I'll do whatever you ask of me. I know you like your own way."

He finished with a smile and a wink.

"You cheeky sod."

His reaction was what I needed, and I'd a feeling he was exactly the right person for the job as we were about to enter the murky underworld of prostitution, violence and drug dealing. I felt better now that Tony and I understood each other.

The incident room was busy with people I didn't recognise. There were definitely more than yesterday and Tony was eager to introduce me to as many as he could before the briefing. But I declined. I wanted time to consider and decide on the most urgent lines of inquiry for the investigation team now that we had a positive ID. As we began to discuss what needed to be done, there was a knock at the door. It was DCS Jordan. I wasn't expecting him. Tony stood to attention and asked him if he wanted a drink.

"Thanks Tony. Coffee, white no sugar."

"No problem, boss."

DCS Jordan had been my Divisional Commander until fairly recently. He'd spent his career in uniform up to the rank of Chief Superintendent but, to everyone's surprise, chief officers decided that he might benefit from a spell as head of the CID. It didn't make any sense to me. If DCS Jordan asked for the move, then he was a brave man because it was a position traditionally held by someone with years of experience in the CID, someone who could advise chief officers, support SIOs on difficult cases, and command the respect of the entire CID. I knew he'd feel out of his depth, through no fault of his own. He was well spoken with boyish looks and a mop of sandy-coloured hair. If I hadn't known that he was a policeman, I would've guessed that he was a bank manager or an accountant.

But as my Divisional Commander, he'd gone out of his way to support me on a particularly nasty case involving the anal rape of a 92-year-old lady. I was convinced that the person I'd arrested was responsible, and I wanted to charge the suspect so that he'd be remanded in custody. The problem was the time it'd take for a DNA semen profile to be checked against his DNA to confirm his guilt. Without it, the evidence was thin and purely circumstantial. I remember DCS Jordan very calmly asking me if I was sure that he was guilty. I said that I was and he replied,

"That's good enough for me. If we're wrong and he sues us, so be it. I'll make sure the force pays the costs. Now go on and charge him and let me know what happens."

He'd put his trust in me and a few days later, I received a call from the forensic scientist at Wetherby assigned to the case. I'll never forget her words.

"I'm going to make your day. It's him. I've got a full profile and there's no doubt it's his."

The case taught me a valuable lesson as a SIO and that was not to underestimate the power of gut instinct. We'd arrested the male in question based on the only thing the poor victim could remember about her attacker – he was wearing shorts. He was caught on CCTV in a shop in the area wearing shorts. That's all we had, nothing more. The elderly lady hadn't wanted to go into detail about the attack but my instinct was to have both vaginal and anal swabs taken, although she'd intimated that intercourse hadn't taken place. It turned out that his DNA profile was discovered on the anal swab.

After I'd briefed him on the results of the post-mortem, I asked if he could tell me why I'd been given this opportunity to be SIO on this case. He told me that it was his idea.

"The force is struggling due to the three other prostitute murders so they needed a SIO from Division. I managed to persuade the ACC to give you a chance. I think you deserve to be given a chance."

I didn't know what to say other than thank you.

"Don't thank me just yet. This looks to be the most complicated of them all and you're going to be up against it.

Don't let me down or else the ACC will be after me. I won't stay for the briefing. I know you're busy. Good luck."

I sat for a moment trying to take in what had just happened, a compliment from a senior officer. I was absolutely delighted. Tony came in and said.

"You look pleased with yourself."

"DCS Jordan persuaded the ACC to give me a chance and paid me a compliment."

"Bloody hell boss, makes a change from getting a bollocking. What's it like, I've never had a compliment before."

I was feeling much more self-assured following DCS Jordan's visit, and I launched into the briefing in high spirits. I could see some officers looking nervous and apprehensive. It was understandable in the circumstances if they'd no experience of working on major incidents.

"Morning everyone. For those that don't know me I'm DCI Davison. This is Inspector Tony Burke, deputy SIO. Let me begin by saying that until we know any different, this is a full-blown murder investigation. The deceased is Natalie Clubb and she was a working prostitute. No matter what she did for a living, she deserves the most thorough investigation possible."

I delivered my soapbox-type speech that I always included at the beginning of a major inquiry. It was designed to set some ground rules so that each and every one of the team knew exactly what I expected from them as the SIO. I hoped that they'd be motivated by my plea for them 'to act with integrity at all times', to be 'first-class ambassadors for the force', and 'to go the extra mile for Natalie', because I knew that I'd be asking a great deal of them.

"Should you fall below the standard expected, you'll be sent back to Division. If anyone wants to leave, now's the time."

You could hear a pin drop, but nobody left.

"You'll all be aware that there are two other undetected murder inquiries on the go. Samantha Class and Hayley Morgan. Detective Superintendent Taylor's the SIO for Class and Detective Superintendent Dickens for Morgan. They're being run from Courtland Road. It's too early to tell whether they're linked."

I spent the next thirty minutes providing details of the pumping station and post-mortem. I needed to leave soon to get back to the scene but before I left, I set three main lines of inquiry for Tony to action: Natalie Clubb's background, family and associates; last sightings and movements of Natalie Clubb; and background of Darren Adams, Clubb's boyfriend. At the end of the briefing, Tony followed me into my office. A queue of people lined up outside.

"Can I leave you to get on with sorting the inside HOLMES staff. And I want good DSs in charge of the main lines of inquiry. If you need me, I'll be on my mobile."

Tony was beginning to impress me more and more. Lisa pushed her way in with Sam Jordan, the FLO.

"Boss, I need five minutes. I'm being swamped by calls from TV, radio. You name it. They're already linking Class and Morgan with ours."

"Lisa, come in. Is it Sam or Samantha?"

"Sam's fine boss."

"Lisa, we can't put anything else out until Natalie's family have been informed."

It was agreed that Lisa would arrange interviews with the press after Natalie's family were told. I left the building by the back stairs to avoid bumping into any of the chief officers. The Chief had been here for about five years. He was the spitting image of Postman Pat. It was uncanny and I often wondered if he knew, probably not, because it would take a very brave person to tell a Chief Constable that he looked like Postman Pat. His claim to fame in the force was known as the 'night of the long knives', when he decided to slash the power of the CID by posting a third of detectives back to uniform. A date was chosen not long after he arrived. Demoralised supervisors had to decide who should go and who should stay. Hard-nosed experienced detectives sobbed uncontrollably at the news - it was a sight I'd never seen before or since, thankfully.

My only meeting with him was to be formally promoted from DI to DCI. I was lucky to stay in the CID on promotion and so I was in high spirits as I nervously made my way to the chief officers' corridor. To be fair, he wasn't at all what I expected him to be as he put me at ease with stories of his younger days as a constable in North Yorkshire. But then, without warning, he looked straight at me and said,

"Corrupt. The CID is corrupt. It's high time all detectives were put back into uniform."

I didn't know what to say. There I was being promoted from within a CID he considered to be corrupt. This was supposed to be an opportunity for the Chief to inspire me to deliver his vision for policing. Suddenly, he stood up, shook my hand and wished me luck. I felt anything but inspired, and I remembered someone warning me a few years ago against pursuing a career in the CID. Their point was that uniform was the place to be to get promoted, not the CID, and I was beginning to understand why.

Driving back to the scene, I thought about the impact of the 'night of the long knives' and how the balance of power had shifted about as far away from the CID as possible. The previous Chief liked the CID and it was afforded an elevated status. Its higher ranks were strong characters with a collective, powerful voice that effectively ran the force, but those days were long gone. I was brought back to reality by a call from DI Chambers.

"Good news. We've found some more body parts. Too early to tell what they are. They're wrapped in bin liners again though."

"I'm on my way."

This was good news. I was grateful for the call because I didn't want to think about how the power of the CID had been diminished anymore. It was too depressing. When I arrived, Chris showed me the new discoveries. As far as they could tell, there was a torso wrapped inside two bin bags that were unsealed, and the upper parts of both legs contained within two separate, sealed bags. Russell and Hugh were busy taking samples, DC Long taking photographs and video footage.

"Any idea of cause of death?"

"Sorry. Have to wait till the post-mortem. I don't want to disturb the bin liners too much."

I knew what Russell's answer would be but I thought I'd

ask anyway. I walked over to see Sergeant Downs who was stood by the side of the drain near to the pump turbines.

"Boss, I've started the search of the river. Just need to set some parameters. I'd suggest the underwater search team go two hundred yards upstream and my officers walk the banks. Is that OK?"

"Sounds good to me. Have they all been briefed? Do they know what they are looking for?"

"Yes. Body parts, bin bags, knives, saws, pretty much anything at this stage."

I got a call from Sam to say that she'd made contact with Natalie's mother in London and arranged to meet her. Lisa already knew and interviews with local TV, radio and newspapers were set for mid-afternoon. Finally, I'd be able to appeal for information. What Lisa didn't know was that the press had turned up at the scene. I couldn't stop them or blame them for wanting to see first-hand where the body parts were discovered. Fortunately, the pumping station was protected by high metal-gates, and the press had no option but to congregate outside. I agreed to do interviews because I wanted them on my side. I didn't give much away apart from new information confirming Natalie's identity, the discovery of other body parts, and that there would be a second post-mortem later today. I expected to be asked about the possibility of a serial killer and I was. I politely declined to comment.

FOUR

'Nobody said a word as Russell began to gently remove the first bin liner'

The second post-mortem was scheduled for five that evening and so I left Tony to do the briefing at HQ. On the way to the mortuary, I wondered whether I'd be lucky and get a cause of death. Without an obvious cause it would be almost impossible to prove how Natalie died. There wouldn't be the remotest chance of anyone in Natalie's world of prostitution and drug abuse co-operating with the police. My head felt like it was going to explode thinking about what tonight might bring, how Fi and the boys were doing, where could I get some food from, how I should go and see my Mum again soon, and what my Dad would say to me now if he were still alive. I missed him and thought about him every day, but it was always worse when I was under pressure and needed a friend.

I was ready with my aftershave as I walked into the mortuary. This was going to smell badly and I had to prepare myself for seeing more dismembered pieces of Natalie's body. Russell was already in the theatre with DI Chambers and Hugh Blunt. They were stood over what we assumed to be her torso laid on the table, still wrapped in bin liners. DC

Long had two of his SOCOs with him to assist. I'd seen them before but didn't know their names. We gathered around the mortuary table and I put my arm soaked in aftershave up to my nose. Nobody said a word as Russell began to gently remove the first bin liner. The second one beneath was stuck to the rotting flesh, and it was impossible to tell whether it was the front or back due to the level of decomposition. There was no skin left. Russell broke the silence.

"Looks like the back to me, nothing to indicate how she died here. I'm going to turn her over to examine the front. I'll need a hand. It'll be a dead weight I'm afraid."

There was an air of expectation as we struggled to lift Natalie's torso onto her back. Russell carefully peeled back the second bin liner. I couldn't believe my eyes. We all moved closer to get a better look: there were what appeared to be multiple puncture wounds grouped closely together around the chest area. It was obvious but I wanted Russell to give us his opinion to somehow make it official. He didn't speak for what seemed like hours but was, in reality, only a few seconds.

"I think there are at least eight stab wounds to her chest. Looks like there's one to her abdomen. I'd say the ones to her chest are ante-mortem. The other one could be ante or post-mortem."

To say this was a lucky break would be a bloody understatement. According to Russell, there was less decomposition due to the bin liner being tightly wrapped around the chest and stomach and that's why the stab wounds had remained intact. Inside, I was overjoyed, elated, excited, punching the air. I tried not to show it given the circumstances but as the SIO, the discovery of the stab wounds was more than I could've hoped for and was exactly what the investigation needed. To charge the killer with murder, though, I knew that I'd need a cause of death, and I was hoping that he'd conclude that the wounds were responsible.

"Bad news I'm afraid, although whoever did this used considerable force, enough to pierce through bone, the vital organs are all decomposed so I can't tell exactly how she died. All I can do is give you the angle the weapon entered the body for each stab wound."

My heart sank but Chris responded in his usual cool, reserved and understated way.

"Shouldn't be too difficult to show that they would've led to death if she hadn't received medical attention. We could approach Professor Green to get an expert opinion."

Russell didn't reply, but he did say more about other injuries to the torso, apart from the stab wounds.

"Looks interesting. There are at least four areas of deep tissue bruising to the chest wall. They're blunt force injuries probably caused by blows from fists or kicks with a shod foot. Ante-mortem, so she was alive when they were inflicted."

I formed a mental picture in my mind of a brutal and frenzied attack on a defenceless female using kicks and punches, followed by a knife of some kind. When Russell had completed his examination of the two femurs, he asked for the arm and head from yesterday. He slowly and methodically arranged the body parts to see whether there was a natural fit, and he concluded that they were female and from the same person. Given that we already knew it was Natalie's right arm, then it had to be her even though DNA tests would still need to be carried out to prove it beyond doubt.

The last sight of Natalie is something that I wish I'd never seen: hopelessly decomposed with her left arm, lower leg bones and feet missing. The emaciated body of poor little George was, up to now, the most upsetting thing I'd ever witnessed, but this was something else. And I wondered how the others were feeling, including Russell, and how they'd cope with the memory of this evening. I felt like talking about what we'd all just experienced from a human perspective, to show some empathy for Natalie and her family, but it wasn't the way in the police. The fear of being branded weak was enough to discourage any outward display of emotion. It was something I learned when I joined some sixteen years ago: the culture of the police was different to any other I'd ever come across. Accordingly, it was a strange atmosphere in the room as Russell delivered what he was prepared to say, which was conservative to say the least.

The moment passed as we all went our separate ways. I drove away from the mortuary and headed for home. Tired and emotionally drained, I was more determined than ever to find Natalie's killer. I turned over in my mind, given the very unique circumstances of this case, how difficult this was going to be to solve. There would be no quick and easy resolution as TV detectives would have you believe. No admission of guilt by the killer or killers. Forensic opportunities would be limited due to the degree of decomposition of Natalie's body and the absence of a scene, apart from the pumping station. Determining the date of her murder would be challenging. And, the number of suspects might run into hundreds given Natalie's occupation. After all, it looked as though Samantha Class was murdered by a punter and dumped in the river, and I knew that the stranger element was making it much more complicated for the SIO to solve the case.

Where would the evidence come from? The more I thought about it, the more convinced I became that I'd have to assume the worst: what if there's no forensic evidence to link the killer or killers to Natalie, what if the murder weapons never found, and what if the instrument used to butcher her body is never discovered. And if all that proved to be true, then the investigation would have to focus on presenting a purely circumstantial case against those responsible at Crown Court. Easier said than done, I thought, when I'd never done anything like this before and absolutely no idea how to begin.

When I got home, Fi and the boys were asleep. I hadn't seen them for the best part of two days. I sat for a while in the darkness with a glass of whisky for company, and I wondered how I'd get to sleep with images of Natalie's rotting corpse flooding my mind. I couldn't stop thinking about what a circumstantial case would look like, and so I sat at the kitchen table, pulled out my notebook, and began to write down ideas about how to move the investigation forward.

I listed everything we didn't know - which was just about everything - before concentrating on what we did know: the cause of Natalie's death. We knew that she'd been punched or kicked and stabbed multiple times in the chest and so would those responsible. I realised that I had to use that information to my advantage but how? I tried to imagine how Natalie's killer or killers would react when we released to the press the identity of the dismembered body parts. They'd be thinking that they were safe, given the passage of time. But what if they'd made a mistake and confided in somebody, or enlisted the help of a friend to get rid of the body. What if we were able to find that somebody and persuade them to give evidence. It was a long shot, a really long shot and, to have any chance of success, I realised that I'd have keep the cause of death a secret from the press and the public. At least it was a start, I told myself, and it seemed like a very logical thing to do, although I knew that withholding how Natalie died, wouldn't be easy. And even if I was able to do so, how on earth would I determine whether the killer or killers had made an error of judgement by disclosing what they'd done to a third party? It was a question that I didn't have the answer to because there wouldn't be the remotest chance of anyone in Natalie's world of prostitution and drug abuse cooperating with the police. By now, it was three in the morning and so I poured myself another whisky before falling asleep on the sofa.

FIVE

'What's the best chance of us detecting this?'

My head ached from too little sleep and too much alcohol. Not the best start to a day that was going to be fast-paced, exhilarating, exhausting and challenging, I thought. On the drive into HQ, as expected, the old familiar enemy returned with a voice chattering away telling me that I wouldn't be able to cope and wouldn't be up to the job. I put on Dylan's 'I Want You' and just listening to the opening drum sequence, made me feel brighter.

When I got to work, Tony was waiting for me in my office. With a broad grin on his face, he shook my hand in celebration at the result of the second post-mortem for what seemed like forever. We both knew that we were lucky given the circumstances and, no matter what challenges lay ahead, at least we had a pathologist willing to say that Natalie had been stabbed repeatedly.

"Before you bring me up to date with what you've been doing, I've had some ideas. Want to know what you think. Now we know for definite she was stabbed, what's the best chance of us detecting this?"

"Bloody hell boss, that's a good question. Could be anybody. We know that her boyfriend Adams was her pimp and their favourite MO was to rip punters off at 119 St John's Grove. She'd bring them back to their place and he'd rob them. They think Class was killed by a punter. Still not detected."

I showed him my notebook and all the stuff I'd written down last night. I hadn't realised that I'd scribbled so much. Maybe the whisky had something to do with it. It took him a while to scan the pages and after he'd finished, he just looked at me and smiled.

"What do you think. Why are you smiling?"

"Just trying to figure out how to keep the cause of death a secret. The press'll find out sooner or later. This is the police after all. But there's something you should know. There's been leaks to the press. Somebody on one of the incidents is talking out of turn."

Tony's news changed things and I knew that I'd not only have to keep it out of the media, but I'd have restrict knowledge of how Natalie died to the investigation team and a few senior officers. We tried to work out how it could be done, and it was clear that such a move would be controversial and make it look as though we didn't trust people. With the briefing only minutes away at eight, we decided to tell the team just enough for now to give us more time to think. After all, we didn't know who was talking to the press; it could be somebody on my team.

I called Lisa in to my office to ask her advice. Her response was refreshingly positive and her eyes lit up at the thought of doing something a bit different. You could almost see her brain going into overdrive at the implications of the decision.

"The fact that she was dismembered will be enough to get the nationals interested, never mind talk of a serial killer. The press will try every trick in the book to find out how she died you know."

Lisa was right, and I realised that I hadn't thought this policy through. It would be one thing asking people not to divulge how Natalie died, but how would I know for sure that they'd kept their word?

The incident room already had its own identity. It was full of life with phones ringing, people busy sat behind desks looking at computer screens and numerous conversations happening at the same time across the room. It felt familiar. It somehow had a purpose, a sense of direction, and it generated in me a feeling of belonging. I knew this was going to be my home for some time to come. But as I walked down the corridor towards HQ bar for the briefing, my stomach churned again at the thought of what I was about to do. It made me bloody angry because a big part of my job as a SIO was to deliver briefings. It didn't make any sense to be filled with dread at the thought of standing in front of detectives who would be looking for leadership. And yet that was how each day began for me.

HQ still had a bar, thankfully. There used to be one in every station across the force but they were being closed due to a number of reasons, the main one being that chief officers didn't think they sent out the right message to the public. I entered through the swing doors and walked past the full-size snooker table. It brought back memories of my old Inspector when I was a probationer. In those days, he liked to think that he was a top-notch player and he spent most shifts taking on junior officers. The better the player, the more time they'd spend at the snooker table. Needless to say, I spent very little time in his company but others would literally come on duty never to be seen again until going home time.

It was a typical police station bar, sparsely furnished with dark wooden seats covered in red threadbare cloth, thick red curtains and cream-coloured metal window frames. It hadn't been decorated in years and it showed. It wasn't the most inspiring venue to hold a briefing; even the morning sunshine struggled to brighten the dingy surroundings. I looked around at my slightly nervous looking assembled team. There were a few more detectives than yesterday but not nearly enough to cope with the scale of the inquiry. It was good to see DC Dave Hopkin as he acknowledged me with a broad, friendly grin. He used to manage a football team I played for and he was a true gentleman. I liked him immensely, everybody did, and I trusted him. He was the kind of person you'd want as a brother.

"Morning everyone. For those of you who weren't here yesterday, I'm DCI Davison and sat next to me is Inspector Tony Burke, deputy SIO. After the second post-mortem late yesterday, I'm certain that Natalie was murdered, although the pathologist, Russell Walker, is putting the cause of death down as unascertained due to the complete decomposition of her internal organs. For reasons I don't want to go into now, I'm not in a position to tell you how she died. What he is prepared to say is she died a violent and traumatic death, probably about three months ago, and that it looks like the body parts are from one female. At this stage, we're assuming they all belong to Natalie, although we'll need DNA to prove this. We're still missing her left arm and lower parts of both legs including her feet."

The experienced detectives looked bewildered and so did the rest of my team. It was obvious that they were confused as to why I hadn't told them how Natalie was killed. I knew that I wouldn't be able to keep this from them for long. I quickly turned my attention to Tony and asked him to provide an update on progress made with the lines of inquiry I set yesterday. I could see he was bursting to speak. His eyes lit up as his commanding, unmistakable scouse accent filled the air. Tony was the kind of person who spoke loudly regardless of the circumstances. It didn't matter to Tony where he was or who was listening, and I admired him for his confidence. I, on the other hand, was the complete opposite, and as he began to talk, I'd a feeling that I was going to enjoy working with my flamboyant deputy.

"Can I start with DS Rob Walker. Rob's been given Natalie's background to look at."

I didn't know DS Walker. Slightly built, with dark brushed back hair, his goatee beard suited his long thin face and sharp features.

"I'm DS Rob Walker for those who don't know me. I've got a small team working with me on Natalie's background, family, associates, movements and last sightings. I think the best thing I can do is hand you over to Karen from plainclothes. She's been responsible for making enquiries into Natalie as a missing person."

"Natalie was born on the fifteenth of February 1973, in Kingsbury, London. She came to Hull in March 1996, with her two daughters, Charlotte and Caroline. Her eldest child, Liam, stayed with his father, James McAlister. Basically, she met Darren Adams not long after she arrived and then her life became a sad tale of shoplifting, prostitution, heroin abuse and violence at the hands of Adams. He exploited her. She was his meal ticket to fund his heroin addiction. Adams is a nasty piece of work. He's got over eighty convictions for burglary, assault, and robbery. You name it he's done it. They lived together at 119 St Johns Grove. Adams reported her missing twice. Once at 1321hrs on the 14th of April, this year from a public phone box in Hull, after she'd left him to live with Nini Thompson and Tony Beaumont. It's believed that Natalie and Nini had a lesbian relationship. They got back together though, and he reported her missing for the second time at 2027hrs on the 14th of May, from a public phone box on Exeter Grove. I've been back to 119 St Johns Grove loads of times since. I believe Adams has been staying with Michael Larvin at 13 Leven Grove. Shall I carry on, Sir?"

"Please do."

"Well, according to my notebook, I went around on the 4th of June. The front door was locked. I got in by the backdoor which was unlocked. There were signs that someone was living there. The electric fire was on and so was the TV. The place was a mess. Clothes everywhere, needles on the floor. I left a note for Adams or Natalie to call me. I never received a call from either of them. I went again on the 8th and 18th of June. The TV was gone. The fire was off."

I was impressed by the officer's account and attention to

detail. Although understandably nervous, her delivery was articulate and precise, and it was obvious that she'd a lot more information to give about Natalie's lifestyle and her relationship with Adams. I asked her to continue, and she painted a sordid picture of how they lived in squalor, both addicted to heroin with Adams depending on Natalie to fund their habit through prostitution. Their MO was for Natalie to bring punters home, where Adams would be ready and waiting armed with a baseball bat and a knuckle duster to rob them. He knew that punters wouldn't report it to the police for obvious reasons. Tony continued.

"DS Goddard's got Adams to look at."

"As Karen's already said, he's got over eighty previous for pretty much everything involving dishonesty. He's been staying with his brother, Shaun, at an address in Morpeth Street, although he gives 119 St John's Grove for the purposes of bail. He's got a sister, Stacey Elliott who he keeps in contact with. Looking on the system, he's got over seventy friends and associates. Pimps, prostitutes, dealers, criminals. Most of them are into heroin. Now that he's got no source of income, he'll be out committing crime to fund his habit."

"Staying with Adams. What do you all think about him as a suspect?" I said.

There was an unexpected silence from the team. I understood that people would be nervous, uncomfortable and unwilling to give their point of view for fear of embarrassing themselves. DS Goddard broke the silence.

"I think we should lock him into an account. Get him to commit his movements on paper as soon as possible so we can check his story. In terms of motive, I don't know why Adams would want to kill his source of heroin. He's going to have to get another prostitute to replace Natalie or go out burgling."

"What about where it could've happened?"

Tony responded.

"All we've got is 119 St John's Grove to go at. It's where she was living mostly before she was killed. I've already made arrangements for it to be boarded up today. I know there's no continuity but I thought it was the right thing to do."

"I'll speak to DI Chambers and get them to give us an opinion as to whether she could've been killed and dismembered in there."

The atmosphere in the room reminded me of school with me as the headmaster talking to pupils on their first day.

"Look, you're all going to be here for some time to come. We're a team. We have to work as a team. I know I'm the SIO, but it will be you as individuals who'll solve this case and we'll solve this case no matter how long it takes. Trust me it'll be your attention to detail, ability to question and think, readiness to work harder than you've ever worked before, that'll be the key to solving this. You all need to start thinking 24/7. When you're at home having a beer or taking a shower. Think motive. How, why, where? And don't be afraid to speak. I don't care how daft a suggestion might seem. I've never dealt with such a complex case so I'm pretty sure none of you will have either. I warn you now, I'll be asking for your ideas every day at briefing. And it'll be no good telling me that you haven't had any."

There was absolute silence. Yes, I would lead the team,

but I knew from experience that my best chance of success would be to create a supportive and positive environment, where individuals felt that they'd an important contribution to make and that they'd be taken seriously and listened to. The police didn't operate like that. Senior ranks rarely asked lower ranks what they thought, and this was obvious from their reaction, which was to look at me in disbelief. From their perspective, most of them didn't know me, most of them had little or no experience on major incidents and yet here was a DCI saying that he wasn't going to solve the case, they were. To be fair, if I were in their position, I'd be confused and disoriented too, and I'd be questioning whether or not the DCI was really up to the job.

But then the contributions came. Slowly to begin with, but it wasn't long before officers realised that they were able to give their opinion without fear of being ridiculed. I smiled because this was how it was supposed to be: quick fire responses with ideas flowing - some inspired, some off the wall, some plain daft. It was better than I could've hoped for in the circumstances. The rest of the briefing covered theories about where Natalie was killed, motive, how her body parts ended up in a rubbish heap at the pumping station, forensic opportunities and much more. The amount of information put forward was staggering. Before the briefing finished, Tony announced that he expected everyone to go for a beer after the teatime briefing.

"The boss is paying."

Even though it was going to cost me, I thanked him for arranging the drink after work. It would give us all a chance to relax and get to know each other. Tony walked back with me to my office. I wanted to have a meeting to discuss progress and priorities for the day.

"How do you think it went?"

"It went well. You've got them thinking and contributing. Some of them weren't made-up not knowing how she died, though."

"I know and I've been thinking about how we can handle it. If I make a policy decision to restrict the cause of death to the team, DCS Jordan and the ACC, they'll each have to sign my book to declare that they won't disclose it to anyone. I'll tell them at the teatime briefing. DI Chambers and his SOCOs will have to sign and the pathologist. Something tells me this isn't going to be a popular decision with those above."

"What about the SIOs?"

"I don't know any of them that well apart from Mr Taylor. He's OK. Mr Dickens isn't my biggest fan and I don't blame him. I need to apologise to him over my review of the Hayley Morgan case. It's a long story. They'll have to promise not to tell their teams. I'm not sure how that'll go down. We're going to have to trust them to keep it to themselves."

"What about 119 St John's Grove. Thanks for getting on with boarding it up. You read my mind."

"That's sound. It'll cost though. I've gone for the metal option rather than wood. The locals will only set fire to wood or rip it off for firewood."

"I want to go down and have a look for myself later. You coming?"

I called ADI Steve Holding into my office and told him

about my policy on cause of death. Steve was a serious individual. I never saw him smile but I believe that was just the way he was. Beneath the dour exterior though was a person who cared passionately about the job, and I knew that I was lucky to have him as office manager in charge of the HOLMES team. It was only right to let him know so that it wouldn't come as a surprise later on at the briefing. He was the kind of person who liked to know what was going on, and he liked to know more than anyone else. He asked about the PDF policy and, without waiting for a reply, he suggested males and females aged fifteen and over. I agreed. There would be no point in setting the age lower. The type of person likely to be encountered on the inquiry – associates, punters, prostitutes and drug dealers - would be older and to set it any lower would create too much work for such a small team.

Before we were able to leave, Lisa rushed in looking flustered.

"Boss, the press has gone mad. They knew there was a second post-mortem last night. I put out a press release saying more body parts had been found as agreed. It's gone national. BBC, ITV, Independent, Guardian. Radio 4 has been on and they want you live tomorrow morning."

"What's their angle, why so much interest?"

"Serial killer steps up a gear to dismember prostitute. Prostitutes frightened for their lives, pretty much sums it up. I've said you'll be available at eleven in the conference room. Hope that's OK."

"It'll have to be. We need to discuss what I'm going to say. Steve, give us a minute please."

"What do you think?"

"I'd play down the serial killer aspect and say we're keeping an open mind. I think we should give some reassurance to working prostitutes. I've heard they're running scared."

Tony agreed. He'd already arranged extra uniform patrols in the area. I walked into the conference room with Lisa. TV crews, reporters, tape machines, microphones, cables and lighting umbrellas, filled the room. I almost didn't recognise it. Lisa and I sat together facing the audience of reporters. I hated this part of the job, although I never turned down the offer of free airtime to ask the public for help.

"Morning everyone, I'm DCI Davison and this is Lisa Hodson, who most of you will know I'm sure. Before you ask any questions, I want to bring you all up to date. Last night, we held a second post-mortem on some other body parts that we found at the pumping station. We'll have to wait for DNA tests to confirm that they belong to Natalie Clubb. But assuming they are Natalie's, she met a violent and brutal death. I'm not in a position to say how I believe she was killed for operational reasons. Any questions?"

The questions came one after another. I was prepared to be patient and repeat myself over and over again until they got the message that I didn't believe there was a serial killer on the loose. After all, from their perspective, this was big news, almost like watching some far-fetched detective story on the TV. But if I'd learned anything from other SIOs, it was to get your own message across, even if the press cut out most of what you said.

"Look, I'm going to have to leave soon but before I go,

can I make an appeal to anyone out there with information that might help us catch Natalie's killer or killers. I want to appeal particularly to the criminal fraternity to come forward. I know there's still honour amongst thieves and dismembering a body is evil, there can be no justification to protect those responsible. Anonymous calls are welcome or you can call me directly. Although Natalie was a working prostitute and heroin addict, this must in no way detract from the gravity of this crime. She was a mother and a daughter and she didn't deserve the brutality that I believe led to her death. Thank you."

Lisa and I left quickly as camera flashlights exploded in our faces, and reporters followed us down the corridor hoping for one last comment. Back in my office, Tony joined us to see how it'd gone.

"Bloody hell Tony, it's taken off now. There's massive press interest. It's taken me by surprise. I'm used to local reporters now they want me on Radio 4. Mad."

It was obvious that Tony and Lisa were relishing the challenge. You could almost see the adrenalin coursing through their veins. I had to admit that, although I was operating purely on instinct not really knowing what I was doing, I felt more alive than ever, like I could see for miles.

"Come on Tony, time to get out of here."

SIX

'The smell would be familiar to any police officer'

We drove out of HQ and headed towards the east of the city, over the River Hull via Myton Bridge and onto Holderness Road. It was a familiar road for it led, eventually, to where I grew up. So many memories came flooding back as we chatted. I used to bike for miles from home to buy the latest Dylan or Hendrix release from Sydney Scarborough record shop that'd now disappeared as if it'd never existed in the first place. I remembered, like it was yesterday, clutching my copy of Hendrix's 'The Wind Cries Mary' single and pedaling home as fast as I could to listen to it for the first time. Magical.

Holderness Road was dreary at the best of times, and even though it was supposed to be summer, dark clouds sat gloomily above the sprawling network of council housing estates that defined the east of the city. As a kid, I lived on an estate not far from Preston Road and St John's Grove. I knew what to expect: depressed looking houses and depressed looking people. There was an air of hopelessness that descended once you entered as if everyone had given up, consigned to a life with little or no ambition. To be fair, there were a number of houses that stood out from the rest that'd probably been bought from the council, with their well-kept gardens and smart outward appearance. At least they were trying to rise above the burnt-out cars, boarded up houses and menacing, gaunt looking youths stood on every street corner, I thought, as we pulled up outside 119 St John's Grove.

It was a semi-detached council house with a small garden at the front boarded by a wooden picket fence that'd all but disappeared. It was covered in weeds, rubbish bags, cereal packets, a rusty old bike and much more. Next door, by complete contrast, was neat and fresh looking with white lace curtains decorating the windows. Tony shook his head.

"What a bloody shame. Can you imagine living next door to this shithole."

It still wasn't boarded up and so we walked around the back. I gave Tony a pair of overshoes to wear and we went into the house by the back door that was slightly ajar. It led straight into the kitchen. The smell would be familiar to any police officer - a product of years of neglect caused by unwashed clothes and urine-soaked furniture. The only way to get rid of the smell would be to burn the house to the ground and start again. There was a sink unit beneath the only window, a fridge and a work surface. Blood stained clothes, an old suitcase, black bin bags full of rubbish, empty cereal boxes, used syringes and a Hull Daily Mail dated 18 May 1998, covered the dirty linoleum floor. Tony pushed the living room door open to reveal the same smell, filth, and squalor. There was a bathroom off the living room. Disgusting. But the bath looked to be cleaner than the rest of the house, which seemed odd to me. Tony commented ironically that maybe it'd never been used.

"What do you think, could she have been killed and cut up in here?"

"I honestly don't know. If she had been what would we expect to find?"

It was a good question. I tried to imagine what it would take to dismember a body and leave no trace behind. If the body was placed on large pieces of plastic sheeting, surely that would capture any blood and body fluids. If whoever did this had planned it and been careful, would there be anything visible? Probably not, but this was early days and I had to keep an open mind. At least I'd know that from today, nobody else would be able to enter the house without my permission. I called DI Chambers.

"Sorry to bother you on a Saturday but I'm down at St John's Grove with Tony. We've had a brief look round and I'd like your opinion on whether Natalie could've been killed and dismembered there. The place is a mess and it stinks. Problem is it's been insecure for ages and anybody could've been in and out."

"OK, I'll get one of my DSs to have a look tomorrow. I'll get him to call you."

On the way back to HQ we talked about what we'd got so far and it wasn't much, apart from the stab wounds. But what else did we have? A scene at a pumping station, miles from anywhere that might yet reveal more. A thuggish pimp of a boyfriend who forced Natalie into prostitution but needed her to provide his daily heroin fix. And the bin bags discovered with the body parts that might provide a forensic link to the killer or killers. If it was a stranger, then it could be any one of her previous punters and there were many. The SIO for the Class case had a full DNA profile from semen inside her but it wasn't on the database. Hayley Morgan was strangled prior to her death, even though she died from an overdose of heroin and then dumped with a bag over her head. Could there be a link between the three deaths? Class's murderer was still on the loose and whoever dumped Morgan, was still out there. The scale of the challenge ahead was overwhelming, and I was pretty sure the force hadn't faced anything like this before.

"Let's go for a drink. Give us time to think. Make some decisions."

I parked the car at HQ and we walked through Queens Gardens, an area lined with flowers, trees, park benches and ponds with fountains, all set within vast lawns. Somebody once told me that it'd originally been the first dock to be constructed in Hull, and had been subsequently transformed to provide a picturesque garden space in the heart of the city. It was indeed a sight to behold and I often spent time here thinking and on a warm day, eating a packed lunch. We headed towards the Olde White Hart Pub on Whitefrairgate in the Old Town. It was my favourite part of Hull, with its cobbled streets and majestic buildings. As a young constable, it had been my patch. It stretched about a mile south to the River Humber, and I used to love walking down to my regular tea-spot, a café close to the water's edge, smell the sea air and share a coffee with Madge, the owner. People would stay there for hours looking out to sea and beyond. Madge would point out the old sailors who'd made a living on the trawlers until the heart was ripped out of the fishing industry as a result of the cod wars in the mid-1970s. My Dad was a seaman in the Merchant Navy and a trawler man, and so I somehow felt like there was a bond between us, although I didn't know any of them.

"What can I get you?"

"Suppose we shouldn't have a proper bevvy. Bugger it, I'll have a pint please."

We sat down in a quiet corner. The Olde White Harte was a typical Old Town pub with its odd shape, low-beamed ceilings and stone fireplaces. It was the kind of pub that you feel at home as soon as you walked in.

"We need to really think about how we're going do this. The more I think about it the more it makes sense to keep the stab wounds a secret. My gut feeling is that we're going to have to rely on whoever killed Natalie to tell somebody. But even if that happens, they're not going to tell us. And then there's the witnesses, how are we going to deal with them?"

"How do you mean?"

"There's going to be a load of people to see. They'll probably all be either coming down from heroin or high on it. Look at that place today. How could you go and see a witness in a place like that and take a statement? I know we've all done it before but when this case goes to trial, the defence would have a field day accusing us of all sorts. We need a way of taking them somewhere neutral."

"We could bring them into a police station. I don't know how we'd get them to come, though."

"It's a good idea but I agree I can't see them volunteering to come to see the police by appointment. They wouldn't recognise the front entrance, only ever been brought in handcuffs by the back door."

I told him about a colleague in another force who'd done some work on recording statements on a tape machine. He asked officers to tape record conversations with witnesses whilst taking a written statement. When he compared the written statements with the tape recordings, he realised that, on average, officers failed to accurately record what witnesses had said. They'd missed about fifteen pieces of relevant information. In one case, a couple that had been robbed mentioned that the getaway car had a different coloured passenger side door compared to the rest of the car. For whatever reason, the officer failed to record it on paper but it was there on the audio recording.

"Are you on about significant witness interviews? I know they've just started to do them but they're for witnesses who actually see something like a crime being committed."

"No, this would be on a much wider scale. I've been thinking about videoing all of our witnesses. It just seems like a logical thing to do. And if my mates right, just think about the missed information. Gone forever. We could hire one of the video suites they use for child protection. Pick up the witness and take them to be videoed. I can't think of a reason why we shouldn't. What do you think?"

"I've never heard of it being done before. Will the bosses let you? There must be some kind of policy that says you can't do it. There always is in the police. We're already going to keep the cause of death a secret and now this. If that's what you want do though, I'll back you all the way. I've got a feeling we're going to have some battles ahead."

Back at HQ, I called DCS Jordan.

"Sir, it's Paul. Sorry to interrupt your Saturday but I thought you'd want updating."

"I've been expecting you to call. How did the second PM go?"

"She's been stabbed eight, maybe nine times in the chest. Pathologist is sitting on the fence because her internal organs are completely decomposed. But we can sort that. There are a couple of things I need to discuss with you. Policy decisions I've made that might cause a few raised eyebrows, and you might get caught in the middle."

"Doesn't sound good. Do you want to talk now or I can come in tomorrow?"

"Tomorrow's fine. But I want to keep how she died a secret known only to a few people so, with respect, can I ask you not to tell anyone else."

"I'll have to tell the ACC. He's going to want to know."

"It's OK to tell chief officers but they'll have to sign my policy book to agree not to discuss with anyone other than people on a list I'll produce for you to see tomorrow."

"Sounds very mysterious. Is it necessary?"

"Yes, it is in my view. I hope you'll agree when I brief you tomorrow, Sir."

I made some entries into my policy book. I was careful to include as much detail as I could about the reasons for making the decisions because I knew they'd be open to intense scrutiny in the future. I might have to stand in Crown Court to justify why I'd made them for a start. Restricting knowledge of the stab wounds felt like the right thing to do, videoing all witnesses felt like the right thing to do, but there was nobody I could ask for advice. There was no book to read on what to do in these circumstances, each murder was different. I certainly wasn't looking forward to explaining my decisions to chief officers and the other SIOs as I slumped back in my chair, tired and hungry. There was a kind of madness about the early days of a major inquiry when the adrenalin rush seemed to elevate everyone to a higher place, a place where you didn't need food or sleep. But after a while, you always came down and I recognised that feeling now. Time for a strong coffee.

I made my way to the canteen on the same floor. A few of my team were there, and I sat at a table with PC Sam Jordan and the familiar figure of DC Phil Barber. They were partnered together as the FLOs. Phil used to work for me before he moved to child protection. He was an absolute gentleman and we had one thing in common, we both had prematurely grey to silver hair. I was pleased he was working on the case because he had bags of experience, and he was about as nice a human being as you could ever wish to meet.

"How's life in child protection?"

"Love it boss. I miss CID, though, and the old team. We had a great time together."

I got straight to the point and told him about my idea to video all witnesses, and I asked him, given his vast experience of videoing children in child protection, how it could be done.

"Boss, yes I've got loads of experience but I've never heard of routinely videoing witnesses. Videoing significant witnesses is just starting to happen but I thought the definition of a significant witness was quite narrow."

"Yes, I know the definition and you're right. But forget the policy for a minute. Can you give me any reason why we shouldn't?"

"Who's going to do them for a start? You need to be trained and accredited. Somebody has to listen and watch the entire interview and summarise it into a written statement for the witness to sign. It takes ages. Where would you do them? We don't have many video suites and they're used a lot for child protection, as you know. How many witnesses are we talking about? What if they won't come voluntarily?"

Phil was right. I hadn't thought this through properly. But I enjoyed the challenge of doing something different, particularly if it was for the right reasons, and the more I thought about it, it was for the right reasons. Although Phil was right to point out the practical difficulties of implementing such a policy, I was in no mood to give up now.

"I don't know how many witnesses, but if it could be done, what do you think?"

"I'm a great fan of videoing. It'd protect your team from taking statements in druggie's houses, but I'm still trying to get my head around how to do it."

"I want you to come up with a policy for videoing our witnesses. I don't care what it takes but don't take no for an answer. If you come across any difficulties let me know. I'm going to need it by Monday. Got to go now. See you at the briefing."

I didn't stay long enough to see Phil's reaction. I trusted him to do the best job he could in the circumstances and I knew he would. I held the teatime briefing in the bar again.

Better get used to the tired surroundings, I thought, as I opened with an apology.

"I don't often do this but I'm going to apologise for not telling you at this morning's briefing how Natalie died. Don't get used to it, though, because it's not likely to happen again."

People shifted nervously in their seats. I admit that I was being overly serious but I needed their attention and I got their attention. You could tell they knew something interesting was about to happen. And, after I'd finished recalling in elaborate detail what I'd witnessed as the pathologist had peeled away the bin liner to reveal how Natalie died, there were some puzzled looking faces. I carried on.

"The problem is you can't share this with anyone. There are two main reasons why. First, somebody's leaking information to the press from inside and we don't know who it is. And second, my gut feeling is that Natalie's killer or killers will confide in somebody, and so we need to keep it out of the public domain. This is really important. I need to trust you all. Does everybody understand?"

I could tell people were uneasy. Tony chipped in.

"It means that you can't tell detectives on the other inquiries, spouses, friends. Basically, anybody other than this team. You're going to have to sign the boss's policy book. If the stab wounds get out to the media, we'll find out who's responsible."

"There's more," I said.

"You'll all be getting actions to see people. Associates, friends, family etc. The majority will be prostitutes, drug dealers and pimps, living in squalor. I've asked DC Barber from child protection to come up with a way of videoing witnesses instead of taking written statements. It's never been done before. I've asked Phil for a policy by Monday."

The questions came thick and fast. From their perspective, this would be a major shock having grown up being taught to take written statements. I decided to explain by way of an example and I told them about a sensitive discipline case I was working on. A constable was being accused of attempting to pervert the course of justice by putting pressure on kids from a care home to admit to committing burglaries they hadn't done. I'd decided to video the appropriate adult acting on behalf of the youths, so there'd be no arguments about what she'd said. It worked better than I'd expected. She came out with information about the officer's poor conduct towards her of a sexual nature that took us all by surprise. I realised then the power of capturing a witness on video. No arguments. Every detail captured forever, just as it happened for all to see. The debate that followed could have lasted for ages. But it was getting late and we were all tired.

"We'll pick this up at tomorrow's briefing. Don't forget I'll be asking for your ideas in the morning. Time for a drink. It's the White Hart pub near Drypool Bridge. I'm buying."

SEVEN

'A slim figure walked towards me out of the shadows'

I drove to the pub on my own. Right onto Wilberforce Drive and left along Alfred Gelder Street. I could see the distinctive shape of the White Hart up ahead. I loved the Old Town pubs, they'd a unique character and this was as good a place as any to start bonding the team. It looked like I was the last to arrive. The welcoming sound of 'Hey Jude' met me like an old friend. There was a definite buzz in the air, and I made a point of talking to officers from the south bank of the Humber. They probably wouldn't know many of their colleagues from the north bank, and I wanted to make them feel welcome. The team comprised of officers from all corners of the force: child protection, uniform, CID, surveillance, plainclothes, intelligence, Special Investigation Squad and Special Branch. I hadn't worked with many of them. I wondered whether I'd be able to trust them and whether they cared about catching Natalie's killer or killers. Only time would tell.

It felt good to relax for a while, and although I was no good at small talk, others were. They seemed blessed with the confidence to speak to anyone, anytime, anywhere. Then the music stopped and I tried to guess what might come next. I was wrong, it was 'Everybody Hurts' by REM and my thoughts turned to Natalie. The song could have been written for her. The sight of Natalie's torso laid on the mortuary slab would stay with me forever and was still very much on my mind. Every time I closed my eyes, it was all I could see. I wondered what her killer or killers were doing now, and I wondered how the other prostitutes in Hull were feeling. The press were doing their best to scare people into thinking there was a serial killer on the loose. Another Ripper.

Everyone seemed to be in high spirits, so I slipped away quietly. I drove towards Waterhouse lane where the local prostitutes plied their trade. I parked on the side of the road not far from the Earl De Grey pub and turned my lights off. Back in 1985, whilst I was seconded to the CID for a brief spell, I remember one of my colleagues investigating a burglary at the Earl De Grey. Thieves broke in to be confronted by the landlord's pet macaws, Cha Cha and Ringo. They were known for mimicking the voices of drunken regulars: pimps, prostitutes, criminals and many of the hard men of Hull. The thieves must have jumped out of their skin when Cha Cha and Ringo suddenly broke the silence amidst the darkness with, 'Last orders please. Let's be having you'. Sadly, the burglars stabbed Cha Cha to death. Ringo was so distraught, he never spoke again.

The streetlights seemed to be dimmer than the rest of the city as if the local prostitutes had struck a deal with the council. A slim figure walked towards me out of the shadows. I lowered my window and she leaned forward to speak to me.

"Looking for company?"

I showed her my warrant card. Her expression changed instantly.

"Fuck off. Bastard coppers, don't give a shit about us. There's a fucking ripper madman on the loose and what you lot doing about it?"

She started to walk away.

"I need a word. Get in the car or I'll lock you up myself."

"Fuck off."

"Alright, have it your way."

I called control to send a patrol.

"There's a riot van coming for you," I shouted.

As luck would have it, a uniform patrol was in the area. It was my old colleague, PC Dick Graham.

"Now then, boss. Bloody hell you've come a long way in a short time. What you doing down here?"

"Good to see you again, my friend."

"What can I do for you? That Clubb job is a bad business. Is that why you're here?"

"Can you just hang around here for a while. I want to talk to that prostitute up there in the doorway."

The sight of the patrol car must have changed the girl's mind. She approached and got into the passenger seat.

"I recognise you now. You're that fucking grey-haired copper on the tele. You lot are bad for business. Scaring the fucking punters off."

I turned towards her face that was partially lit by the street lamp. She couldn't have been more than twenty with dyed blonde hair parted down the middle, wearing a tiny black skirt, and thigh-length black high-heeled boots. There was bruising to her right eye and a cut to her upper lip, almost healed. I had to admit that she was pretty, but with her decaying front teeth, cheap perfume, and breath smelling of stale cigarettes, she was about as far away from the role portrayed by Julia Roberts in the film 'Pretty Woman' as you could get.

"What's your name?"

"Maxine. Look is this going to take long? I've got a living to make."

She looked nervously towards the Earl De Grey, no doubt looking for her pimp.

"Did you know Natalie?"

"Yes, we all did. She was off her face on smack most of the time. Silly cow. She was always with that shithead of a boyfriend of hers. Can't you hurry up and find out what happened to her. Business is fucking crap with you lot swarming all over the streets."

"Who do you and the other girls think is responsible?"

"There's all sorts of fucking rumours going around. Could be anybody, there's some really weird fuckers out there I can tell you."

"What about her boyfriend, Adams?"

"Violent bastard all right but can't see it myself. He's a lazy cunt. Nat earned him money. I've heard he's had to go out robbing for his heroin."

I thanked her for her time and then she was gone, disappeared into the darkness, probably hoping for a few more punters before the end of the night. I wondered how she'd come to this miserable place. If I had to describe the opposite to all that is good in life, then this would be it:

prostitutes stood in the shadows looking for a few quid from Hull's brigade of shabby, grubby, kerb-crawling men.

I walked over to see PC Graham.

"Thanks Dick. I'm off home now."

"No problem, boss. Just remember I taught you everything you know. Stay healthy my friend."

As PC Graham drove off, I remembered my first day as a police officer, 10 September 1982, Hull Central. I was paired up with Dick. He pulled up in a Mini Metro at the front of the station. It was a ridiculous sight; his huge frame looked like it'd been poured into the dinky toy of a car. I wondered whose bright idea it was to think that the tiny Mini was fit for purpose as a police patrol vehicle as I managed, eventually, to squeeze into the passenger seat with some difficulty. He didn't say a word for what seemed like ages, but then he suddenly turned towards me as we waited at traffic lights. With a serious expression on his face, he said.

"I go sniffing."

I waited for him to elaborate but he just glared at me.

"What for?"

"What do you think my friend, fanny of course."

It was the strangest conversation I'd ever had with anyone prior to joining the police, and the day turned out to be more like a scene from the keystone cops than the routine day out on patrol I as expecting. Later, we received an assistance call whilst in the station canteen and we ran outside to our waiting Metro. Two other burly officers asked for a lift and I was the smallest of the four of us by far. It took forever to shoehorn ourselves into the pocket-sized vehicle. Off we went as fast as we could, but as Dick screeched around the first corner, the car suddenly dropped on the passenger side with a metallic clunk. The rear wheel had parted company, and we watched in amazement as it rolled past ahead of us. I smiled as those memories came flooding back – truth was absolutely stranger than fiction. But Dick was a character and for that he was worth his weight in gold. The force was in danger of becoming too politically correct and soon, there'd be no place left for the PC Graham's of this world.

EIGHT

'You could always get a second opinion, if you're not happy'

I arrived at HQ early. Tony was already waiting in my office with a coffee.
"Where did you slip off to last night?"
"Waterhouse Lane."
He was about to fire a sarcastic comment my way when DCS Jordan arrived. Tony left my office and closed the door. I spent then next thirty minutes bringing DCS Jordan up to speed with the investigation. I knew that he'd have to brief the ACC and so I gave him as much detail as possible. It was awkward in a way because this was not his world and I didn't want him to feel uncomfortable. He'd been kind to me and seemed to believe in me, but to suddenly be thrust into this position would be the very steepest of learning curves for someone with a uniform background. I explained my reasoning behind the policy decisions to withhold the cause of death and to video witnesses. I could be very persuasive and passionate when arguing my case, and I admit that I wanted to convince him that he could trust me and that I wouldn't let him down. I hinted at the likely resistance there might be from the ACC and the other SIOs to my policy decisions, and how this might affect his position stuck right in the middle. Rather him than me, I thought. I could see he

was thinking hard about everything I said and was trying to make sense of it all. He looked uncomfortable and I knew that he'd be searching for a past experience with which to compare this with, so he could offer some advice. I'd want to help if I was in his position but he couldn't, and to be fair to him, he just listened, asked questions and offered his support.

He walked with Tony and me to the briefing in the bar. The team looked nervous when he entered.

"Morning everyone. I know it's Sunday but we've got work to do. I want to start with when Natalie was last seen alive. Any progress?"

There was good news. Following some inspired detective work by DS Walker and his team, they'd recovered a form from the benefit office in Alfred Gelder Street, signed by Natalie on 28 April, bearing her fingerprints. Accordingly, it was agreed to stage a reconstruction on Thursday, 6 August, seven days after the discovery of the arm, using a prostitute to walk the route that Natalie would probably have taken to Alfred Gelder Street. Although it was accepted practice, given the passage of time, I wondered whether it'd be successful. Nevertheless, it'd be an opportunity to generate publicity. I offered Maxine, the girl I'd met last night on Waterhouse Lane, as a likely candidate. She was the spitting image of Natalie.

The briefing moved on to what seemed like a million other aspects of the investigation: possible suspects, including Natalie's pimp boyfriend Adams; 119 St Johns Grove as a potential scene; motives for her murder; reasons for dismemberment; whether fingerprints would be found on the bin bags; the TIE policy; and theories of how the body parts could have found their way onto the rubbish heap, based on the assumption that she was killed somewhere else.

DC Weir had clearly given the last issue a great deal of thought, and to his credit, he wheeled a mobile white board into the bar with a map of the area surrounding the pumping station, drawn in felt tip. He identified three locations where it would be possible to drive to the drain upstream of the pumping station: Carlamhill Bridge, Commom Lane Bridge and Lumbercote Bridge. If the body parts were dumped at any of these locations, would the power of the four pumps capable of moving tons of water per minute, be sufficient to move them downstream as far as the pumping station? It was a question that generated a number of actions: to consult an expert on water flow in drains and rivers, and to conduct enquiries at those locations, particularly with residents living near to Carlamhill Bridge, in the search for witnesses.

We tried to second guess the intention of those responsible. Had they simply dumped the bin bags stuffed with Natalie's dismembered body in the Holderness Drain, hoping that they'd never be discovered, or had they counted on the pump's gigantic turbine blades crushing Natalie's body into pulp, leaving no trace as the drain's contents fed, eventually, into the River Humber. I could see that more and more members of the team were getting the hang of being able to voice an opinion without fear of being ridiculed. From my perspective, I'd a complex problem to solve; they were part of my team and so it was their problem to solve as well. I wanted them to feel personally responsible as if they were the SIO with all the pressure and expectation that came with the role. And, as if to prove my point, PC Humphrey raised an important issue and asked the question: what if the body parts were dumped downstream of the pumping station in a drain on Preston Road Estate? Up to now, we'd assumed that they were dumped upstream. Some were quick to question her argument, but she stood her ground and explained that the council often cleared debris from other parts of the drain and deposited it at the pumping station for burning. The team had to admit that it was possible. Well done Karen, I thought, still in your probation and making a telling contribution.

DCS Jordan didn't say a word until the end of the briefing.

"Can I just say that I'm really impressed with the way that you've all contributed today. The amount of information coming from you all was simply staggering. I couldn't do what you do. I wouldn't be able to store that much detail and this is just one briefing, so well done. Good luck."

I admired him for his words of encouragement and I could see that they had a positive effect on my team. We'd just witnessed a high-ranking officer showing a fair degree of humility, something I'd not seen before in my sixteen-year police career and it wasn't something I was ever likely to see again. We left the bar together, and he told me that the ACC wanted a meeting tomorrow with me and the other SIOs to discuss progress. He must have sensed my unease at the news and told me not to worry. In police terms, that usually meant there was something to worry about. I wasn't looking forward to justifying some of the decisions I'd made to senior officers. There was every chance that, collectively, they saw me as a pain-in-the-arse that needed bringing down a peg or two.

My thoughts turned to DS Pickering. I called him and he was already on his way to see me having carried out a preliminary forensic assessment of 119 St Johns Grove. When he arrived, Tony joined us in my office at HQ. I was hoping it was good news.

"Les, good to see you again. Thanks for having a look inside the house. What do you think?"

"It depends what you mean. DI Chambers just asked me to have a look to see if I thought Natalie Clubb could've been killed and dismembered there. I'm not really sure what you wanted."

"I didn't get chance to call you. Sorry. I just wanted your professional opinion to see whether it's worth a more thorough forensic investigation as a possible scene."

"It would take forever to do an in-depth job you know. The place is a mess."

It wasn't what I'd wanted to hear, but deep down I knew that it was my fault for not being more specific about what I wanted from him. I was the first to admit that I was no expert in the field of forensic science. What I'd learned had been gathered by attending numerous scenes as a SIO and gradually raising my knowledge and understanding from experienced SOCOs. There were no training courses on how to be a competent SIO, you had to learn on the job. He had me at a distinct disadvantage due to his undoubted expertise, but all I had was 119 St Johns Grove.

"Look, I understand. I've been inside to have a look. All

I'm asking is, based on your years of experience, do you think it likely Natalie could have been killed and cut up there."

"No, I don't think so. But I'm not sure, the place just looks as if nobody's lived there for ages. I would've expected to see signs of cleaning up for example but I couldn't see any. That's my opinion anyway."

"OK, another question. What do you think I should do? What are my options?"

"I'd talk it over with DI Chambers. You could always get a second opinion, if you're not happy."

After he left, we considered our options with 119 St Johns Grove. My instinct was to press for a second opinion. This was too important to get wrong. I wanted the place taken apart methodically and scientifically so that I could make an informed decision. To declare it a possible scene would focus the inquiry on Adams or a punter who'd been robbed at that address and wanted revenge. To rule it out as a scene, would give some support to the theory that whoever killed Samantha Class might be responsible and dismembering Natalie was an escalation in their gruesome behaviour. We'd nothing to lose and everything to gain. I couldn't care less if a forensic scientist agreed with DS Pickering's initial assessment because it wasn't about who was right or wrong. I called DI Chambers at home at home.

"Sorry to interrupt your Sunday……"

"Les's already called me about getting a second opinion. I'm not sure what difference it'll make but I'm happy to give Wetherby a call. I'll let you know what they say."

"I hope that Les hasn't taken this the wrong way about

getting a forensic scientist in. It's nothing personal but I'm really struggling here."

He put the phone down abruptly and I formed the impression that I'd upset them both. From their perspective, it probably looked like I didn't trust them and if I'd been in their position, maybe I'd feel the same way. I pulled out my policy book and made an entry stating clearly why I wanted a forensic scientist to give me a second opinion.

Tony lightened the mood with one of his stories as he made me a coffee. The one thing most police officers had in common was that they'd usually been divorced at least once, and I often thought that the force should invest in a full-time marriage guidance counsellor. It would be money well spent. Accordingly, the most popular topic of conversation in the police, by a mile, was the latest person to go 'over the wall', who'd they left home for, how much it was costing in child maintenance, and whether their spouse was going after their pension. Tony talked about a friend of his who was questioned by his wife following a so-called CID course he was supposed to have attended in Wakefield in the depths of winter. His friend had in fact taken his girlfriend, affectionately referred to in the CID as 'auntie', to Spain for a week. The problem was that he'd returned home with a healthy but suspicious looking suntan. Despite blaming hours spent on a sun bed, his wife ended the marriage and left his worldly belongings in bin bags scattered over the front garden. We shook our heads at his friend's misfortune. His wife would see things differently, however, and no amount of explaining that it was just the culture of the CID to have an 'auntie', justified his behaviour to her or anyone else for that matter.

On the way home, I thought about my own 'going over the wall' experience. I was a detective constable at the time, and for many reasons, my wife and I had drifted apart. I knew I had to tell my DS who would pass it upwards to the head of the CID. I was nervous because I could be posted back into uniform. It'd happened to others and so why not me, I thought, as I took a deep breath and told him. As it turned out, I needn't have worried, he'd left home the same day as me and as luck would have it, so had our DI. We'd all left home on the same day. I was summoned to see the Detective Superintendent fully expecting the worst, but all he did was give me some words of advice. With a stammer almost as pronounced as PC Graham's, he shouted,

"Sort your fucking life out or else I'll have you pounding the beat for the rest of your career. Now fuck off out of here."

NINE

'All progress depends on the unreasonable person'

The following day, I left Tony to take the briefing as I headed along the corridor towards the chief officers' suite. I wasn't sure what to expect from a meeting with the ACC, DCS Jordan and the other SIOs. I knew that DCS Jordan would've already briefed the ACC and the other SIOs about progress on my case. I felt apprehensive but surprisingly confident and ready to stand my ground over some of the more contentious decisions I'd made. I reasoned that they would surely understand and want to support me once they'd listened to what I had to say.

I walked in and sat down. The atmosphere felt anything but supportive. I couldn't be certain but it looked to me as though they'd had a meeting before I arrived. The ACC sat at the head of the table. I knew him mainly through playing football for the force. If you were a half-decent footballer in the police, the stiffness of the rank structure seemed to soften in your favour. It allowed you to get time off to play for the force, usually on a Wednesday afternoon, even though your shift couldn't do without you. He'd never done me any harm, but since his promotion from chief superintendent to ACC, some said that he'd changed. It was hard to imagine because as a more junior officer he was well liked and one of the boys. He looked anything but happy and the SIOs didn't look too happy either. They were all a rank above me and they were sat next to each other on the opposite side of the table. I was intimidated by their collective breadth of experience. They'd all built solid reputations leading major inquiries at force level. There was Mr Taylor, Mr Dickens, and Mr Statham, who was leading the investigation into the murder of Karen Tomlinson. She was a prostitute killed by her boyfriend, who was on remand awaiting trial.

The meeting didn't go well from my perspective. This was new for me to be operating at force level, and I felt very much like an outsider looking in. I could feel my confidence slipping away as I began to speak. My mouth went dry, and it reminded me of the first briefing I'd given on the case when I'd mumbled incoherently, like a gibbering idiot. It was a familiar feeling. I could see by their faces that they were uncomfortable at my awkward, nervous performance. I managed to recover some of my lost composure, but my insistence that the cause of death should remain confidential and the request for them all to sign my policy book accordingly, was met with a collective shrug of the shoulders. Their response was something like, 'So you're pinning your hopes on solving the case by keeping the cause of death a secret. Well good luck with that'. There was simmering tension in the room that was diplomatically diffused by DCS Jordan, who suggested that I leave my policy book and he'd make sure that it was duly signed. But when the issue of videoing witnesses was raised, I had to face some difficult and searching questions. Whilst I could understand their concerns over implementing something that hadn't been done before on such a wide scale, by now, I was in no mood to back down. I was the SIO. I believed in the decisions I'd made. If they proved to be the wrong decisions, then I knew that I'd have to accept the consequences.

Detective Superintendent Taylor caught up with me as I headed back to the incident room. He told me that I'd done really well in front of the ACC. We chatted together in my office over a coffee and he did his best to make me feel better. I hoped to look upon him as a kind of mentor, but I knew that he had enough to cope with swabbing thousands of known clients of prostitutes in an effort to solve the murder of Samantha Class. There was nobody else. I didn't really know Brian Statham, I'd already annoyed Detective Superintendent Dickens over my review of his case, and DCS Jordan was a gentleman but out of his depth. I did feel better, but as I looked at him, I wondered whether he'd been made aware of the issue over 119 St Johns Grove. SOCO came under his command. I decided to leave that for another day.

Tony came in as he left.

"How did the meeting go?"

"Bloody brilliant. Better than expected," I replied with lashings of sarcasm.

"Only kidding my friend. The SIOs think I'm naive to think we can keep the cause of death a secret. Maybe I am but I don't know what else to do. And they weren't too impressed with the policy to video witnesses either. Do you think they'll take me off the case? Wouldn't be surprised if they did."

"No, I'm sure that won't happen. After all, there's no one left," he said with a broad grin.

"Bastard."

"Only joking. I agree with you and the word from the team is they agree with you as well. Better to have them on your side, they're the ones you keep saying will detect this, not the ACC or the other SIOs."

"You're right. I'll just have to tread carefully. Pissed off senior officers can do your legs. We've all seen it happen. But I'm not going to change the way I do things for anyone."

"That's more like it. Come on. Lunchtime."

I could hear the words coming out if my mouth about not changing. I'd move heaven and earth to catch Natalie's killer, but I knew that not only would I have to work tirelessly to do so, I'd have to be careful not to alienate the other SIOs. I'd already been warned that they were struggling with their own investigations, and the videoing of witnesses wasn't helping due to the amount of time it took a typist to turn a video into a written statement. There were only so many typists and they were shared between the various inquiries. I hadn't properly considered how my policy would impact on the other SIOs, and I was challenging the way the police recorded witness statements. Was I being unreasonable, I wondered?

I recalled George Bernard Shaw's famous quotation: 'The reasonable man adapts himself to the world; the unreasonable one persists in trying to adapt the world to himself. Therefore, all progress depends on the unreasonable man'. In my world, I understood his words to mean that I could either continue to stand my ground to give me the best chance of success, or conform to the old way of doing things for a quiet life. I knew that I wouldn't change direction though, however unreasonable that might seem to my colleagues. I'd a feeling that my team, Tony and me, had better get used to being treated as 'unreasonable' given the circumstances.

Paul Hodgson from the National Crime Faculty arrived after lunch. I was hoping that he'd be able to offer some help and advice, given his role as a national advisor on serious crime. Although he wasn't a SIO, he introduced himself as an experienced Detective Inspector. I'd no way of knowing or testing his expertise, but I'd nothing to lose by keeping an open mind. To his credit, he was pleasant, approachable and he listened carefully as Tony and I briefed him on the case. The fact that he listened made a favourable impression on me from the start, and I wondered what he'd make of my decisions to withhold cause of death and to video witnesses. I explained my reasoning in some detail and, to my surprise, he not only understood why I'd made them, but considered them to be logical and reasonable given the circumstances. It gave us a well-needed boost. I asked him about possible motives for dismembering a body.

"Could be sexual. There was a case of a heroin addict who killed his prostitute girlfriend, dismembered her and buried her body parts in bin bags in a wood. He didn't do a very good job though. The bags were found by walkers. The killer appealed on the grounds that she fell and hit her head causing her death. He'd panicked, cut her body up just to get rid of it. The judge rejected the appeal on the grounds that he displayed a 'higher level of criminality' by cutting one of her feet in two and removing both nipples."

"What about Operations Enigma and Lynx I've heard about?"

"Operation Lynx was set up fairly recently to try and catch the so-called travelling serial rapist. He abducts women in city centres, beats and rapes them. In one case, he dumped a victim in the river with a bag over her head. She survived. There are similarities with the murder of Class. Enigma was set up in 1996, over fears that police forces might be missing links between about seventy unsolved murders. The Ripper case is always at the back of everyone's minds."

"Should I be looking locally or further afield in my case?"

"I don't know. It's not something we've come across recently. The case I mentioned earlier was in another country. Cutting a body up to me suggests somebody local with time and a place to carry it out. But that's just my opinion."

For the next few hours, we speculated over motives, likely suspects, latest forensic techniques and whether the deaths of Morgan, Class and Clubb could be attributed to the same killer or killers. And we came to the conclusion that, although the MOs were very different, anything was possible given the circumstances. They were all heroin addicts and they were all prostitutes.

He left us with the feeling that he was impressed by our approach. I thanked him for his advice and for being so receptive to the decisions we'd made. The meeting with him was enjoyable and provided me with some much-needed relief from the tensions in force, and it made me realise that, although there were no words to describe the horror of Natalie's untimely death, there was no denying that a case like this only came once in a SIO's career.

"Tony, I think we ought to get all the supervisors together before the teatime briefing. I need to bring them up to speed and sort out getting Adams on video."

"Good idea there's loads for you to catch up on. They're starting to see friends and associates of Natalie and Adams. All addicts either high or rattling."

We held a meeting in my office. There was DS John Goddard, DS Rob Walker, DS Kev Scarth, Acting DS Mark Chapman and Acting DI Steve Holding.

"Thanks for coming at short notice. I'd a meeting this morning with the ACC and the three SIOs. It didn't go well. I explained why I made the decision over cause of death but the SIOs considered me to be naive to think we could keep it quiet. Maybe they're right but it shouldn't stop us from trying. I'm telling you all this because I get the feeling that I'm very much the outsider."

DS Goddard responded.

"Boss, I've already had detectives from other inquiries asking me how Natalie died. They were angry and puzzled when I refused to tell them. I think the team is going to be on the outside as well. I can see a load of tension coming between us Class and Morgan and then there'll be detectives at Division."

"Anybody else?"

The response from the others was exactly the same. Apparently, the decision was already the talk of the force, and there were critical comments over the decision to video all witnesses.

"I've upset the SOCO DI as well. DS Pickering took a quick look inside 119 St Johns Grove and he doesn't believe Natalie was killed or dismembered there. I've asked DI Chambers to arrange for a forensic scientist to take another look. So, it seems that we've already pissed off most of the force and we've only been at it since Thursday. Must be some kind of record."

"We'll be OK we just need to keep out nerve. Does anybody disagree with the boss's decisions? If you do, now's the time to say."

There was a moment of reflection at Tony's comments. It was another way of asking for their loyalty and support in front of me. I knew that I maintained a certain distance from lower ranks during major investigations, and I was grateful to him for giving them the opportunity to speak. I was pleasantly surprised by their positive response summed up by DS Goddard.

"I think it's a brilliant inquiry to be on and I'm behind you completely. I couldn't care less how much crap I get over the cause of death issue. It's the right thing to do."

I could tell that the rest agreed with DS Goddard. They didn't need to speak as I could almost see the bond between us grow stronger. They were placing their trust in me and I couldn't let them down. Then it was down to business. We had to get Adams locked into an account as a witness. There were no grounds to treat him as a suspect, although he was an obvious place to start. DS Goddard was responsible for researching Adams's movements and background. He'd a way of speaking that made you want to listen and trust in everything he said. It was a kind of understated intelligence coupled with a healthy degree of humility. I was glad he was part of my team. But as he talked about Adams, it was clear that we were going to have problems getting him on video.

"Boss, I've seen Adams at Larvin's house. Karen came with me. He's either rattling or high. He's agreed to go on video and only way we'll get anything out of him is if he's scored when we collect him."

"OK, we'll just have to declare it from the start of the video. Nothing else we can do."

After the meeting, I felt deflated and tired. It'd been a long five days since Natalie's arm was found. Seemed more like five months. The familiar voice of negativity returned whenever my confidence waivered, which was most of the time. 'What if you've got it wrong Davo? Won't look so bloody clever then will you, smart arses always get what's coming'.

A thank you for all the hard work from the ACC would make all the difference but I knew that would never happen. I didn't blame him. The culture of the police was just the way it was. No emotion, no thanks. The rewards came in different forms: solving a crime or a guilty verdict at court, and that got me thinking about a case I dealt with as a young DC. A well-dressed man had been abducted, robbed, and beaten up by a gang of youths who forced him into their car before eventually dumping him miles from anywhere. The man couldn't remember a thing about his abductors, only that there were four of them, and they drove a white car with four doors. I asked uniform patrols to look out for four likely youths driving around in a white car. Before long, a keen PC stopped a car fitting the very loose description I'd given and obtained their names and addresses. It turned out that tapings from the car seats, matched those taken from the man's suit he was wearing at the time. The youths were subsequently convicted of robbery and received lengthy prison sentences. I was absolutely over the moon at the result and so was the victim. I'd got a result from virtually nothing to begin with, and the feeling was an adrenalin rush on a grand scale like no other I'd experienced in life.

It taught me a valuable lesson though - you had to make your own luck by making things happen, by taking positive action, even if it turned out to be the wrong thing to do. And that's how I felt right now. Yes, a thank you would make me feel better for a moment but what good would a thank you be, if I subsequently failed to solve the case and failed to convict Natalie's killer or killers? It made me call Tony anyway and thank him for doing such a good job as deputy, because I'd a feeling that judgment day for the killer or killers was some way off in the distance.

TEN

'Natalie loved to be loved'

There was a knock at my office door the next morning before briefing. It was Karen Humphrey and John Goddard.

"Come in, sit down. Karen, I'll get straight to the point."

She glanced nervously at John for reassurance.

"Karen, don't worry it's nothing bad. On the contrary, I've been hearing some good things about you. The video interview's been arranged for tomorrow I understand. We'd like you to do it. DS Goddard has every faith in you and that's good enough for me. What do you think?"

"I would absolutely love to do it Sir, thank you for your belief in me."

"Good, that's settled then. I can't stress enough just how important this is. We'll only get one chance to lock him into an account. And you don't need me to tell you he'll be drugged up during the interview."

After the briefing, I closed the door to my office and settled down to read the pile of statements sat on my desk. I wanted to know more about Natalie's life when she was growing up, and I found the statements from her mother, Linda Purdy (nee Clubb), and James McAlister her ex-boyfriend and father to her three children Charlotte, Caroline and Liam. They were good statements taken by PC Sam Jordan the FLO.

I started with Natalie's mother's statement. She gave birth to Natalie on 15 February 1973, in Kingsbury, London following a brief sexual relationship with Terry O'Connor. I was hoping that Natalie had enjoyed some happiness as a child, but I wasn't surprised to learn that her start in life was a sign of things to come. Linda Purdy's father insisted that Natalie be adopted at birth. Accordingly, for the first three months of her life, she was cared for by a neighbour, and the bond between mother and daughter was formed based on daily visits from Purdy. Eventually, Natalie was allowed home but at the age of three, Natalie and her mother moved into a flat on the Chalk Hill Council Estate, Wembley, London. Unfortunately for Natalie, her mother met and married Edward Purdy, who had three well-behaved daughters from a previous marriage. This proved to be a highly significant event – it caused jealousy in Natalie and drove an everlasting wedge between her and her mother. Natalie's behaviour deteriorated beyond her mother's control, and she was placed into the care of Wiltshire Social Services.

I tried to imagine what it would be like to be put into care by your parents. Linda Purdy's perspective was real but at the same time very sad: 'It is believed she tattooed the word CHAOS onto her arm because that's what she caused wherever she went'. From here, Natalie's life was influenced by the care system until happiness arrived in the form of a relationship with James McAlister. They set up home together in Salisbury and Natalie became pregnant at eighteen. They had three children in quick succession between 1992 and 1994. According to Linda Purdy, the last contact Natalie had with any family member was in February 1997, when she telephoned one of Linda's sisters, Christine Morgan. Natalie said she was in Hull, had a drug problem and wished she'd never met her current boyfriend, Adams.

I wondered why Natalie left Salisbury for Hull. McAlister's statement didn't help much other than to say that their relationship broke down for no particular reason. But it did offer a valuable insight into Natalie's personality and character whilst free of drugs: 'Attention was a big part of Natalie's life, if someone thought she was good she loved that. It was a very funny type of attention seeking but Natalie loved to be loved, loved to be wanted but also hated it at the same time. I wouldn't say she was schizophrenic but she was definitely not all quite right. She was a very frightened little girl with a very big chip on her shoulder who decided that her way of facing everything that came along was to shout louder than the person who shouted at her. I've also seen her at her weakest point, she would hate for anyone to see that. She would be easily led and that used to really annoy me'.

Could McAlister be responsible for killing Natalie? Perhaps he followed her to Hull, found that she was a drug-taking prostitute, that their children Charlotte and Caroline were in care and killed her following an argument. But why dismember the body? He could have hidden it somewhere, disappeared back to Salisbury and arranged an alibi to cover his movements. And where would he have been able to carry out such a gruesome task without being discovered? He'd have to be seen again. Definitely.

I reflected again for what seemed like the millionth time today on the lack of progress in the case so far. We had the stab wounds and it looked as though we'd managed to keep it from the press and from the other inquiries, but there was no scene other than the pumping station, and it was looking increasingly likely that it was a deposition site, as opposed to the scene of the crime. And, there were no suspects other than maybe Adams and McAlister. I studied schematic diagrams of Natalie's friends, associates and known clients on the wall of my office. Tony came in for a chat.

"Do you know any of these?"

"FIB's done a good job. Yeah, some of them have been RCS targets in the past. Amadi, Mohamed, Pattison. There're some big hitters there. Evil bastards. They'll be her dealers, probably. Anyone of these could be capable of murder."

"Just what I wanted to hear. Thanks."

"Sorry boss. I've got some news you're not going to like. A DC from one of the other inquiries had a go at one of our team. They were on a night out in Hull. Both been drinking and apparently the DC demanded to know how Natalie died. When our DC wouldn't tell him, a punch was thrown."

"Bloody hell. What happened? Did they get arrested?"

"No, don't worry. I'll deal with it. You don't need to know who it is. If it looks like going any further, I'll let you know."

"OK, but if it gets as far as the rubber heals in Discipline, I'll need to know. They'd have a field day with something like this. Do I need to post our DC back to Division?"

"No. He wasn't to blame as far as I can tell. He's a good lad."

"Have you ever thought what the public would make of all this? I expect they'd want us to concentrate on catching those responsible for killing Natalie, not fighting over demanding to know how she was fucking murdered."

I could guess how this had happened and it wasn't entirely unexpected. When I joined the CID in 1987, it was pretty much a closed shop. About ninety percent were detectives who'd been there for years and there was a certain hierarchy to be observed. SIOs had their favourites and they were always the first to be seconded onto a murder inquiry. The problem was that it bred a type or elitism amongst the detectives and they believed in their own legends – affectionately known as 'big hitters'. You could see why our current Chief didn't like the CID. And so, when I became a SIO in my own right, I kept an open mind when it came to judging individual competence to investigate. 'Big hitters' were welcome, but young in-service officers like Karen Humphrey were not to be underestimated.

I asked Tony to give me his opinion about the officers working on our case. I'd pinned a list to the wall next to Natalie's friends and associates.

"If we were a football team would we be pushing for the title or struggling to avoid relegation?"

"At the beginning it didn't look good but I've done a bit of wheeling and dealing with Division, called in a few favours and we've got some stars who can play a bit. Shaun Weir and Rob Walker are a dead experienced pair from Tower CID. John Goddard and Andy Marshall from surveillance, I've worked with both of them in the past and they're sound. And we've got big Mark Chapman from your

Division. I could go on but I think we've got a strong team. It's got a good feel about it."

"I've been thinking about picking a couple of detectives to do the interviews and the file. Who would you suggest?"

"I like your confidence. Can I think about it and let you know?"

"Of course, but I've been impressed with Shaun Weir and Rob Walker. I've watched them both and they seem very professional, hard-working and committed."

"Good choice. I agree. You need somebody who's done a murder file before and I know they have. I'm not sure about the other DSs."

"That's settled then. Let them know. They're going to have to get their heads around all the information coming in. It could be a long time before they get the chance to interview whoever killed Natalie. But it's going to happen. And they need to be prepared."

It was getting late in the afternoon. I cancelled the teatime briefing and told everyone to go home early and see their families. The team had worked hard with really long days. I got to thinking more and more about tomorrow and Adams's video statement. I called Paul Hodgson at home and asked him if he could put me in touch with anyone who'd be able to give advice about the approach to take with Adams. I'd read about advances being made by psychological profilers in assessing whether or not someone was telling the truth from body language. Adams would lie on video, even though he wouldn't be under caution - it was a way of life for him. Although it wasn't an exact science, better to be prepared, I thought. He told me to leave it with him and he'd get someone to call me.

About an hour later, a professor from Leicester University rang me. He'd worked on other criminal cases and achieved some success advising SIOs on whether or not individuals were being truthful. His advice was to observe Adams whilst talking about things he wouldn't have to lie about, such as his family and what his childhood was like, in order to provide a baseline for his body language, before asking him about Natalie's disappearance. This kind of thing interested me. I knew that I had to put Adams either in or out as a suspect, and I was counting on his video to help me make a decision.

I took a drive to the pumping station. I'd already released it as a scene because I was satisfied that every inch of the grounds had been meticulously and forensically examined. Sergeant Downs and his team had done a great job extending the search for Natalie's missing left arm, feet and lower parts of both legs without success. The drains feeding into the large pumps had all been either swam or walked, together with the drains downstream leading to the River Humber. Had Natalie's killer dumped some of her body at different locations? If they were dumped downstream, could they have reached the Humber? And if they had, where would they be now?

I stood by the giant turbines deep in thought. A small terrier jumped up, tail wagging. It had a kind face and, as I knelt to return the warm welcome, a man's voice called out.

"Ella, come here. Now."

"Is it Mr Snowden? I'm DCI Davison. SIO on this case."

"Hello, yes, it is. I know who you are. I've been away for

a few days while all the fuss died down. I saw you on the television. They said body parts were discovered in bin bags. This is Ella. She found the arm."

This must have been the last thing he wanted, and I could understand his desire to get away from all the attention and intrusion into his daily life.

"Do you think those responsible dumped the bags here or upstream somewhere?"

He seemed surprised by my direct approach.

"I don't know. I've been thinking about nothing else since it happened. Not many people come here. If they knew about the pumps and thought they'd grind stuff like a giant blender, they'd be mistaken. The turbines are protected by weed screens. My guess is that the bags were dumped upstream somewhere. The pumps can shift a lot of water. Those small diggers clear the debris that builds up in front of the weed screen and dump it over there where you've been digging."

I thanked him for his time as he wandered off with Ella trotting faithfully behind him. I stood for a while on the bridge that sat above the giant pumps and connected both banks of the drain. It gave me time to think. Appeals for witnesses and help from the public had been disappointing. It was time to put pressure on Hull's kerb-crawlers.

I went back to my office and called Lisa, and to her credit she came in to see me on her day off. She'd worked for a local newspaper before switching to the police. I always found her to be approachable and respectful but she'd a way of letting you know that she was there because she wanted to be and not because she had to be. There was a difference and I understood the difference - it was as if she resented being supervised and I felt the same way. It was, I think, something to do with pride. It meant that she'd tell me exactly what she thought.

"What do you think about putting a press release out asking for punters to come forward for elimination and if they don't, we'll come knocking on their door. We'll follow it up by doing an operation down Waterhouse Lane stopping everything that moves."

"It should put the fear of God into them. Class and Morgan did something similar with limited success. If it doesn't work you could use details of punters on the other inquiries. They've had a head start on you. We've got nothing to lose and it'll reassure the public that we care."

"That's a good point. I want to blame heroin. I want the public to have some sympathy for Natalie. There's a danger they'll see her as just another prostitute and not worth bothering with. I want either me or you all over the press 24/7 so people get sick of seeing us."

"OK, I'll get onto it right away. And by the way I agree with your approach."

Time to go home. I always enjoyed the drive from the city to open countryside. But thinking about the drug-dealing underworld that flourished like breeding rats and seemed to operate with impunity, made me angry. If the public only knew just how many so-called pillars of society were involved in distributing heroin, cocaine, amphetamines, they'd be utterly amazed and disgusted in equal measure, I thought.

I remembered being asked by my old Detective

Inspector, Gary Scaife, who was now the drug squad DI, to help them catch a major criminal responsible for everything from armed robbery, fraud, human trafficking, drug dealing and just about anything else that would fund his lavish lifestyle. The problem was that they knew very little about him other than his name, the identity of some of his criminal associates and where he lived. They'd been after him for years but couldn't get near him. But they got lucky when an informant told the drug squad that a man connected to the target was in the market for a chemist to manufacture drugs. That's where I came in. Gary asked me to play the part of the chemist, given my background in chemical engineering.

I was to meet the man in a pub in a village on the outskirts of Hull. Gary reassured me that the place would be crawling with drug squad detectives, either drinking or serving behind the bar. I hired a beat-up old car and drove to the pub. Inside, I saw a man stood at the bar alone sipping from a half-pint glass. I recognised a couple of detectives and ordered a pint. I needed it to calm my nerves. The man approached me and said,

"Is it Dave by any chance? I presume it's Dave and you're the person I'm looking for."

"That depends. I've just come back from Canada having worked at the University of Toronto as a post-doctoral fellow lecturing in chemical engineering. I understand you may have a proposition for me."

"That's what I was told. Word perfect. We can relax now."

I felt confident because everything I'd said was true. And, as he spoke about a plan to manufacture amphetamines for sale in Manchester and Liverpool, I baffled him with science on the process I'd use, the amount and type of chemicals required and the purity I'd be able to produce. I could tell he was impressed but then he asked me to go with him to meet the person who was going to fund the operation. It wasn't what I was expecting. Gary's brief was not to leave the pub, under any circumstances. I refused and told him that I'd be happy to meet the man but he had to come here. To my surprise, he excused himself to make a phone call. Whilst he was away, a couple of drug squad detectives looked at me puzzled. I was enjoying myself. Maybe the four pints of beer had something to do with it. I hadn't meant to drink so much but going under cover wasn't easy.

When he returned, he asked me if I'd mind if his client came to meet me at the pub. I couldn't refuse. It would be a chance for Gary to get more intelligence on his target. As we waited for him to arrive, I kept looking nervously towards the door. The target would, more than likely, be accompanied by a bodyguard for protection, and it would be just my luck if they turned out to be someone I'd arrested in the past. I kept my fingers crossed. Bodyguards usually carried guns. Eventually the target arrived with a bodyguard I didn't know, thankfully. I managed to convince the target that I knew what I was talking about and he could trust me. After we'd agreed to work together, he moved his face close up to mine, looked me in the eye and his mood changed from being friendly to deadly serious in an instant and said.

"If you fuck me over, I'll kill you. Do you understand?"

I didn't reply. I wanted to take him outside and show him just what I thought of his threat. He stood for everything I hated and I hated criminals with a vengeance. But just as quickly, he became friendly again and told me something I've never forgotten.

"Once this is all over, I'll invite you to a party at my house and introduce you to all the people who help me deal drugs. You'll be fucking amazed. Politicians, judges, barristers, bankers, top police. You'll be fucking gobsmacked."

Gary was delighted at the operation and it led to the eventual arrest and conviction of the target for a bank robbery. I thought about Haden Caulfield in 'Catcher in the Rye'. Whilst he pictured saving thousands of little kids playing in a field of rye from falling over a cliff, my wish would be round up all those parasites responsible for spreading misery by dealing drugs and do the opposite. I'd herd them to their deaths over a cliff edge into the sea, to be washed away forever. Now that'd be a sight to behold, I thought, as I pulled into the driveway.

ELEVEN

'He moved as if in slow motion, eyes black and vacant'

Adams was the main topic of discussion at the morning briefing. Everyone was keen to offer PC Humphrey and DC Barber advice but, as Phil rightly pointed out, it wasn't meant to be an interview it was an opportunity for him to give us his account as a witness. They left early to collect Adams from his brother's address in Morpeth Street. After they'd gone, I decided to shake things up.

"We've got to start making our own luck, make things happen. I'm stepping up the press appeals asking punters to come forward. We're going to do an operation down Waterhouse Lane this week. Adams will be on video by the end of today. But I've already said this before, this case will be solved not by me but by your attention to detail, your ability to think, question. The answer is out there somewhere."

There was frustration in my voice and I could see why people thought I was intimidating. But this wasn't a popularity contest. Convicting those responsible for Natalie's brutal murder was all that mattered. My approach certainly forced people to make contributions but I wasn't sure that they believed in themselves enough to unlock their own potential. The team had swelled to about twenty-five outside staff and ten inside, plus Tony and me. Still it was early days, I thought, and I just had to keep reinforcing the message that this was an opportunity for each and every one of the team to be outstanding. I had to create a positive atmosphere where people felt valued and respected for this to happen. Back in the real world, I knew only too well that I'd be fighting the negative police culture they'd all grown up with. Good luck with that, I thought.

I watched from the window as Adams got out of the car at the back of HQ. PC Humphrey and DC Barber brought him in by the rear entrance. I waited in the corridor near to the video suite. As he came towards me, I was struck by the way he walked, stiff and rigid, like a robot. Maybe it was the heroin. It must have been unusual for him to be in a police station and not be inside a cell, and he looked anything but comfortable as he shifted his gaze between Karen, Phil and me. His hands were covered in tattoos, with badly bitten fingernails, and his skin looked like it'd never seen the light of day. He moved as if in slow motion, eyes black and vacant, speech slightly slurred. I couldn't wait to hear what he had to say.

I watched Adams sit down opposite Karen on the TV monitor from the room next door to the video suite. It was clear that Karen got on well with Adams. She was young and attractive, and Adams acted as though he was in with a chance. Karen was obviously aware and used it to her advantage. The camera gave me a good view of the front of Adams. He seemed relaxed as Karen chatted about nothing in particular, whilst Phil checked the video camera recording levels.

"Darren, for the purposes of the tape can you confirm that you're happy to be videoed as a way of taking your statement and that you are making it of your own free will."

"Yes."

"I have to tell you that there are other officers watching this from a room next door. Are you OK with that?"

"Yes. I've got nothing to hide. Don't care who's watching."

"Can I also confirm that my colleague DC Barber and me picked you up from your brother's address and that during the journey, we didn't speak about Natalie or her disappearance."

"Yes, we spoke about fuck all."

"Darren, it's important that you understand you're not under caution. The boss just wants to find out what happened to Natalie. He doesn't want you to worry about dropping yourself in it. You can tell us anything if it helps the investigation."

It was obvious Adams didn't understand.

"OK Darren, let me give you an example. We know you must've taken heroin before we picked you up. Now that's a crime as you know. But we're not interested in that or whether you've been out burgling or dealing if it helps you remember details about your time with Natalie. Do you understand now?"

Adams looked completely lost and confused. He'd spent most of his life trying to evade capture and lying to the police, and yet here he was sat in a police station being told that he could talk freely about the crimes he'd committed to a pretty detective and no action would be taken. He must have thought this was some kind of wind up or that he was dreaming. It was a tactic I'd learned from Mr Taylor on the Samantha Class inquiry. It was an inspired decision on his part and it came with the full support of the CPS.

"OK, if you say so, doesn't sound fucking right to me though."

In an afterthought he said.

"Oh, sorry for swearing."

He really was trying to impress Karen.

"Can I just confirm that you're a heroin addict and that you've scored today?"

Adams shifted in his seat and looked from Karen to Phil as if he didn't know what to say. But, eventually, he held his nerve and nodded.

"Does that nod mean yes?"

"Yes, yes."

If he'd expected a load of hairy-arsed coppers to burst through the door and arrest him, he must have been pleasantly surprised when Karen continued.

"Darren, let's make a start and see how we go. We're only interested in your time with Natalie. But can we start with you. Tell us about your family and childhood."

"It was fucking shit. Sorry, it was shit. Me and Shaun lived with my Dad before he stuck us in foster care. Stacey stayed with our Mam. He was a nasty bastard. Sorry again."

"Look Darren, swear if you want to. Don't worry about offending me. Really."

"Me and Shaun ended up at Stockton."

"That's an approved school near York isn't it?"

"Yes. Left as soon as I could. Got a flat on Spring Bank in Hull."

Karen was doing really well. All her questions gave him the opportunity to tell the truth and his body language was open, relaxed and he sat upright as he spoke confidently about his relationships with women. He remembered their names - Patricia, Susanne, Davina, Johanna, and Sarah - but not surnames or dates. Occasionally, his concentration wandered and his head drooped as if he was about to nod off. Karen brought him back by raising her voice slightly, and I wondered how long we had before he'd need to score again. We'd have to get him back home before then. Karen must have read my mind.

"Darren, can you tell us about Natalie."

He painted a picture of their loving relationship, how they met at William Booth House and immediately fell for each other.

"I really loved her. I used to beg her not to go out. I didn't like it but she needed to earn money for her habit."

With those words, his body language changed remarkably. He was obviously lying. We knew he was violent towards Natalie and that she was his means of funding his massive heroin addiction. This was no love affair, no great romance. I was no expert but even I could spot the change in his behaviour as the lies poured out of his mouth. Karen then hit him with the bombshell question.

"Who do you think killed Natalie?"

"Jodi Amadi. I ripped him off over some drugs. He must have killed her as revenge for the drugs I owed him."

"What about punters? We know you both ripped off punters at 119 St Johns Grove."

"Maybe, I don't know. Can't think straight."

He started to drift again but Karen hadn't finished yet.

"Darren, tell us who your friends are."

This should be interesting, I thought, as I looked at the never-ending list of friends and associates prepared by FIB.

"You tell me. Nini and Tony Beaumont until Natalie fucking left me for her. She came back but it was out of order. Fucking bastards. I called you lot to report her missing. I didn't know where she'd gone. I thought something had happened to her."

"How did it make you feel when she left you for Nini?"

"I was fucking angry. Wouldn't you be? I missed her, I loved her."

"Angry enough to kill Natalie yourself?"

"No fucking way. I loved her, why would I kill her? I've told you it was that sick bastard Amadi. Why don't you lock the fucker up?"

"You reported her missing again after that according to our records."

"Yes, it wasn't long after we got back together again. She left one night for work and didn't come back. I went to Nini's to see if she'd gone back to her but they hadn't seen her."

"Where were you living before Natalie went missing?"

"With Ian Armstrong at his place in St Johns Grove."

"And afterwards?"

"With me brother Shaun and off and on at Mick Larvin's. I didn't want to be on me own. Armstrong moved out as well."

"Has anyone else been staying at St Johns Grove since you last saw her."

"Don't think so. Last time I looked it was boarded up."

Adams was clearly starting to rattle and so Karen closed the interview down. After Karen and Phil took Adams back to Morpeth Street, they joined Tony and me in my office to discuss his performance. Karen looked slightly nervous and flush in the face, which was understandable given that she was still young in service and had just conducted a video interview with someone who was of crucial importance to the investigation. Telling her that she did a first-class job, though, brought a smile to her face and her nervousness turned to pride in an instant.

"Karen, what do you think?"

"I think I did what you asked, Sir. Getting him to talk about stuff that we knew he wouldn't be lying about first was a good idea. When I asked him about Natalie his body language kind of changed, he stopped looking at me, his head went down and he began to shuffle."

We all agreed that Adams had been lying throughout most of the video apart from his hatred of Nini Thompson. Had he killed her because he was jealous over Natalie's relationship with Nini? Was there any truth in his accusations about Jodi Amadi? Anything was possible. I knew that we needed a break, something to give the investigation positive direction. The forensic search of 119 St Johns Grove would either rule it in or out as a possible scene. If DS Pickering proved to be right, then I'd no idea what to do next.

PART 2

THE GATHERING

MOMENTUM

TWELVE

'DC Long designated the discovery exhibit TML/4'

I met DC Long outside 119 St Johns Grove around eight-thirty. He arrived in a white SOCO van. A marked police van pulled up behind him driven by a young constable. I'd arranged for a uniform presence to make sure that our vehicles weren't set on fire or stoned by the locals.

"Morning, boss. This is Martin Eddows, the scientist from Wetherby I told you about."

"Good to meet you, Martin. I'm Paul the SIO."

Martin gazed for a moment at the house we were about to enter. The ugly patchwork of thick metal guarding the front door and windows, and wasteland of a garden, made it look more like a prison than a dwelling.

"It's a bloody mess inside and the smell will turn your stomach, I'm afraid."

We put on white protective suits and overshoes and entered via the back door that led straight into the kitchen. The stench was still the same. We each took a room to search. I made my way carefully upstairs to start on the bedrooms holding a powerful flashlight to guide my way through the rubbish, knee deep in places. The ventilation holes in the boarded-up windows looked like an expert marksman had pierced the shutters. There was a bed in one of the rooms that had a filthy, badly stained mattress perched on a metal frame. No furniture, nothing but blood-stained clothing and used needles strewn about the bare floorboards. The dark staining on the walls looked like blood, and I wondered how many punters had been up here with Natalie, how many turned over by Adams.

I carefully bagged each item of clothing and each needle ready for forensic examination. It seemed to take hours, but it was important for me to experience as much as I could. Being briefed about something had its limitations. I knew that I had to make a decision whether or not to formally designate this place as a scene. As I breathed in the desolation of my surroundings, why couldn't it be here, I thought, as I made my way downstairs. And then, half way down, Tim shouted for me to come to the kitchen. He sounded excited.

"Look what we found in the kitchen. Got a newspaper dated 18 May. Looks like blood spots to me on the front page. Might help. Loads of clothing with maybe blood staining. Now I don't want you to get too excited yet but just take a look at this. We found it amongst all the rubbish."

He showed me what appeared to be a small piece of human tissue with what looked like head hairs clumped together. It was maybe the size of a ten pence coin, and it was stuck to the surface of a plastic bin bag. My heart skipped several beats, and my gut feeling was that this could be a piece of scalp ripped from someone's head. It wasn't like anything I'd seen before.

"What do you think? Looks like hair similar to Natalie's. Dyed similar to hers."

"We both agree it could be."

"Mind you both don't get too excited."

They were both calm and collected. I was the exact opposite.

"Early days yet boss, but I think we were right to keep an open mind and conduct a proper search otherwise it would've been missed. I'd like to take this place apart from top to bottom. There're some new techniques I'd like to try out. I'll work with Martin on the detail and let you know if that's OK."

I couldn't help it, I felt like punching the air. Could this be the break I was waiting for? Fast track DNA would give me the result in the next couple of days. Tim and Martin continued as if nothing had happened. I expected nothing less from true professionals. He also showed me three pairs of female ankle boots recovered from a larder off the kitchen. One pair was cut open down the middle of each boot. I looked at Tim and he knew what I was thinking - if Natalie was wearing them when she was killed, it'd be the only way to remove them. Pulling them off would be difficult due to the degree of bloating after death. Martin agreed to take them back with him for testing. There were still hours of work to do. I thanked them both before heading back to HQ to break the news to Tony and the team.

On the way, I thought about what to tell them. I didn't want to get their hopes up just as Tim and Martin had rightly cautioned, but I'd a strong sense that it would be Natalie's

DNA and when I briefed everyone on the search, I couldn't hold back my absolute joy at what we'd found. Tim designated the discovery as exhibit TML/4.

A couple of days passed. Surely the result would be back soon, I thought. Whenever the phone rang, my stomach churned hoping it was Martin Eddows with the result of the DNA test. Everyone else kept looking at me through the office window whenever I picked up the phone. I couldn't blame them for hanging around the incident room. They were on edge just as much as Tony and me.

On the morning of 20 August, I answered the telephone and it was Martin.

"I'll get straight to the point. I've tested item TML/4, the piece of tissue we found the other day. Good news. It's definitely Natalie Clubb's DNA."

"That's brilliant. You know what my next question's going to be. Can you tell me exactly what it is? Looks to me like a piece of her scalp that's been ripped from her head. What do you think?"

"I don't know yet. But I am in a position to say that the hairs attached to the piece of tissue have bare root ends and were therefore actively pulled out and not lost by natural shedding or cutting. I'll need to carry out mitochondrial DNA testing on the hair to see if matches hair from the post-mortem. But I've visually compared them both and they show similar patterns of dying. Looks like she dyed red and blonde at different times. I'd say her natural colour was a dull dark brown."

"Are you able to say if you think it was torn from her head in a struggle of some kind? I just want your opinion off the record."

"My guess would be yes, but that's all it is, a guess."

I didn't press him further. I knew he wouldn't be prepared to commit himself without hard evidence. I understood and respected him for that, but it didn't stop me from using common sense to speculate on how a piece of Natalie's scalp had found its way onto a bin bag inside 119 St John's Grove. I knew I'd a mountain to climb to prove a connection between her murder and TML/4, but it was a start.

"What about the bin bag for fingerprints? How long will it take?"

"I was going to suggest we have a case conference to discuss a forensic strategy for the items recovered. There's twenty-eight pieces of clothing that all look to be heavily bloodstained, a newspaper with spots of blood, thirty black bin liners, a blood-stained glove inside a Weetabix box, I could go on."

"I agree. I'll set one up but, in the meantime, can you fast track that bin bag. I could really do with knowing who's handled it."

"Of course, I understand. Will do."

I could see Tony hovering until I put the phone down. I went out into the incident room. Everyone had miraculously assembled and they all looked towards me waiting for news. I put on a really glum, miserable face for effect.

"That was the forensic scientist. You're not going to believe it but that piece of tissue we found on the bin bag's human and you're not going to believe it but it's bloody well Natalie's. Fucking amazing, fucking amazing. And to think we could've missed it all together."

Tony was the first to speak.

"You're kidding. I don't mean to gloat but I'm going to. We were right all along to trust our instincts about the house. Are you ready for some more good news? We've been dead busy doing house to house and this morning we've got a statement from a neighbour who says she saw a blue Sierra arrive mid-afternoon sometime in May she thinks. Adams was with two other males. They disappeared round the back of the house and came out carrying bin bags, put them in the boot and drove off at speed. And Larvin's got a blue Sierra."

"Is the witness reliable?"

"Looks like she is. She's a cleaner at the local school. Do you want me to get the officers who took the statement?"

"No, it's OK. We've got enough for me to formally policy Adams as a suspect based on TML/4 alone. I know the house has been left insecure and anybody could've been in and out. What do you think?"

"Definitely. I know we're going to keep an open mind but it gives us something to focus on at the teatime briefing."

We sat and chatted with the team for a while over a coffee to enjoy the moment, and discuss what action to take now that Adams was a suspect for the murder and dismemberment of Natalie. We knew we'd have to make our own luck by putting pressure on Adams, his friends and associates. Tony came to life clearly relishing the idea of taking the fight to Adams. His RCS experience would be useful, and it was agreed that he'd take responsibility for putting 24/7 surveillance on Adams. I wanted to know every move he made from now on. If he did kill Natalie, would he lead us to Natalie's missing left arm and parts of her legs? Did he have another prostitute to provide money for his heroin addiction or was he committing crime instead? If he was committing burglaries, was he doing it alone or with someone else? Adams was already on bail for house burglary and a further arrest would keep him in custody on remand.

The phone call had changed everything. There was an air of heightened expectation as the team prepared themselves to get onto the streets and unravel the mystery surrounding TML/4. The investigation now had clear direction, and it was time to put the pressure on Adams and those who had access to 119 St Johns Grove. It was also time to conduct a proper and thorough forensic search of the address.

Back in my office, DC Long called to see me with a bloody great smile on his face. I knew that he'd been given a hard time by some of his colleagues for being the one to prove DS Pickering's initial assessment to be wrong. I understood why. It was just the culture of the police. But I knew that what I was about to say would brighten his day.

"Look, I want you to take responsibility for the forensic search of 119 St Johns Grove. Adams is now a suspect after TML/4. I'm really interested to hear what you think."

His eyes sparkled as he confidently began to brief me on how he proposed to tackle 119 St Johns Grove. Armed with the latest forensic techniques available to SOCOs, this opportunity for him to prove his worth must have seemed like a gift from heaven. But it presented a very real challenge. The house had been left empty for some time and so any half-decent defence barrister would argue that anyone could have had access. And they'd be right. I knew we'd have to literally take the house apart, based on the belief that Natalie was murdered and dismembered inside, or at least dismembered there even if she was killed somewhere else. If the house was the scene of her murder, what physical evidence might be waiting to be discovered and how would we go about recovering it?

"Boss, my plan is to search for latent blood and fingerprints on items recovered from inside the house. I'm sure there'll be numerous prints from anyone who's been in the house together with those from Armstrong, Adams and Natalie, but I think we should do all the exposed surfaces, including walls and doors. I've not done anything like this before on such a big scale. It's going to mean spraying with two reagents, Luminol to detect blood and DFO for fingerprints. It'll take some time I'm afraid."

It was a judgement call. We'd no option but to try and identify every person who'd been inside the house from blood and fingerprints. Although Adams was now the number one suspect, I had to keep an open mind. I couldn't rule out Amadi, an angry punter, or some other low-life with a score to settle with either Natalie or Adams.

I made myself a strong coffee. It was getting late and I was tired. My in-tray was piled high with numerous statements to read. The team had conducted sixty video interviews already from mainly friends and associates of Natalie and Adams. Each statement taken generated more and more actions for my outside team to complete. I didn't have the latest figures but there'd be hundreds of actions already on HOLMES. I always worried about missing something. It could be the smallest detail that could make all the difference at a subsequent trial.

I stood up and wrote on the white board all of the things I'd want to tell a jury if they were here now, all the stuff they'd never be aware of during a trial. It would be ordinary people sat on a jury who'd need to be convinced beyond reasonable doubt about the guilt of Natalie's killer or killers, based on the evidence presented. And if it turned out that the evidence was purely circumstantial then, more than ever, they'd need to trust those presenting that evidence - from the barrister to the police officer, from the pathologist to the SOCO. They also needed to trust the SIO and the integrity of the investigation.

I imagined what my answer would be if they asked what I meant by the integrity of the investigation. I'd probably begin with the decision to video all witnesses. It was one that I was proud of because it demonstrated a desire to be as open and transparent as possible in our dealings with witnesses, who some might judge to be vulnerable and untrustworthy, given their addiction to hard drugs and desolate lifestyle. And if they understood why I'd made the decision, then maybe they'd have confidence in the prosecution case as a whole. But above all else, I'd want to somehow make them understand that it's the calibre of both my inside and outside teams that ultimately defines the outcome of an investigation.

Back in the real world, I felt a tingling sense of contentment because I knew that, regardless of what the future might hold, I was blessed with outstanding individuals that would always try to do the right thing. This is what I loved about being a SIO, I thought, and it was at times like these that I remembered why I'd left my career as a chemical engineer behind. It was for me the highest privilege to investigate the death of another human being. Nothing else came close. But as I closed my office door and headed for home, I knew there was a very long way to go before Natalie's killer or killers would be stood before a jury. I didn't doubt for one second that it would happen. I couldn't imagine ever giving up, no matter how long it took.

THIRTEEN

'She opened her naked legs wide and pointed to an open wound'

I wanted to know more about Nini Thompson and her relationship with Natalie, and so I met DC Andy Marshall and DS Kev Scarth outside 29 Ellerby Grove on Preston Road Estate, around four. It'd also give me the opportunity to judge whether we stood a chance of presenting her to the Crown Court as a credible witness, should she be called upon to do so.

"How do you want to play this boss?" asked DS Scarth.

"You two do the talking, I just want to meet her for myself. Will she be alone?"

"No, don't think so. Tony Beaumont will probably be there. He's a druggy as well."

They were both quiet, unassuming detectives. I was impressed with their contributions during briefings. DC Marshall was the more talkative and he'd grown in confidence since his arrival on the second day of the inquiry. I wondered how he'd manage the transition from watching people from the relative comfort of a surveillance squad vehicle, to the squalor we were about to encounter. I didn't have long to wait to find out.

Andy knocked on the front door. The curtains were

closed at each window. The door opened slowly to reveal a man in a filthy looking string vest, with his arms and neck covered in tattoos and numerous unhealthy-looking track marks.

"Tony, I'm DC Marshall, this is DS Scarth and DCI Davison."

I looked inside into the hallway. Most of the floorboards were missing and then the familiar smell hit me. Warm, sickly, smoke-filled, tinged with urine. He showed us into the living room. There was no furniture, no carpet, no comfort, just cigarette ends and used needles littering the floor. A small female figure sat motionless in front of a gas fire, with a dirty duvet wrapped around her shoulders. It looked to be covered in blood stains.

"Some coppers here to see you, Nini."

"Tell them to fuck off."

Nini was shaking and looked ill. Maybe she needed to score again but she didn't seem to be in the mood to talk, neither did her partner. Andy, without a moment's hesitation, sat down on the dirty floor next to Nini, put his arm around her and gave her a cuddle. It was a rare moment of compassion and understanding, and I watched in admiration as Nini opened up to Andy. She even apologised for her behaviour. It was like watching two old friends chatting about old times sat around a campfire, except for the trickle of blood visible on her left inner thigh. Andy noticed and asked her if she was OK. She just opened her naked legs wide and pointed to an open wound about the size of ten pence piece at the top of her groin.

"Fucking needles. Running out of places to score. Tony, I

need something soon. It's a fucking shame what happened to Nat. Hayley and Sam already gone."

"Can you tell us why Natalie came to stay with you a few weeks before she died?"

"To get away from that cunt of a boyfriend. She had a massive cut on her head where he smacked her with a metal coat hanger for not earning enough. She was high and dozing when he fucking smacked her and told her to get out and earn some money."

Nini looked worse, shaking more and sweating and so we decided to leave. I knew the sight of Nini and Andy sat on the floor together would live long in my memory for it was something I hadn't seen before. He was blessed with a rare gift, one that allowed him to somehow instantly connect with another person, regardless of their circumstances. I was really impressed.

On the way back to HQ, I thought about the haunted, drug-ridden pathetic figure of Nini, with her life ruined by addiction to heroin. Every day the same - sleep, score, prostitution. No wonder Natalie, according to her friends, weighed barely six stone when she died. When she'd arrived in Hull in search of a new life, Natalie had been a healthy twelve stone. And, after meeting Nini, I knew with absolute certainty that videoing witnesses on neutral ground, was exactly the right thing to do. But what would a jury make of her? It was a question I didn't know the answer to.

FOURTEEN

'How's the car Archie? Still going strong'

It was about two in the afternoon when Tony called.

"Boss, I'm at Queens Gardens. We've banged up Adams for burglary. No choice. I'll come up and see you when he's in a cell."

It wasn't long before Tony swept into my office looking really pleased with himself.

"You're not going to believe what happened. We followed him from the benefit offices in Hull to Albany Street. Without warning, in broad daylight, he barged into a terraced house, picked up a telly from the living room and calmly walked out onto the street. It was that big he couldn't see where he was going. The woman and her kids were watching it at the time. She chased after him with a baseball bat, but he put the telly down and told her to fuck off or else he'd stick the bat up her arse. We'd no option but to lock him up. The job never ceases to surprise me."

This was good news. At least we had him where we could keep an eye on him. I was just about to call DCS Jordan with the news when he walked through the door.

"Sir, I was just about to call you. Adams has been locked up committing a burglary."

I told him the story and he laughed. It was a moment of light relief before he got down to business.

"The ACC wants a review of your case conducting as soon as possible. He wants a meeting at five today to decide who's going to do it and suitable terms of reference. He wants you there."

"Sir, do you know who's in the running?"

"Can't say, I'm afraid."

I wasn't looking forward to the meeting and so I changed the subject and asked him how he was enjoying being the head of CID. By the way he looked at me, he knew that I was asking a great deal more than that. He knew that I was really asking if he was coping, given the extraordinary circumstances facing the force with unsolved prostitute murders and talk of a Ripper-style serial killer on the loose. And then there was his personal position having to supervise strong SIOs with far more experience than him, and keeping his fingers crossed that his faith in me with the most complex of them all, wasn't misplaced. It's a wonder how he slept at night, I thought. His face was less boyish than I remembered. He seemed to have aged in just a few weeks and he looked tired. I formed the impression that he wanted to say more before he left but he didn't. The police force was no place for such a gentleman, I thought, never mind the head of CID.

I took a deep breath as I made my way to the ACC's office. It was a strange atmosphere on the chief officers' corridor. Quiet and stuffy, and I wondered if any of them realised just how far removed they were from reality, from the public they were supposed to serve. I saw that the door of Chief Inspector Archie Jenkins' office was slightly ajar, and my spirits lifted for a moment, hoping to see the friendly face of the Chief Constable's staff officer. Archie was completely crackers and not at all like any other senior officer I'd come across. Short, with dark hair and a magnificent moustache that seemed to dominate the features of his face, he was known for wearing crumpled white police shirts that had never felt the heat of an iron. He went jogging at lunchtime every day, and his tiny office became a kind of airing cupboard for his running gear. His filing system for important documents was his desk that was perpetually piled high, almost to the ceiling. I knocked on the open door and Archie's face appeared from behind the pile of papers on his desk. He had to stand up to see me.

"Still not heard of filing cabinets, I see."

"Paul good to see you, cheeky sod. Filing cabinets would spoil things. I know where everything is. All at my fingertips."

I couldn't disagree. They were certainly all within easy reach but one wrong move and they'd all come crashing down around him.

"How's the car Archie? Still going strong?"

Archie owned a bright green Morris Minor and its claim to fame was an occasion when he went to a conference with the previous DCC, who prided himself on his immaculate appearance. They went separately but, at the conclusion of the day, the DCC asked Archie for a lift to a formal function hosted by the High Sheriff at County Hall. Archie panicked. He realised that the DCC was dressed in his very best uniform, and he formed a mental picture of him climbing into the passenger seat of his beloved Morris. The problem was that his car hadn't been cleaned for years: old apple cores, dog hairs, and half-eaten chocolate bars, covered the seats and carpets. He'd tried to wriggle his way out of the DCC's request but it was no good.

He feared the worst when the DCC opened the passenger side door and looked inside, but he appeared not to notice what he was about to sit on. The subsequent journey passed with Archie encouraging the DCC to talk about his favourite subject, himself. When the DCC finally got out of the car, he must have looked an odd sight: front - immaculate, back - covered in dog hairs and chocolate stains from shoulder to ankle. To Archie's relief, the DCC never asked for a lift again.

"What brings you up here?"

"Come now, you must know why I'm up here. You know everything that goes on. Time to go. Don't want to keep the ACC waiting."

He disappeared back behind his walls of paper. It was good to see a friendly face. Being a SIO was the best job in the world as far as I was concerned but it was also a lonely one. It was no surprise to discover that I was the last one to arrive.

"Paul, come in. Just about to start."

Superintendent Bland and Superintendent Dalton were sat opposite the ACC and DCS Jordan. I assumed that they were both in the running to conduct the review. They didn't look at all comfortable and neither would I if I was in their position, with absolutely no detective experience between them, never mind serious crime.

"I'll get straight to the point. I've talked it over with DCS Jordan and I want one of you two to review Paul's job. Who wants to do it?"

The news that they were being asked to review my case appeared to take them by surprise. They looked at each other for a moment and to his credit, quick as a flash, Superintendent Dalton volunteered. Superintendent Bland looked relieved. It was one of the shortest meetings I'd ever been to. Outside the ACC's office, I took Superintendent Dalton to one side. I didn't know him that well, but I knew that he'd need a great deal of help from an experienced SIO to even know where to begin the review, never mind be of any help to me. He must have sensed my frustration at what had just happened.

"I take it you're not happy with me doing it."

"It's not that Sir, it just doesn't make any sense to put you in such a position. I don't think it's fair on you given your uniform background. It's just not your area of expertise. With respect, can I suggest you ask an experienced SIO to support you? Maybe Grahame Bullock, you'll need some help."

"I understand and thank you for the suggestion. No offence taken. It's a good idea."

After he'd gone, I hoped that he'd take my advice and ask DCI Bullock to help him. I wanted someone of his expertise to scrutinise what progress I'd made to make sure I hadn't missed anything. Grahame was far more experienced than me and, if I received his approval, then the ACC would be reassured that DCS Jordan's faith in me hadn't been misplaced. I reflected on the short meeting and how revealing it was to watch two officers of the same rank react so differently in difficult circumstances. Superintendent Dalton accepted the task with good grace, and although it would be a massive and steep learning curve for him, the experience would increase his awareness of how the force investigated serious crime. He'd chosen a different career path in the police and looked to be far more at peace with the world than I was. But his path wasn't mine, and I'm pretty sure he wouldn't want to swap places with me if he were able to spend a day in my shoes right now. It was a missed opportunity for Superintendent Bland, I thought, one that may not come again in his career.

When I got back to the incident room, I was more than surprised to see the Chief Constable chatting to staff. I'd never seen a chief officer in any incident room, never mind my own. My immediate thought was negative, as usual. Had I done something wrong? It was a feeling that turned my stomach for a moment but I decided to approach him with an air of confidence. His reaction was not what I expected. He was friendly towards me, shook my hand and asked to be briefed on progress with the investigation.

After he left, Tony came in for a coffee.

"What did the Chief want?"

"Just wanted a briefing on progress. He was OK to be fair. He was the last person I expected to see."

"I know. We didn't get any warning he just walked in. It was good for the staff to see a chief officer interested in the job. Any road, any news about the review. Go on who's doing it?"

"Superintendent Dalton. It was between him and

Superintendent Bland. To his credit Mr Dalton volunteered straight away. I've asked him to consider getting Grahame Bullock to help him with the investigation side of the review. I'm going to do a fairly in-depth report about progress to date to help the review team. Can you let me have a breakdown of all the relevant stuff I'm going to need. Number of statements, actions generated and so on. You know HOLMES inside out better than anyone."

"Will do. When do you need it for?"

"As soon as you can. The review date has been set for early September."

FIFTEEN

'What colour is that red bike?'

The journey into work gave me time to think. Although it was a bright September day, there were signs that autumn was on the horizon and I realised that summer had passed me by. I was apprehensive about what the day might bring. This was my first major inspection conducted by my peers; all my previous cases were solved fairly quickly, without the need for them to be reviewed. But I felt confident about presenting my report to an audience that would include the ACC, DCS Jordan, Superintendent Dalton, and DCI Bullock. I'd spent many hours writing it because I wanted to do justice to the progress made by my team, and I imagined that if Natalie were watching over the investigation, she'd be happy with what had been achieved so far.

Since the meeting with the ACC, Superintendent Dalton had managed to enlist the help of Grahame Bullock. I smiled as I recalled Grahame's nickname, Banana Boots, given to him by Ted Grantham, who used to be one of my sergeants. It was one of the things I liked about the police, nobody was ever called by their real name. Grahame's came from playing football. He remained under the impression that he was a top-flight footballer and to be fair to him, he was pretty good, but try as he might to kick a ball straight, he didn't have much success. It invariably tracked a course the shape of a banana, which caused his teammates to have to guess where on the pitch the ball would land, to their obvious frustration. When Ted saw this for the first time, Grahame's nickname was born in an instant and it'd stayed with him ever since.

I arrived at the conference room early. I was always early for everything. I reasoned that it was better to be there before everybody else, so that I wouldn't have to enter a room and be looked at. How ridiculous, I thought, for a supposedly strong SIO to suffer from such an unreasonable character flaw, one that I'd grown up with and hated. At school, it'd caused me to stutter badly if I'd to read aloud in class. As a consequence, I avoided asking questions of teachers at all costs, which often led me to soldier on in blind ignorance over something I didn't understand rather than seek help.

I shook my head at just how much I was influenced in later life by those early years. I contributed very little at meetings or conferences, even if I'd something worthwhile to say, and here I was again sat alone waiting nervously for others to arrive. Would I ever be able to break the cycle? I had to believe that I would, because I spent far too much time each day dwelling on how best to tackle any contact or interaction with my fellow human beings. It was funny in a tragic kind of way as I calculated in my head just how much time I'd wasted over the years in a state of almost permanent anxiety for no good reason. It didn't make any sense to me, and I'm pretty sure it wouldn't make any sense to my colleagues and peers, if they knew.

The morning sun streamed through the windows overlooking Queens Gardens. I'd looked out onto the same gardens many times during my career. The first was when I'd come down from Aberdeen for an interview to join the police. I was working for a firm of consultant chemical engineers at the time. I didn't like being a chemical engineer and looking back, I couldn't understand why I'd studied for God knows how many years to become one. But as I travelled on the overnight coach to Hull, I hoped that it wasn't too late to change direction. The interview went well but my medical didn't. In those days, a female police officer assisted a doctor to carry out medicals. When it came to the colour-blind test, I failed to the absolute delight of the female officer, who could have given most burly rugby players a run for their money. Upon learning of the outcome of the test, the doctor peered over his glasses and summoned me to the window overlooking Queens Gardens.

"What colour is that red bike?"

"Red."

"Very good. Now what colour is that green tree?"

"Green."

"Officer, it appears that this young gentleman has passed the colour-blind test."

The doctor clearly enjoyed seeing the officer's face turn from delight to the appearance akin to a bulldog chewing a wasp. I couldn't believe what'd just happened and I've never forgotten the doctor who changed the course my life. That wouldn't happened today, I thought, with our strict health and safety mad policies that seemed to infiltrate every aspect of the force.

Superintendent Dalton brought DCI Grahame Bullock and a small team of individuals to help probe different aspects of the investigation. The ACC was accompanied by DCS Jordan. Tony, ADI Holding and DC Long were my support. I opened my presentation full of confidence, although I knew that DCI Bullock had way more experience as a SIO than me and I'd have to be at the top of my game to impress him. Tony gave me a reassuring glance. It felt at that moment like we'd something to prove.

"Today is the forty-third day of the inquiry. The investigation has progressed from the discovery of a right severed arm to a position of strength. There is a number one suspect in Darren Adams and a likely scene at 119 St Johns Grove. This is a challenging case and we look forward to a robust and forensic examination of the lines of inquiry I set and we welcome any assistance you're able to give me and my team."

The ACC replied,

"I'll hand you over to Superintendent Dalton now. I've another meeting to attend."

"Paul, we've all read your very comprehensive report and so I'd like to get straight to the point. How confident are you that you'll solve the case?"

I told them that I was sure that we'd get a result. I recalled the time after the second post-mortem, when I'd sat in my kitchen at home and thought about how to use the information that only we and Natalie's killer or killers knew – the cause of her death. I went on to explain in elaborate detail why my initial gut instinct to keep the stab wounds out of the public domain, has been the main focus of the investigation.

"Some of you are aware of the covert operations we've put in place as a consequence of that policy. Their best chance of success is if we can be pretty sure that any information we receive is pure and can only have come from the killers or killers."

I couldn't talk openly about the nature of those operations; they had to be kept secret so they wouldn't be compromised. Detective Superintendent Taylor, who was in overall command of the policy on covert policing, had agreed to the specific tasking of informants to seek information from the criminal fraternity about Natalie's murder. This approach hadn't been used before. It meant snouts being paid to grass by their detective handlers. It was a long shot and fraught with problems. Trusting criminals was never a good idea. The Chief had also agreed for us to bug a number of homes, including Michael Larvin's and Ian Armstrong's. They seemed a logical place to start: Larvin was Adams's closest friend and they'd a long history of committing crime together, and Armstrong was also a friend and associate of Adams and he'd sublet 119 St Johns Grove to Natalie and Adams.

I wondered whether I'd live to regret my confident words in the future. Would I become to be known as the inexperienced DCI with potential who didn't quite make it? If I didn't gain a conviction, would I be moved back into uniform and be put out to grass? But as I looked across the table, I knew that even DCI Bullock with all his experience hadn't dealt with anything like this before. It didn't stop them giving me a hard time though as they probed in some depth every aspect of the investigation.

The review seemed to go on forever and by late afternoon, I was exhausted. DCS Jordan ended the day by raising the issue of whether or not there was any evidence to suggest that Natalie's murder could be linked to Class, Morgan and Tomlinson. It was an issue that must be keeping him awake at night, I thought. When he'd agreed to have his career developed as head of CID, I'm pretty sure that he got much more than he'd bargained for, thrust into the national media headlights over talk of another Ripper on the loose. But he'd acquitted himself with an air of confidence and came across as articulate and trustworthy. His posh accent helped. He didn't suffer from the local Hull dialect that was unmistakable and unfortunately made people 'sound' less intelligent than they were. I was pleased for him, and you could almost see the relief in his expression as collectively we all came the same conclusion: there was no evidence to link any of the deaths. The MOs were all significantly different. The only common factors were heroin and prostitution.

Given DCS Jordan's skillful denials over rumours of another Ripper, there was a problem keeping the press interested. Apparently, the other SIOs had faced the same waning of interest over time. The tragic death of Princess Diana a few days earlier, was worldwide news and would be for some considerable time to come - there'd be no loss of interest, ever. In complete contrast, Natalie was just another working prostitute in the eyes of the media judged to be less worthy than the rest of us. It was my job and the responsibility of my team, not to let Natalie be seen in that way by the public. Even though it was turning out to be an uphill struggle, Lisa was doing a first-class job in keeping my face on the TV, and there'd been a moment of light relief when Superintendent Dalton had asked about the media strategy. With a grin on his face, Tony offered,

"What's the difference between DCI Davison and Emmerdale? Emmerdale's only on three times a week."

Apparently, that was the joke being repeated across the force with a healthy degree of sarcasm. But I couldn't care less. All that mattered was keeping Natalie in the public domain. We'd had to concede that there was very little information coming in from the public, despite the staged reconstruction in Alfred Gelder Street, and the appeal for punters to come forward. The operation on Waterhouse Lane to stop vehicles did identify a number of regular customers, but they'd been subsequently eliminated from the inquiry. We'd used Maxine to point them out, and when questioned, it was funny how they'd all made a 'wrong turn' into Waterhouse Lane by 'mistake'.

Grahame caught my eye before we left.

"Fancy a coffee?"

He walked back to my office with Tony and me. A few of the incident room staff said hello to Grahame in a very warm and friendly way. He was popular, particularly with the ladies. He possessed a kind face and an infectiously positive attitude that was uplifting to be around. His only problem, as far as I could see, was that he appeared to have it all: good looks, intelligence, confidence and bags of ability. Normally, that'd mean he'd be destined for high office but not in the police.

Grahame had about twenty-five years' service and was still only a Chief Inspector. I say only a Chief Inspector because in my opinion, he should've been an ACC by now. He'd missed out on promotion a few times and I knew he was frustrated. They'd stuck him in Community Safety to write force policy on the recently introduced Crime and Disorder Act to further his career. In reality, it meant being moved sideways to get him out of the way.

"That was impressive my friend. How do you think it went?"

Tony brought in the drinks and closed the door behind him, as he left us to talk.

"OK, I think. I'm confident about the way the investigations going but I don't know who to trust. Something just doesn't feel right. I feel like an outcast fighting the way things have always been done."

"I know what you mean but you'd better get used to it, you look the part, you're competent, and you thrive on challenging the old way of doing things. I don't fit into their view of how a senior officer should behave and neither do you. It's nothing personal, it's just that you make them nervous."

Grahame stayed in the incident room for a while flirting with the female staff. He once told me that he never suffered from nerves and thought it likely that they'd been removed at birth. I'd give anything to be more like him, I thought, as I imagined his every waking moment being filled with an inner confidence from knowing that he was at peace with the world. It was like he'd figured out how everything worked, how one thing affected another. I remember once asking him about the new Crime and Disorder Act and its purpose. His explanation was simply breathtaking - his understanding of the key issues was as if the Act was his idea in the first place. Impressive.

Tony came in for a chat about how the day had gone.

"Bloody hell Tony, it was like the fucking third degree but it's been really useful. Grahame's not found anything we've missed, which is a good sign."

"Mr Dalton was only doing his job. He was right to give you a hard time. Knowing you, you'd have been disappointed with anything less. You'd have done the same if you'd been asked to review another case."

Tony was right, of course. What goes around comes around sprang to mind as I thought about my review of the Morgan case and how critical I'd been.

"I hope you don't mind me saying so but you're demanding, you expect everybody to meet the standards you've set for yourself and you get disappointed if they don't meet them. I'm afraid you're going to be disappointed a great deal."

John Goddard appeared at the door and before long, my office was full. People were anxious to know the outcome of the review. In hindsight, I should have arranged a briefing but I didn't know how long we'd be. I was pleased to be surrounded by so many of the team. I didn't feel like being alone and I wasn't ready to go home. There would be no better time than now to have our own review. The problem was that the investigation had generated a staggering amount of information and we needed to stand back and reflect on what to do next. I recalled DCS Jordan's bewilderment at the briefing he'd attended as he tried to keep up with, and make sense of, what was being said. He couldn't but I'd no choice. I was the SIO and today was a timely reminder that I was responsible for every aspect of the investigation. I couldn't think of a more demanding or exhausting job, with the vultures circling for the kill, should I put a foot wrong. It was easy to understand why most senior officers avoided becoming a SIO like the plague. They were probably at home now, I thought, and I'd be here for God knows how long. But I wouldn't swap places with any of them, not for anything.

We started with when we believed that Natalie had been murdered. It'd proved to be one of the most difficult things to determine due to the putrefied state of Natalie's body parts. I'd received the pathologist's report and his estimated date of death was early to mid-May. The forensic entomologist was, as I'd expected, unable to help. As he'd told me, there are too many variables: don't know where Natalie was killed, how long her body parts were in the drain, and what temperatures were involved. I knew that I needed a more specific date than early to mid-May. There were only two reliable corroborated sightings of Natalie before her disappearance: uniformed patrol officers stopped Natalie in a taxi on 5 May, and an independent and drug free witness, Angie Moore, discovered Natalie in bed with Ian Armstrong at 66 Ryehill Grove on 12 May. This was verified by Moore's social worker. There were no corroborated sightings of Natalie after this date and, because Adams reported her missing from a public phone box two days later, we had to go with our best guess in the circumstances. She must have been murdered sometime between 12 and 14 May. That's all we had.

We moved on to Natalie's friends and associates. There were over sixty. All had either been seen or were in the process of being seen by detectives working in pairs. Apart from probation and social workers, the rest were fellow prostitutes, drug dealers or pimps. They all had their story to tell about Natalie and her relationship with Adams. It was bleak, cruel and violent. No wonder Natalie tried to escape by going to live with Nini Thompson. The FIB had identified numerous friends and associates of Adams, all criminals, all thoroughly dishonest with no moral code. How on earth would we be able to believe a word any of them said?

"Boss, to give you an idea of the kind of people we're dealing with. Dougie McKenzie burgled his own house to feed his habit. Sold his own kid's PlayStation he'd got from his Grandma for Christmas. Kid was heartbroken."

Whilst DC Marshall's comments made me almost want to give up on the human race, they showed that the policy of granting immunity to criminals who admitted crimes in an effort to help the investigation, was working. In McKenzie's case, Andy wanted evidence of his movements at certain times and dates and the reported burglary to the police provided the necessary corroboration. But I wanted to know how he'd managed to get him to admit the crime.

"I've known him for some time. Always been able to talk to villains. I'll admit it took a long time to gain his trust but I just talk to them like I'm a mate. The bit about immunity if he helped me came as a shock to him but it's one of the best things we could've done. It's really made it a lot easier. Without it, we'd be getting nowhere."

Everybody agreed and I had to take my hat off to Detective Superintendent Taylor for coming up with the idea in the first place. But it was unfamiliar territory for everyone including the experienced detectives. It just didn't feel right. In normal circumstances, you'd be lucky to get a criminal to reveal their name, never mind admit to committing a crime.

I remembered bringing a prisoner into the charge room as a young probationer and presenting him to the custody sergeant. Custody sergeants in those days tended to be ex-army without much of a sense of humour. When the sergeant asked for his name, the prisoner cockily replied.

"Donald fucking Duck."

"So, you think you're a bit of a comedian. I'll ask you nicely one more time. What's your name?"

"Donald fucking Duck. What's the fucking matter you bastard deaf?"

The sergeant calmly stopped typing, walked purposely from behind the counter, got hold of the prisoner's head with both hands and smashed his face down hard onto the wooden surface. His nose exploded, blood everywhere.

"Now, I'll ask you one more time, what's your fucking name you little shit?"

"Fuck off, you fat twat," came the reply.

Eventually, after three or four more bangs to the head, the prisoner had a change of heart and gave up his name. It was the first time I'd seen anything like it in the custody suite. Unfortunately, the Inspector came in for his usual cup of tea just as the prisoner was about to be taken to a cell.

Upon seeing the sorry blood-soaked state of the prisoner, he asked how he'd come by his injuries. The sergeant explained that the prisoner had, for no reason, suddenly and repeatedly banged his head on the counter and that they were powerless to stop him.

"Well done for trying lads. Usual please, milk and two sugars," as the Inspector yawned and settled down to read the paper.

It was a good thing for everyone concerned that routine videoing of custody suites, although inevitable, was still some way off. The odd assault on a prisoner wasn't the only thing that shouldn't have been allowed to happen in the cells but it did. It wasn't just prisoners that considered themselves to be comedians, most of my shift did too. Two of my colleagues in particular possessed a razor-sharp eye for seeking out any opportunity to spread their brand of humour.

I recalled one occasion when 'eye' was the operative word. They taped a very authentic looking glass eye to the small round inspection hole in one of the cell doors. From inside, the poor prisoner would've seen what looked like a person's eye looking right at them, never blinking, just staring. It drove the prisoner mad and he screamed and screamed for the 'person' to stop spying on him. The two officers responded by singing as a duet, 'I Fought the Law and the Law Won' by the Clash as they danced arm in arm outside the cell door. Looking back, it was a hilarious episode for those of us working at that time. Although it would be frowned upon these days and rightly so, it still brought a smile to my face whenever I thought about those lost times.

As much as I enjoyed reminiscing, it was getting late and the optimism generated by proudly justifying my policies all day at the review, seemed to evaporate as we summarised the progress made so far. It sounded like a lot in terms of the lines of inquiry set by Tony and me: media appeals; forensic examination of both scenes; toxicology and histology tests following the post-mortems; videoing all associates of Natalie and Adams; POLSA led searches of local rivers and drains; and tasking informants and bugging houses, to name but a few. But in reality, all we had was a piece of Natalie's scalp discovered in 119 St Johns Grove, and the belief that it must have been ripped from her head with a fair degree of violence. It certainly wasn't shed naturally.

"OK, so from everything you've heard, it's time to decide, Adams or somebody else? I think we all know this case is unique, different, complex. Shaun, can you give us your perspective, you probably know more than anybody."

I asked Shaun because I was impressed with him and Rob Walker and the way they'd responded to being tasked with the demanding but prestigious role of interviewing officers. There were other equally talented detectives I could have chosen but from early in the investigation, Shaun in particular demonstrated the ability to memorise and recall detail at will.

"Boss, Rob and I have gone through just about everything, read everything that's come in so far. Adams has to be either ruled in or out. He's our only suspect and although there's no continuity at 119, we've got TML/4, the neighbour seeing bin bags being put into Larvin's car sometime in May, and his less than convincing video statement when he's clearly lying about Natalie's disappearance. We need somebody to come forward. If Adams is our man, there's no way he'll admit it. Never in a million years. Problem is how do we get somebody to talk. There's very little coming from any of the covert stuff or informants."

After Shaun finished, DC Marshall spoke with a fair degree of optimism and common sense.

"I believe it's Adams and I think somebody'll talk eventually. He must've had help from somebody, maybe Larvin or Armstrong. We just need to keep chipping away and keep an open mind. If you take Neil Pattison for instance, he knows more. I'm sure of it. And there are others who've got a lot more to tell. I think it's just a matter of time."

I could see DS Chapman with his hand raised waiting for the chance to speak. I knew him well from working together at Division and he was in every sense a gentle, friendly giant. From the very first time he'd knocked on my office door and entered as if in slow motion, I was impressed by the way he conducted himself: respectful, shy, articulate with bags of humility. Everybody liked him, with good reason, but I knew that it'd be difficult for him to make himself heard amongst his more confident colleagues.

"Mark, can you give us all your view on Amadi. Adams has done nothing else but blame him."

I hoped that he would summarise what he had to say. Brevity wasn't his strong point. I'd often hinted at the benefits of getting to the point but it just wasn't in his nature.

"Boss, thankyou…"

To his credit, although his contribution lasted for some time, he gave us all an impressive and detailed account of all the drug dealers he'd been looking into and Amadi, just like the rest, claimed to have a watertight alibi for when Natalie was killed. And then I put Mark on the spot.

"Could Amadi be responsible?"

He didn't look at all comfortable being the centre of attention. I'd seen it so many times before back at Division, there'd be a long pause before he spoke as if he needed time to prepare himself to deliver precisely what he wanted to say. He never said anything that couldn't be proved or corroborated and so I knew what was coming next.

"Well boss, I'm not sure. Difficult for me to say. There's no evidence linking him to the murder. Do I think he's capable of killing someone? Yes, I do. But I don't know why he'd want to kill Natalie. And in any case, if we're right about when Natalie was killed, then I don't see how he could be responsible. I've spent loads of time on his movements between the 12th and 14th of May, and he was in Bradford. No doubt I'm afraid."

Mark said much more and reminded us of the brutal and unforgiving sub-culture of violence that lived beneath the radar of reported crime. It was a world not seen by routine policing, and one that could only ever be exposed by this type of thorough and in-depth investigation. The beatings, kneecappings, and stabbings, occurred with alarming regularity but they were never disclosed to the police - they were accepted as an occupational hazard. And the more he spoke, the more it became clear that I was going to have to make a decision about who was responsible, based purely on gut instinct.

By now it was gone eight, and Mark's contribution seemed like a good place to end the discussion that still had Adams as our number one suspect because of TML/4, but not much more, and a question mark over whether I should rule out other possible suspects. Some headed off to the pub for a drink. Tony asked me but I declined. I wanted to get home to see my family. It'd been a very long day and I needed time to think.

I drove out of the station and through the city centre. the streets were alive with loud music booming out of the pubs and bars. It hadn't changed much since I patrolled the same area back in the early eighties, and tonight would probably be no different, I suspected. The alcohol-fuelled atmosphere would build throughout the evening and then, for no reason, there'd be an explosion of violence. I'd dealt with it so many times before. Extreme drunkenness led to the most horrific acts of aggression. A broken glass or bottle in the throat or face and stabbings, were commonplace every weekend.

On one occasion, I was called to a fight outside a pub. A male was sat on top of another pounding his face with his fist over and over again. When I eventually managed to drag him off, he admitted that he'd wanted to kill him because he didn't like the colour of the battered male's shirt. No wonder the average member of the public avoided the city centre like the plague.

It got me thinking about how most people spent their lives having to suffer things being done to them by others. Whether or not Adams killed Natalie, the moment they met, her life was destined for degradation, drug addiction and prostitution. Adams had no right to inflict his dark and menacing influence on a loving mother, who'd travelled to Hull for a new life with her children. But he'd done it anyway, without her permission, there was no one to stop him, no guardian watching over her to keep her safe. In life, her only purpose in the end was to earn money to buy heroin every day for herself and Adams. In death, at least Adams was behind bars and he'd be experiencing how it feels to have the tables turned on him for a change.

My head ached as I left the outskirts of the city behind and headed home. It was a dull, sickly, tired feeling caused by being emotionally and physically knackered. Every waking moment was spent trying to figure out where the evidence would come from. Usually, there'd be something conclusive that linked the criminal to the victim or scene, but not in this inquiry. In many ways, as the SIO, I felt helpless, frustrated and powerless. Although I'd done as much as I could to lead the investigation, I knew that the next few months were critical and it would be the detectives who'd shoulder the responsibility for getting people to talk. I hoped that they possessed the ability to operate within the criminal underworld, and somehow produce credible witnesses from heroin-addicted users, dealers, pimps and prostitutes, capable of testifying at Crown Court. The prospect of success didn't seem at all likely as my headlights lit up the country roads.

SIXTEEN

'I was pretty sure they weren't destined for greatness'

DCS Jordan came to see me a few days later armed with a copy of Superintendent Dalton's report. On the whole, it was good news. It concluded that my investigation was going in the right direction in treating Adams as a suspect but at the same time keeping an open mind. There were a few recommendations but none to say that we'd missed anything. It was a massive relief given the circumstances. I knew I'd be left alone now to get on with it. Reading the report, I could clearly see Grahame's influence and whatever chief officers thought about his promotion prospects, they respected his professional opinion when it came to serious crime.

By now the team had assumed its own identity. Officers had come together from the far corners of the force to work on my investigation. It didn't exist prior to the discovery of Natalie's arm and, in less than two months, it was something to behold, something I was immensely proud of. It wasn't what I'd expected at the beginning when I'd feared that most of the experienced detectives had already been seconded onto the other murder inquiries. And yet, for some reason, I'd been blessed with talented, humble and in many ways, extraordinary individuals. I'd demanded the highest standard of integrity and transparency from the outset, and their response was far beyond what I could've hoped for.

The next few months were spent methodically and painstakingly concentrating on Adams, his close family, friends and associates, and 119 St Johns Grove. If Adams was responsible, then Larvin would be the person most likely to have helped him to get rid of Natalie's body. He very quickly ended up in prison on remand for burglary, which is exactly where we wanted him. Bugging his house was disappointing because nothing was said about Natalie's murder and so, like Adams, Larvin was better off in prison safe from overdosing on heroin. He'd be sharing his cell with other criminals and the plan was to hope that he talked. I decided against putting paid informants in to share cells with Adams and Larvin for the time being. I didn't trust informants and presenting evidence gained by them at court wasn't easy.

Two significant things happened to increase suspicion that Larvin was involved. The results came back from forensics showing that seven of the nineteen fingerprints found on TML/4 were Larvin's, although one belonged to Dougie McKenzie, and eleven contained insufficient detail for identification. And police divers recovered a wallet from Holderness Drain, just upstream from the pumping station, discarded following a burglary that occurred in Beverley on 21 July. It contained a receipt bearing a fingerprint of Larvin's, which showed that he'd detailed knowledge of the location where the body bags could've been dumped.

Armstrong was next on the list. Following his release from prison on 28 August, he moved into a flat on Marfleet

Lane. Again, listening to his conversations revealed very little although it did capture his proposal of marriage. To celebrate the happy occasion, his future bride agreed to buy fish and chips. Whilst she was gone, another female arrived at his door offering sex in return for heroin. Armstrong agreed without hesitation. Eventually, his unwitting partner returned none the wiser, no doubt looking forward to a bright future with her faithful husband to be. If Armstrong's lifestyle put a smile on the faces of the detectives listening, Larvin's certainly didn't. On one occasion, he was busy injecting heroin into his veins slumped against the front door. His young children asked to be let in and he was heard to shout, 'Fuck off and play you little bastards or I'll fucking batter you both'. Fortunately for the children, his wife, Debby, made an effort to look after them, even though she was a working prostitute and fellow addict. I wondered what would become of the children. I was pretty sure they weren't destined for greatness.

The plan to get Armstrong remanded worked better than I expected. Undercover officers engaged on another operation in the city successfully bought heroin from Armstrong and, because he'd been released from prison in August for dealing, Magistrates had no hesitation in sending him right back again. With Adams, Larvin and Armstrong safely locked away on remand and not likely to be released for some time, the process of gradually and relentlessly pursuing witnesses began in much greater depth.

SEVENTEEN

'They were both trembling, beads of sweat glistened on their foreheads'

Neil Pattison emerged as a very close associate of Adams. He'd let Adams and Natalie live with him at Victor Street only weeks prior to her disappearance. The problem was that Pattison had been arrested and charged with manslaughter, following the robbery of an elderly lady called Ada Johnson, that led to her death. He was remanded and would have to be produced from prison to enable us to speak to him. DCI Tom Stewart was the SIO, and he didn't agree with our intention to produce Pattison. It ended up with Tony going to see him to discuss the matter. Tony returned fuming and angrier than I'd ever seen him. He wouldn't tell me what happened due to his respect for senior ranks but it was clear there'd been a serious difference of opinion. Tony said that he'd sort it and sure enough, his scouse resilience eventually led to Pattison being produced. This caused an everlasting rift between both inquiry teams. It wasn't what I wanted, given the already fractured relationships with the Class and Morgan investigations. Whilst I understood DCI Stewart's reluctance to cooperate given the unusual circumstances, Pattison had to be seen due to his connection to Adams and there was no other way of getting close to him.

I'd always liked DCI Stewart because of his refreshingly quirky view of the world that set him apart from other senior officers, and we continued to be friendly towards each other despite this episode. But I didn't underestimate the potential depth of his animosity towards Tony and me for going over his head. It was human nature after all.

Tony accompanied DC Marshall and DS Scarth to the prison the first time Pattison was produced, and I'll never forget them bursting into my office upon their return. Although he'd said nothing of any value, they were convinced that he'd much more to give. Andy in particular was excited. It was as if all of his years of experience in getting criminals to talk and handling informants, had brought him to this.

"Boss, I've never been more certain of anything, there's much more to come from Pattison, I don't know why it's just a feeling. It was the way he said that he'd talk to us if we got him out of prison."

Tony and Kev both agreed with Andy. It was obvious that Pattison had made an impact and they were struck by the way he spoke. It was articulate, demonstrating a clarity of thought that they hadn't expected. It certainly wasn't in keeping with a prolific criminal with a propensity for drug dealing, armed robbery and now, probably manslaughter. Before they left, we discussed the procedure to follow with Pattison when he was out of prison. He'd have to be taped when talking about Natalie.

If Pattison did have more to tell, then why would he want

to help us? Any reasonable defence would look to show that we'd offered him inducements and being produced from prison, could well be interpreted as an inducement. Detectives were under strict instructions not to offer anything in return for information received from witnesses. Normally, criminals wouldn't lift a finger to help the police unless there was some kind of payment for services rendered. Informants did it purely for money. Co-accused did it for immunity from prosecution. The idea of a public-spirited criminal helping the police and wanting nothing in return seemed too good to be true, but we'd nothing to lose by producing Pattison. It was at his request, and we couldn't repeatedly visit him in prison with the eyes of fellow criminals watching.

And that's exactly what happened. Beverley and Hessle police cells were used and he was given an entire wing to himself. It was like a home for him within a police station with a TV, bed, table and chair. Each production usually lasted for a couple of weeks. The officers just talked to Pattison trying to build a kind of understanding between detectives and villain. Most of the time it was nothing to do with the case. Their approach was to treat him as an equal with no barriers between them. And despite the fact that he was a professional criminal prone to committing unbelievable acts of violence towards other human beings, they couldn't help but judge him based on hours spent in his company.

The officers returned to the incident room after each meeting like a couple of excited school kids with secrets to tell. I enjoyed their enthusiasm and looked forward to hearing about Pattison: dreadlocked, clever, cunning, and widely-read. How he helped other prisoners by preparing detailed appeals and writing letters on their behalf. And his sense of pride in the way he'd prepare meticulously by watching a family for days, prior to making his move and burgling their house. This level of preparation set him apart from the average Hull burglar and he knew it. He also gave the officers the impression that he was always one step ahead of them. It was the way he held himself as he walked into the interview room and stared at them with his black eyes and 'you're the detectives, go figure it out', attitude. He was proud of the fact that he was the only white male in Hull with dreadlocks and, even though this made him easily identifiable, he didn't care. Although he only possessed one set of clothes - a pair of trainers, denim jeans and a striped blue shirt - he wore them with a certain distinction as if to demonstrate that it didn't matter what clothes you wore, but it's how they're worn that counts.

Eventually, the day arrived when DC Marshall and DS Scarth burst into my office, and it was obvious from the expression on their faces that they'd some important news. Tony was there with me. DC Scarth advised us both to sit down, and in their excitement, they talked over each other.

"We've just seen Pattison and we've got something to tell you."

They were both trembling. Beads of sweat glistened on their foreheads. DS Scarth took out a handkerchief and mopped his brow as he looked at DC Marshall and said,

"Go on Andy. Tell them what Pattison told us."

Andy cleared his throat. Took a deep breath.

"Adams killed Natalie. He told us that he saw Adams sat on a drain bank near to Flinton Grove looking like a ghost with his head in his hands. He asked Adams what was wrong. He looked up at Pattison and said he'd, 'served her up' after an argument and he woke up that morning next to Natalie and there was a knife sticking out of her chest. Pattison wouldn't say anymore other than it happened in 119 St Johns Grove."

Andy and Kev were brimming with excitement. It'd been a long time coming to get to this point. They'd already conducted over thirty taped interviews with Pattison. Even though they knew there was a long way to go to corroborate what Pattison had told them, they believed him and so did Tony and me. There would be no way that Pattison could know that she was stabbed in the chest unless Adams told him: DCI Stewart's team didn't know, it hadn't been in the papers, on TV or the radio, and 'served up' was a slang expression for stabbing someone.

The news spread quickly amongst the rest of the team. I experienced a surge of about a thousand emotions all at once. It felt like we'd climbed the highest mountain together as a team and the summit, with its magnificent view beyond, was in sight. We all knew the huge significance of what Pattison had said. I couldn't believe that the policy of keeping the cause of Natalie's death a secret had worked. If the cause of death had been in the public domain, then Pattison's disclosure would be worth very little. For the first time since the discovery of TML/4, the investigation had received a well-needed boost, even though it'd come from an unlikely and unreliable source – the mouth of a convicted criminal on remand for manslaughter, with a reputation amongst his peers for being a compulsive liar.

In the light of Pattison's revelation, statements already taken from witnesses to Adams's behaviour after he reported her missing, made more sense. Jeff Pattison recalled a conversation with Adams a few months before Natalie's body was found. It was outside a public telephone box as he waited to call a drug dealer. Pattison was with his brother Neil and Stephen Brewster, when Adams appeared and said that he still hadn't seen Natalie. Jeff Pattison decided to wind up Adams and told him he'd seen Natalie a few days ago getting into a punter's car. Adams said that it was impossible, they couldn't have done and was visibly shocked.

Michelle Wolfe, the prostitute who'd helped us with the reconstruction, told us that she spoke to Adams at her house in Alliance Avenue some four weeks before Natalie's body was found. He made her sit on the floor next to him and said, 'the black bastards think I've killed her. When the police come for me, I'm going away for a long time, will you come and visit me'? Wolfe replied, 'well, what are you on about? You're only up for burglary'.

But despite Andy and Kev spending more and more of their time either interviewing or taking him out to different locations, Pattison skillfully avoided talking about Adams. They took him to the area surrounding the pumping station and walked along the drain banks. Two smartly dressed men in suits either side of the dreadlocked Pattison in handcuffs, must have presented an odd spectacle to the occasional dog walker. On another occasion, they drove him out to Paull, a small village on the outskirts of Hull famous for its location on the banks of the River Humber and its views out to sea. I'd been there many times before when I needed time to think. On a clear day, you could see way across to Holland.

Andy was handcuffed to Pattison when the officer needed to take a piss. Pattison had no choice but to accompany him to a toilet inside one of the village pubs. It created the perfect opportunity for the officer to try a different approach with Pattison. The detective turned towards him taking care not to piss on his trainers, and said that he'd compiled a list of ten things about Natalie's murder he thought Pattison knew but hadn't yet revealed. Pattison, clearly intrigued, agreed to take a look the next day. The officers knew that Pattison liked to solve puzzles of any kind. He spent hours doing crosswords in daily newspapers and became annoyed if he couldn't complete them in minutes.

When Pattison took a look at the list the next day, he grinned at the officers, sat back in his chair and said something that again, made them feel they were one step behind him,

"You need to think about the position I'm in. What would you do if you were me?"

Pattison wouldn't say anymore, despite being quizzed by Andy and Kev over what he meant. During the long sessions when both officers briefed Tony and me on progress with Pattison, we tried to guess what he was up to. Admittedly, he'd given us a vital piece of information but we expected more to come, much more. We tried to look at it from his perspective. Being produced for weeks at a time would definitely be far more preferable than being in prison. With two friendly detectives spending most of their time keeping him company in a police station cell wing all to himself, Pattison was intelligent enough to know that Adams's drain bank confession would be enough to keep their attention. And he also knew that the minute he gave everything, if there was more to give, then the police would lose interest and his trips out of prison would stop. We all agreed that we'd probably do the same thing in his position. There was no option but to continue to produce Pattison and hope that he would, eventually, cooperate fully. But I wondered if it was more than self-interest on his part and more to do with coming to terms with the enormity of grassing on Adams, and betraying the bond of trust between villains never to tell under any circumstances.

It got me thinking about a book I was reading. One of the stories was about Solomon, a wise man who people paid in return for his wisdom. His servant was about to leave to return to his family after working for Solomon for over twenty years. But before he left, Solomon gave his servant three pieces of advice, one of which was: 'Don't meddle in other people's lives'. The story goes onto explain the reason for Solomon's advice. On the servant's journey back home, he sought refuge in a cottage on the edge of a forest owned by a ruthless giant of a man, who kept his wife locked away in a room under the floor, and fed her soup ladled from the skull of her former lover. As the servant was about to criticise the man for his cruelty, he remembered Solomon's wise words and told the giant that he must have good reason for his actions. It turned out that the giant cut the throat of any traveller who dared to interfere, and the servant would've met the same fate if he hadn't remembered the words, 'don't meddle in other people's lives'.

Maybe he did know much more about what happened to Natalie but was reluctant to 'meddle', or interfere, with what had already been done to Natalie and couldn't be undone. Maybe he was worried that he'd already set in motion a chain of events that could spiral out of his control. Pattison might be worried that Adams would somehow get to him in prison, seeking retribution for grassing. If he was frightened of Adams, then Pattison might never give us any more information. I realised that all this stuff about Solomon was speculation on my part, but if I were in Pattison's position, what would I do. It was the cryptic question he'd posed to Andy and Kev. And the more I thought about it, I'd think twice about getting involved, no question.

EIGHTEEN

'Sunman must have wondered whether he was having a bad dream'

The breakthrough with Pattison came as welcome relief for me as the SIO. When Tony and me reflected on the way we'd stood our ground over withholding cause of death, the forensic search of 119 St Johns Grove, and videoing of witnesses, we came to the conclusion that the effectiveness of the police had nothing to do with inspirational leadership, but had everything to do with individuals raising their game in an effort to prove their critics wrong.

DC Long was tapping into a vast well of enthusiasm and energy, partly because that was just the way he was, but partly because he'd something to prove to his peers. Andy also felt that he'd something to prove. From the beginning of the inquiry, he'd wondered whether he belonged amongst his more experienced detective colleagues, and there were malicious rumours flying around questioning his integrity over his dealings with Pattison, putting his hard-earned reputation on the line. When he'd skillfully persuaded Pattison to talk, he must have experienced an overwhelming sense of achievement and the urge to tell everyone to Foxtrot Oscar. I would've done in the circumstances. What

Andy couldn't have known though was that he, along with DS Scarth, would eventually inspire the rest of the team by the example they'd set in their sensitive and painstaking handling of Pattison. It created a friendly rivalry to be the next detective to produce a witness with credible and significant information about Natalie's murder, and it worked better than I could have hoped for.

During October, Adams shared a cell on E Wing at Hull Prison with Trevor Sunman, a career criminal and heroin addict. Following his release, Shaun Weir and Rob Walker visited him at his home on numerous occasions, and his initial hostility towards them gradually turned to an unlikely tolerance of each other's company. Shaun's description of Sunman as a street rat with a drug addict's pale, gaunt face and hatred of the police, made what happened at their last meeting with him all the more extraordinary. DS Walker called as they made their way back to the incident room to make sure that Tony and me were there when they arrived. He hadn't given a reason as to why he wanted to see us both other than they'd something important to say.

And as they walked into my office, I had a feeling of déjà vu as I recalled Andy and Kev doing exactly the same thing a few weeks earlier. Shaun then described in vivid, three-dimensional detail, what happened at Sunman's house. The depth of recall was breathtaking - it brought Sunman's kitchen into my office, so that I could almost see him stood leaning against the sink as he'd broken down and sobbed. The detectives had never witnessed a criminal with the moral code of an alley cat so vulnerable and embarrassed, and Shaun demonstrated how he'd put his arm around Sunman in a rare moment of compassion. Sunman must have wondered whether he was having a bad dream.

Eventually, Sunman composed himself and talked about his time in a cell with Adams. Adams had difficulty sleeping and would often wake up sweating. On one occasion, Sunman apologised for innocently saying that someone 'lost their head'. Adams responded by making jokes about Natalie being 'armless and legless'. But then Adams's mood changed in a moment as he complained to Sunman that it'd taken 'five hacksaw blades man, five fucking hacksaw blades, it took me five hacksaw blades to cut her up 'cos they kept snapping'. And with tears in his eyes, Sunman thrust his hand in the air with fingers and thumb outstretched, inches from the detective's face, to illustrate how Adams had rammed home the number five. Sunman kept repeating that he was only doing this because it was out of order to cut Natalie's body up maybe hoping that, by doing so over and over again, the criminal underworld would hear his words and forgive him for grassing. In complete contrast to Pattison, who seemed more interested in playing a game of cat and mouse with the detectives, Sunman sat with his head in his hands, spirit broken, as if he couldn't cope with what he'd just done. I didn't ask whether they believed Sunman. There was too much detail, too much emotion for Sunman to have made the whole thing up. In his eyes, grassing was the ultimate sin amongst thieves - he'd never be forgiven and he'd never forgive himself - and so he must be telling the truth. At least that was our reasoning as we sat and looked at each other wondering which one of us would be the first to punch the air in celebration.

Sunman's disclosure was massive, but our biggest problem would be keeping him onside so that he eventually gave evidence. The prospect didn't seem likely but it didn't matter for now. There was already a degree of corroboration from the pathologist, who'd already concluded that a thin bladed saw was used to dismember Natalie, a fact that'd never been released to the press. Crucially, it also showed that Adams had confided in two close associates, presumably in the belief that they'd never, under any circumstances, help the police.

In the light of Pattison's and Sunman's revelations, it was time for a meeting with the head of the CPS, Bob Marshall, to discuss the evidence against Adams. He was relatively new in post, and he'd already impressed me over agreeing to the policy of overlooking crimes admitted by witnesses in an effort to help the investigation. It was done over the telephone, and so I was looking forward to seeing him for the first time.

The CPS was affectionately known as the Criminal Protection Society amongst the rank and file, due to their liking for discontinuing seemingly watertight cases with very little or no explanation, at least that's what it seemed like from our perspective. On one occasion, as a DI, I'd demanded a meeting with the CPS lawyer assigned to a case involving a man who'd badly assaulted his oldest daughter leaving her with permanent brain damage. The lawyer had concluded that there was insufficient evidence to charge the male in question, despite there being an eye witness to the assault. He must have sensed that I wasn't about to back down and, to his credit, he listened to my argument. The eye witness was the younger daughter, who was woken by her sister's screams and watched helplessly as her father lost his temper. The CPS judged her to be unreliable, and the father had argued that it was an accident. But the injuries were too severe and his story was full of inconsistencies. Eventually, the lawyer changed his decision, and the father was subsequently charged and found guilty at Crown Court.

We received a warm welcome from Mr Marshall, a small, well-spoken, confident man who looked lost in his huge, expensively furnished office. I thanked him for supporting the policy of overlooking crimes and told him that it was really helping. I could tell that he was pleased. I couldn't imagine someone in his position being thanked very often. On the very rare occasions when it'd happened to me, it made me feel like a million dollars, and I couldn't understand why such a powerful motivational gesture wasn't used more often.

Mr Marshall listened without interruption as we outlined the case against Adams and, possibly, Larvin. His grasp of the evidence, which we accepted was largely circumstantial, apart from TML/4, was impressive. He rightly pointed out some of the problems we faced bringing the case to court: presenting Pattison and Sunman as credible witnesses, the presence of other fingerprints on TML/4, and the lack of continuity with TML/4 at 119 St Johns Grove. But before we left, he complimented us on the thoroughness of the investigation to date and he genuinely seemed to care.

During the drive back to the incident room we both formed the opinion that Mr Marshall had shown a degree of empathy towards Natalie that we hadn't expected, and a willingness to support the controversial policy decisions already made. We told ourselves that it was because we'd hypnotised him with our collective passion and enthusiasm. I imagined him wandering around attempting to convert his junior colleagues into taking a more positive approach when dealing with the police, only to be met with blank expressions. Given that he was new in post with bags of energy, I hoped that he'd try and mend the fractured relationship between the Police and CPS. The public deserved better.

NINETEEN

'It wasn't what I signed up for'

Back at HQ, there was a message to call DI Rick Wilson. I knew it would be to do with a sensitive discipline inquiry I'd been given by the ACC in May earlier this year. My heart had sunk about as far as it could at the news because I'd never had to investigate a colleague for potentially criminal offences before. The alleged misconduct was serious. The male officer in question, PC Lee, was from a minority ethnic background and he had, apparently, attempted to convince the CPS and Magistrates, that four youths from a local care home had committed well over a hundred burglaries, shop thefts and TWOCs. When the juveniles pleaded not guilty to the crimes, Magistrates weren't convinced that there was evidence to support the charges, and the matter was referred back to the force accordingly. It was my job to provide the answer, and it felt like I'd been entered into a race that I'd no chance of winning. Out of my depth again in only a few short months. Consequently, the forthcoming interviews with the officer, were preying heavily on my mind.

At the very beginning of the inquiry, I'd discussed with Rick the need for us to be meticulous and fair and let the evidence speak for itself. Accordingly, we'd videoed all witnesses, and I'd decided against arresting PC Lee, although I was well within my rights to do so. I couldn't have been more transparent and objective if I tried. From the moment I was given the task, I couldn't care less about the officer's ethnicity, but I was naive to think that a skillful, fair and thorough investigation would be enough. It should have been, and I'm pretty sure the average member of the public would agree with me, but what I hadn't bargained for was the ugliness of the political world of police discipline that I wanted no part of. It wasn't what I'd signed up for.

It was a world I knew nothing about. Sure, I was aware of officers falling from grace for various wrongdoings, and back in the early days of my career, it seemed to be a fairly smooth and efficient operation. An officer who breached the discipline code usually accepted his or her punishment, that ranged from written warnings to dismissal from the force. On my shift, we lost two officers for pretty serious errors of judgement in a week.

PC Hartson, a likeable but fiery officer, spent his refreshment breaks visiting a prostitute on his patch. The rest of the shift didn't think it was any of our business how he chose to spend his well-earned refs but one morning, inevitably, his world came crashing down around him. I arrived for an early morning shift and couldn't see PC Hartson anywhere, which was unusual because he was always there before me. When I asked the sergeant where my colleague was, he replied,

"He's in the cells."

"Blimey, he's keen. Locked up already before the shift's even started. Fair play to him."

"No, he was arrested last night for battering his prostitute girlfriend. He's the one actually locked up in a cell."

It transpired that PC Hartson had broken off their arrangement and she'd come looking for him with a knife and tried to stab him. Unfortunately for her, she got more than she'd bargained for and ended up in hospital. PC Hartson went quietly accepting his wrongdoing, and everyone agreed that it was probably for the best.

PC Bloom, the other officer, was black. He was a very friendly, confident individual who was always willing to help and give advice to anyone who happened to be in his immediate vicinity. He always meant well, but believing that he was the font of all knowledge when it came to police work, despite being young in service, proved to be an annoying trait, one that caused his colleagues and senior officers to run for cover when they saw him coming in an effort to avoid his words of wisdom. But in the end, it was his readiness to help others that proved to be his downfall. PC Bloom discovered that the Drugs Squad were about to execute a warrant at his girlfriend's address. In an effort to prevent her from being arrested, he'd recovered her drugs before the raid whilst on duty but was subsequently caught red-handed leaving her house. He took full responsibility and resigned immediately. No trying to keep his job by taking the force to tribunal and accusing the investigators of being racist. No trying to abdicate responsibility for his actions. His colleagues on the shift weren't sorry to see him go but I was. I didn't for one minute condone his involvement with drugs - far from it - but at least he did the honourable thing by going without any fuss. I wondered if he realised that helping others should probably be restricted to non-criminal circumstances though, because he'd paid a high price for attempting to pervert the course of justice for his girlfriend. I heard that they'd split up not long after his fall from grace.

Before I returned Rick's call, Tony came in for a coffee.

"You've been sat staring into space for ages. Is everything OK?"

"Just thinking about the discipline investigation I'm conducting. Never done one before. Can't say too much but I've a feeling the officer in question is going to play the race card. I can't see any way this is going to end well. Any advice?"

"Can I ask is it criminal?"

"Potentially, yes."

"You don't need me to tell you that whoever the other officer is, will be fighting for their lives. The federation will be supporting them and providing funds for an expensive legal defence. And I'm sorry to tell you but they'll probably come after you if things don't go their way. It's not like the old days anymore. I'd be careful."

"Thanks. Just what I wanted to hear."

Deep down I knew he was right. I'd heard of cases in other forces were officers under investigation had turned the table on their investigators by making spurious allegations against them. And I didn't doubt for one minute that my case would be any different. I needed to hear a friendly voice and so I called DI Wilson.

"Boss, thanks for calling. It's about Judy Harris, the officer's brief. Her reputation of being a bloody pain-in-the-arse is spot on. She's nitpicking over everything, particularly disclosure. She wants everything we've got on the officer prior to the interviews or she'll be advising him to go no comment. Looks to me as if she's on some kind of bloody mission. Like she's a point to prove. You can imagine my response. She didn't like it."

I knew that Rick wouldn't have given an inch. Ms. Harris would be sadly mistaken if she assumed that she could outwit my trusted colleague. Although I couldn't think of anyone who I'd rather be working with on this inquiry, I knew that I'd asked a great deal of him. That he'd agreed in a flash to help me, even though PC Lee had already accused him of treating him differently due to his ethnicity, was a measure of the man and his principles. I still wasn't sure that I'd done the right thing though, because the officer might well argue that Rick's involvement showed that my investigation was biased against him from the start. After all, I'd questioned the ACC's decision to appoint me as the SIO for the inquiry, on the grounds that a DCI from a different Division would be seen to be more independent and objective.

"OK, I'll call Gary Shaw and get back to you."

DI Gary Shaw was a big character with a broad Geordie accent. I'd heard of his stature as an expert in investigative interviewing some time ago, and invited him across to address my detectives not long after I'd arrived as the new DI at Division. Prior to Gary's input, it was accepted practice to provide full disclosure of the police case against suspects before interview. But as he told his expectant audience: 'why tell a suspect you've got their fingerprints at the scene of a burglary? They'll say thanks for the heads-up and lie about how they got there. Makes no sense'. His advice proved to be a revelation and shifted the balance of power in favour of the detective.

When I eventually got hold of Gary, he talked enthusiastically about a recent case, R v Imran and Hussain, that justified his approach. Imran was one of four men caught on video trying to break into a shop. When he was subsequently interviewed on tape by police neither he, nor his solicitor, were informed of the existence of the tape beforehand. After Imran lied in the interview, he was told about the video. Imran was convicted and applied for leave to appeal against conviction on the grounds that the police should've disclosed the existence of the tape before Imran was trapped into lying in interview. Leave for appeal was denied. Gary read out what the trial judge said,

"It is totally wrong to submit that a defendant should be prevented from lying by being presented with the whole of the evidence against him prior to the interview. To hold that the police have to play a form of cricket under one rigorous set of rules whereas the suspect can play under no rules whatever seems to lack reality."

It sounded odd the words of a judge being spoken in a broad Geordie accent. I was always impressed by how those in high positions in the legal profession managed to express themselves with such precision, with every word chosen for its exact meaning. When I mentioned this to Gary, all he said was,

"Aye well, they're canny lads them judges, bright as buttons."

Accordingly, Gary's advice was to give written disclosure

before each interview sufficient in detail to give PC Lee no choice but to answer questions put to him. I knew I'd be able to cite R v Imran and Hussain as a reason for not giving full disclosure to Ms. Harris, but I also knew that to give too little, would certainly hand them grounds to say nothing. Written disclosure was a new concept, and if it proved to be successful in this case, then my mind was already fast-forwarding to its use when interviewing Adams.

On the first day of the interviews, the officer strode confidently and purposefully into my office flanked by a wide-eyed and ready-to-do-battle Ms. Harris. My office was long and narrow and so we'd arranged the desks so that he was about as far away from me as possible. Rick had already told me that PC Lee would bring his larger than life personality into the interviews and sure enough, his first comment was to ask for his desk to be moved closer to mine. The officer conducted himself with an air of superiority, and I reflected on whether my decision not to arrest him was the right one. When I explained that DI Wilson was monitoring the interviews from the room next door, he looked like he'd just seen a ghost. He asked why and to be fair, if I was in his position, I'd want to know why too. It was something I'd done before and was becoming accepted practice - it would allow Rick to observe the interview and make sure that I didn't miss anything. It just made the whole procedure more professional in my eyes and was a logical thing to do. Whilst I didn't think he'd be over the moon at the thought of DI Wilson listening to every word that he said, if he'd nothing to hide, then I couldn't see why he'd object. And to my surprise, he let it go without any argument. His mind must have been concentrating on what he was about to say. At the beginning of the first interview, with the tapes rolling, PC Lee asked if he could read out a prepared statement. I wasn't prepared for what came next.

"I wish to state from the outset that I've been the victim of racial discrimination throughout my career. I came here to escape the oppressive behaviour I suffered in my previous force, but I'm disappointed to say that every supervisor I've encountered so far has discriminated against me because of my ethnic background and religious beliefs. DS Myers, DI Wilson and DCI Davison have been particularly open in their racial bias towards me for these reasons. I intend to make formal complaints against all of these officers in due course with the support of the police federation."

I closed the interview down and left the room. I needed time to think about his cleverly prepared words. They knew they'd gained the upper hand. The threat of formal complaints was clearly designed to intimidate my colleague and me. I wondered why he'd singled out DS John Myers, who used to be one of his supervisors in Fraud Squad. I knew John well from our time as DCs together at Tower Grange police station in the late eighties. He reminded me of Rick in many ways - highly principled with bags of integrity. He was also very generous. He'd given me loads of stuff to help me set up home again following my divorce. Red velvet curtains sprang to mind. I still had them after all this time.

When I called DS Myers to find out why the officer was accusing him of racial discrimination, his voice changed from a 'Davo, nice to hear from you', friendly tone, to one that quivered with emotion. I listened as the proud detective struggled to get his words out fast enough. He was angry about how he'd properly tackled the officer over his conduct in Fraud Squad and submitted a thorough, evidence-based report outlining his concerns to his supervisors. But he'd felt let down when, although the officer was duly posted out of the department into uniform, it was made to look like the officer had asked to leave because it wasn't to his liking. I was beginning to understand why John was so disillusioned. His view was that his report had been swept under the carpet because of the officer's ethnicity. There was a deep sense of injustice as he described what happened next: a posting into uniform for him instead of a move to the Major Crime Team he was promised and always wanted, and a prestigious HOLMES course for the officer. It wasn't long though, before the officer was duly disciplined for neglect of duty and making false entries in his notebook, prior to being posted to my Division in June 1997.

"Always good to hear from you Davo. Sorry I've gone on a bit but it really affected me. Hope you have better luck than me. How are those red curtains doing?"

I tried to come to terms with what DS Myers had just told me. I felt like walking away and leaving all this behind. I was angry, deflated and disillusioned. For the first time in my career, the pride I felt at being a police officer began to ebb away. But as I looked across at Rick, he must have read my thoughts because he said something that has stayed with me ever since,

"The only thing that matters, is the truth."

"I'm not sure that'll be enough in this case my friend. I don't see how this is going to end well for either of us I'm afraid. But you're right. All we can do is what's right. I don't know about you but I've had enough of this crap."

I strode back into the interview with steely determination. There'd be no sweeping anything under the carpet today or any other day. From the officer's fixed and direct eye contact with me, he was in a confident mood. Based on previous experiences, he'd be of the opinion that he'd be able to manipulate the circumstances to his advantage. But unfortunately for him, for whatever reason, he'd got me, and I knew that it wouldn't be long before he realised that this investigation had been conducted to the highest possible standard. There'd be no way out for him. I was looking forward to watching PC Lee struggle to answer the questions I was about to put to him.

I told him that his comments had nothing to do with this investigation and that if he wished to make formal complaints, then that was entirely a matter for him. And then Ms. Harris showed her true colours. I tried to ask the first question but she interrupted complaining vociferously about everything: how could this possibly be a fair investigation when her client was going to make a complaint against DI Wilson and me, why were the desks so far apart, why hadn't she been given full disclosure, why had we videoed witnesses, why were we remote monitoring, and how did the issues over sexual harassment come to light. The last question caused me to interrupt Ms. Harris in full flow.

"Ms. Harris, I'm glad you asked that last question. The issues over your clients alleged sexual harassment of a number of females came to light during Jane Freeman's video statement. You'll recall that she's a social worker who acted as an appropriate adult for the juveniles involved in this case. It came as a surprise to us all. Do you want to see the video? I'd be happy to play it for you both. I believe that answers your question over why we videoed witnesses. It was indeed fortunate that it was captured on video, don't you think? In relation to disclosure, I'm sure you'll be aware of R v Imran and Hussain. I've taken the liberty of producing a copy of the stated case for you. I believe that you've been given appropriate disclosure in the circumstances."

Ms. Harris and the officer looked at each other and before either of them could speak, I continued.

"Ms. Harris, I'd be grateful if you would resist the temptation to constantly interrupt me when trying to put questions to your client. I'm conducting this interview not you and so unless you have something to say relating to the reasonable defence of your client's interests, please remain silent."

Ms. Harris's face turned a bright red with rage, and she threatened to make a complaint against me. I told her to get on with it. By now, I was sick and tired of the 'I'm going to complain about you if I don't get my own way', culture. It seemed as though they thought they'd the right to bully their way out of situations like this, like petulant children controlling weak parents. But all they did was put my protective instincts on high alert. I knew now, more than ever, that I'd have to be a model of professionalism. The officer would go on the attack at the conclusion of the interviews, with the full support of the Police Federation, and every word I said would probably be scrutinised and pored over at some future proceedings against me.

The interviews lasted three days. I purposely and properly questioned PC Lee in some detail about each and every one of the crimes he'd claimed the juveniles had committed. He'd no option but to admit that they were unsafe, mainly because there was no evidence. His defence was that he'd been neglectful but denied any intention to pervert the course of justice. If the juveniles hadn't denied committing the crimes before the Magistrates, then he would indeed have succeeded.

TWENTY

'ITV's got Lynda La Plante. We've got Natalie'

It was a relief to get back to the incident room. I hadn't enjoyed the experience of interviewing the officer, having to be in such close proximity to someone whose conduct, in my view, had fallen far below the high standard expected and demanded of police officers. Being around individuals like DC Weir, DC Marshall, DS Goddard, DS Chapman, Lisa Hodson, in fact anyone in my team for that matter, was how it was supposed to be. It seemed to me that they lived by a higher moral code, significantly higher.

Tony had done a good job in my absence. The focus of the investigation was very much on trying to corroborate Pattison's and Sunman's accounts, although DS Chapman was still looking at other possible suspects, including Jodi Amadi, as a line of inquiry. If I were defending Adams, I'd certainly try to convince a jury that Natalie was murdered over a debt owed for drugs. Adams had cleverly put Amadi forward as the person responsible during his video statement, and I knew we had to pretty much prove that he couldn't have done it. DS Chapman was already convinced that his alibi was watertight.

Forensic tests on the black bin bags came back whilst I

was away and they were disappointing. No fingerprints were found on those recovered with Natalie's head, torso and arm, and they hadn't come from the same batch as TML/4, those discovered in 119 St Johns Grove or Larvin's address, 13 Leven Grove. We'd also engaged the services of an expert to examine the knots used to tie the bin bags containing Natalie's body parts, but they weren't able to determine whether they were tied by a right-or-left-handed person. DC Long's search of 119 St Johns Grove for fingerprints was still ongoing. I knew there'd be numerous prints found inside belonging to friends, associates, and punters. They'd all have to be identified and eliminated.

On a positive note, the circumstantial evidence against Adams was building. Tony briefed me on a friend of Adams and Natalie, Jason Blakeley. He'd come across Adams a few weeks after Natalie went missing and asked if Adams had heard from Natalie. Adams said that Natalie 'was in the drain'. Blakeley told the detectives, 'I took his response to be a joke. I was with him at a garage a few days after, and before I could say anything, he said he hadn't heard from her, and there were no other conversations'.

Another friend of Natalie's, Shirley Brady, eventually came forward. She was amongst a group of people, including Adams, when they were talking about the police wanting Adams to get in touch with them. Someone called Dodi urged Adams to go to the police. Adams didn't want to go and said, 'they'll blame me if she's dead or missing'. Dodi replied 'well, how can you say that? You don't know if she's dead'. Adams said, 'it's nothing to do with you'.

Tony told me about an interesting witness called Rebecca

Carroll, who detectives had questioned as they'd made enquiries around the flats in Porter Street. She spent most of her life sniffing glue with her friends. It can't have been much of a life. Porter Street was renowned as a red-light district and the flats were grim and depressing, even on a sunny day. On one occasion, after Natalie went missing but before her body was found, she'd seen Adams on the flat stairs, maybe on the third or fourth floor, with two pieces of cardboard stuck together. Tony read out part of her statement,

"I think I saw him sketching on it. He was sketching an unclothed lady. She was lying on her back, but not straight. She was slanting. There were slash marks on her neck, and a drug needle going into her arm, the kind you inject with - a syringe and barrel. There were bubbles with writing. They said 'Don't take drugs' and 'Drugs kill'. There was a cross, and in it were the letters 'RIP'. There were drips of blood coming out of the wound in the neck."

I was about to ask if there were any further developments with Pattison when I saw Stephen Hodgson, the force solicitor, loitering around outside my office. I waved for him to come in.

"Paul, do you have a minute?"

Tony knew that meant a word in private and left. My heart sank a little for whatever he wanted, the force solicitor never came bearing good news. I liked Stephen. He was clearly well educated and he'd a way with words that set him apart from the rest of us. It was measured and slightly posh but not in an overbearing way, it was just the way he spoke. I always talked far too quickly. It was something I did from early childhood, the sooner I got the words out the sooner people would stop looking at me, I reasoned. I knew it was ridiculous but I hated being looked at, hated being the centre of attention. Stephen, on the other hand, had no such problem. He seemed able to say precisely what he wanted to say, each word carefully chosen for its exact meaning, and delivered in a way that made you want to listen and consider it time well spent.

"I take it this isn't a social call."

"I thought you ought to know that police constable Lee has lodged a formal complaint of racial discrimination. It is in the form of a grievance but papers have also been lodged so that it can be heard at a future employment tribunal. The basis of the grievance is that since his transfer to Humberside, he has been the subject of determined and widespread discrimination because of his ethnic background. You, my friend, together with DI Wilson, appear to be his main targets. But if it is any consolation, there are many others named in his submission, which runs to over one hundred and eighty pages."

Normally, I'd have exploded with rage and sworn profusely at the news that, although I was expecting, nevertheless made me really angry. But he was too much of a gentleman and he'd have been offended.

"Dare I ask why he thinks I've discriminated against him?"

Stephen rarely showed emotion regardless of the circumstances and he never gave opinion, only the facts. I'd tried in the past to prise more from him but he'd a way of letting you know that it wasn't appropriate. I often thought that if I ever wanted someone to keep a secret, I'd turn to Stephen. He looked at me for what seemed like an eternity as if he was turning over in his mind whether or not to answer my question. He must have been in this position so many times before, being asked to give a reason why seemingly corrupt officers were able to deflect attention away from their own conduct by playing the system.

The force had unwittingly, and unfortunately, provided the perfect breeding ground for this to happen by introducing a disciplined service to the grievance procedure. Chief officers must have believed that it would be a simple and effective way of resolving differences between colleagues. In reality, it led to mostly spurious allegations that nevertheless had to be investigated. I remember a colleague of mine, a DS, who was on the receiving end of a grievance from one of his DCs, who'd accused him of treating him differently because he was Scottish. It began with a grievance and ended up at an employment tribunal that cost the federation a fortune in legal fees. The DS won the case because he'd done nothing wrong, but it took months to resolve and caused him a huge amount of distress.

"The officer is claiming that your investigation was conducted to an unusually high standard, one that is not routinely displayed on other investigations. He cites the videoing of witnesses, and the remote monitoring of his interviews by DI Wilson, as examples of this."

I knew there'd be no words of comfort, no reassurance that everything would be OK. There was no point in prolonging the conversation. He wouldn't tell me anything more and so I spared his discomfort by thanking him for his time and making it clear I'd work to do.

"Always a pleasure to see you Paul. One of these days, I will come bearing good news in altogether more pleasant circumstances."

Tony sensed something was wrong. He brought me a coffee, closed the door and sat down. As I told him the story, my heart sank deeper and deeper. His response made me feel better. With a broad smile, he said.

"I've been in the shit more times than I can remember and I'm still here. You know you're not racist and that's all that matters. So, what if they do investigate you. Sounds like they're clutching at straws if they're pinning their hopes on showing you to be racist because of your dog's bollocks of an investigation. Never heard of an investigation being too good before. Usually the other way around."

"Thanks. Means a lot. But I can't help thinking this is serious. You know as well as I do that these things can take on a life of their own."

I asked Tony to leave so I could think. I was angry and frustrated. The mere mention of the words racial discrimination sent everyone rushing for cover to avoid the inevitable fallout. Those unfortunate souls accused of discrimination on the grounds of gender and race were inevitably hung out to dry, regardless of the circumstances. I'd seen it happen many times before and, as I wondered whether I was next, I got call from DI Wilson.

"I've just found out he's accusing me again of being racist, along with just about any supervisor who's employed by the force. It's fucking outrageous. I bet he's done it to attack our investigation before the file gets to CPS. Well, I'm not having it. I'm going to take him on at his own game. He's making false accusations against me. The federation will have to pay for a barrister to represent me. They'll have no choice."

"I'm sorry I got you into this. I should've seen it coming."

"Boss, I knew what I was getting myself into. It's not your fault he's playing the system. Anyway, I like working with you. We have a bloody good laugh don't we."

His absolute disgust at the accusations vibrated down the phone like a bolt of lightning. Although the officer had a fair chance of bullying senior officers and the federation into submission, in DI Wilson, he'd chosen someone who'd never give in. I knew that Rick would see this as a battle that must be fought to uphold his integrity and reputation, and it would be a battle he'd be willing to fight until the bitter end, no matter how long it took, no matter what the consequences.

I recalled Arthur Ashe's opening comments in his book 'Days of Grace'. 'If one's reputation is a possession, then of all my possessions, my reputation means most to me. Nothing comes even close to it in importance'. I felt exactly the same way. My reputation was at stake. I'd worked hard over sixteen years to build a solid foundation as a trustworthy, honest police officer, and all that could disappear in a heartbeat over something like this.

After the phone call, I slumped back in my chair and tried to make sense of what was happening. My Dad would have tried to make me see things from PC Lee's perspective to better understand his motives for making such serious accusations. He'd have reminded me of the need to reserve judgement by quoting the advice given by a father to his son from the opening of F Scott Fitzgerald's 'The Great Gatsby'. 'Whenever you feel like criticising anyone, just remember that all the people in this world haven't had the advantages that you've had'. It was one of my favourite books and I kept a copy with me in my briefcase as a reminder to see the real person behind the police mask. The police service bred a cynical 'who the fuck do they think they are', approach to making initial assessments of people that were invariably wrong, most of the time.

I wondered what it would have been like for the officer to start over again in a new force not knowing anyone. Maybe his perception was that he'd been treated differently, or maybe there was some substance to his claims. But regardless of his circumstances, he'd taken advantage of some vulnerable kids from a care home and attempted to convince the court that they were responsible for committing numerous house burglaries and other crimes. And I, as the senior officer who'd uncovered the extent of his wrongdoing, would be in the firing line. A shiver ran down my spine as I caught a glimpse of my future that looked bleak and uncertain. At that moment, I couldn't have agreed more with F Scott Fitzgerald's observation that 'reserving judgements is a matter of infinite hope'.

When I called my wife about the allegations of racism against me and the likely consequences if they were proven, she asked questions that any ordinary member of the public would ask. She couldn't understand why the officer was allowed to make such accusations against me on the grounds that my investigation was too good.

"Why can't somebody higher up apply some common sense and reject his ridiculous claims today. It wouldn't take long."

Tired and fed up, I went for a walk around the familiar streets of the city. Hull wouldn't be for everyone, but it felt like home to me and I needed time to think. It was rush hour by now, and as I watched commuters making their way home, I wondered if any of their lives were as complicated as mine. I imagined trying to explain to some unsuspecting individual sat next to me in a pub, perhaps, how the officer had, apparently, manipulated and intimidated the force by playing the race card. I felt sure that if the individual was an average member of the public blessed with the ability to determine right from wrong and with an ounce of moral integrity, they'd throw their arms up in disbelief, disgust and anger. My instinct would be to try and defend the force but I knew I'd lose the argument. All I'd ever wanted to do was come to work and make a difference by doing a good job, but right now, it felt as though I was an expendable pawn in some elaborate game of chess, with very little or no influence on the outcome.

I wished my Dad were still around more than ever at times like these. I'd give anything for him to suddenly appear, even for a moment. It would've made me feel better. I missed him, and I didn't realise just what a diamond of a person he was until he was gone. I wished I'd told him. If there were a machine able to measure a person's capacity for human kindness, humility and integrity, then my Dad's reading would have been off the scale. No question. It seemed to me that PC Lee's reading would definitely be way less than zero.

When I got back, Tony burst into my office with a broad grin on his face. It was just what I needed.

"Come on boss, I've got something to show you that'll cheer you up."

"Where are we going?

"St Johns Grove. DC Long's going to meet us down there."

When we arrived, Tim was already inside. The smell hadn't changed. The living room was brightly lit with halogen lamps.

"What've you got for me?"

"I've been wondering for some time why that wall has been recently painted and the rest haven't. Doesn't look right to me. Anyway, when I was looking for fingerprints with the quasar after spraying with DFO, something really interesting happened. Watch."

He shone the quasar light towards the wall and suddenly, words appeared in a scruffy scrawl, 'ITV's got Lynda La Plante. We've got Natalie'. Tim had clearly done his homework and told us that in his opinion, it was a reference to the TV series 'Killer Net', written by Lynda La Plante and shown on Chanel 4 in May of this year. A female called Charlie was found dead in the series, and she was identified by a large tattoo on her back. Although we wouldn't be able to prove who'd written those words, we'd be able to reasonably argue that it was likely to have been Adams. They were obviously never meant to be found, and their discovery was down to DC Long's determination to extract as much evidence from the scene as he could. It was good news, and it took my mind off PC Lee, if only for a moment.

TWENTY-ONE

'Time to make my own luck'

By now it was late January and with so much going on, I'd hardly noticed that Christmas had come and gone. I knew that it was time to fix a date to arrest Adams. I'd hoped that by now, six months into the investigation, Pattison would have given us more information. Maybe he was enjoying his time out of prison too much, maybe he didn't have more to tell or, if he did, maybe he was frightened of deepening his betrayal of Adams.

The day began like any other day, sat with Tony in my office preparing for the briefing, but a call from the DCC was about to change the course of my career and shatter my fragile confidence. Our paths had barely crossed since his arrival in force some two years ago, and I'd no idea what he thought of me, or whether he knew if I existed for that matter. In a watered-down Birmingham accent, he abruptly informed me that I was being posted to Bridlington in uniform.

"But Sir, what about my investigation. It's not finished. I can't leave it now."

"I've asked Detective Superintendent Taylor to take it over. Shouldn't be a problem."

"Can I ask when from?"

"Beginning of April."

"Can I ask why?"

"We think you've spent too long in CID and you need developing. Do you good to do something else."

To say the call was a massive shock, was an understatement. Tony could see something was wrong.

"I'm being posted to bloody Bridlington in uniform from April."

That's all I could say as the DCC's call started to sink in. Tony was in complete disbelief. His first thought was to ask if I'd upset somebody or done something wrong. I knew I'd never know. I'd never be told the real reason for being posted. My heart sank. The DCC's decision would have far reaching consequences for me. I'd never heard of a SIO being moved off a case before it was solved. My mind started racing and I began to panic. Tony tried to put a positive spin on the news.

"Looking on the bright side, they've got bloody good fish and chips at the seaside."

I told him to fuck off but I understood that he felt bad for me and he was only trying to help. We both knew that whichever way you looked at the decision, it wasn't good for me. I was being selfish, no question, but my career and reputation meant everything. A posting to the seaside seemed like a posting into the policing wilderness. It wouldn't be long before I'd be the main topic of conversation across the force, 'haven't you heard, Davo's been taken off Clubb and posted to the seaside, serves him right, arrogant bastard'. I imagined those words being spoken time and again and there'd be few ready to leap to my defence. All sorts of made up, fanciful and ridiculous reasons for my demise would surface. The police culture certainly had a unique way of dealing with those individuals who wouldn't conform. This felt like a subtle form of humiliation. Payback for the long list of people I'd upset, including the ACC, or at least that's how it seemed to me. Whatever the reasons behind my posting, just as football referees never changed their decisions despite being wrong most of the time, I knew chief officers wouldn't change their minds either. All I could do now was look for way of saving my career.

"Tony, I want to get this case sorted before I go. It's our investigation. I'm the SIO. Fuck passing this over to someone else. We've got about two months, maybe a bit longer if I can swing it."

It was time to make my own luck. It would be my decision when to go for Adams, Larvin and maybe Armstrong, but I wanted Tony's support.

"That's more like the boss I know. Fighting talk. You're the boss. You know I'll support you, although it'll be a race against time."

I felt a million times better in a very short space of time: from utter despair to elation in a heartbeat. I was proud of myself in some small way. I reasoned that by charging Adams before leaving for the seaside would bring about a form of closure with most of the hard work done. All that would be left would be the trial and I'd make sure I'd be there. Nothing would stop me. But as I drove home, that old familiar feeling of loneliness returned with a vengeance. I'd no idea what the future had in store for me now.

When I got home and told my wife about the DCC's call and my imminent posting to Bridlington, it was all I could do to hold back the tears. Although I'd put a brave face on in front of Tony, my wife understood the impact the posting would have on me, an impact that couldn't be put into words. All she did was give me a hug. I couldn't sleep because the deep sense of humiliation was very real.

The next morning the briefing room was full. Word had obviously spread quickly. If I was one of my team, I'd want to know what was going on from their soon to be replaced SIO. I pretended to be genuinely bristling with enthusiasm for my posting to the seaside. My behaviour must have seemed odd in the circumstances. I'm sure they'd have understood if I'd taken some time away to digest the shock of my imminent departure. I looked around the room. The majority had been with me from the start and we'd come a long way together. I felt that I owed it to Natalie and the team to be as strong a leader as I could, despite feeling let down by those sat in high places.

When I announced that we were going to make the arrests before my move to Bridlington, I could see Shaun and Rob exchange worried glances as they contemplated the implications of what I'd just said. I'm sure that some of the team must have questioned whether my departure was the right reason for moving on Adams. I'd have done. But in my mind, I didn't have a choice. Only time would tell if I'd made the right call. And it was a relief to see the team openly support me; if they'd any misgivings, they hid them well. After a lengthy discussion, it was agreed to arrest Adams for the murder of Natalie, and Larvin and Armstrong for assisting Adams to dispose of her body. The grounds for arresting Larvin would be documented in my policy book as his fingerprints on TML/4, and for Armstrong, they were comments he'd made to friends and associates indicating that he'd helped to dispose of Natalie's body.

I held a meeting in my office with Tony, Shaun and Rob after the briefing. I knew what was coming and to be fair to Shaun and Rob, they presented a cogent argument for delaying the arrests and interviews to give them more time to prepare. But my mind was already made up and they knew that it was a waste of time trying to get me to reconsider. I called my old friend Gary Shaw and asked him to come across and help with planning the interviews. It was an absolute pleasure to hear his disarming Geordie accent once again and he agreed without a moment's hesitation. Gary's advice would be invaluable in such a complicated case and it would be good to see him again. Shaun and Rob left my office to the sound of me singing Gary's praises. They hadn't met him but I knew they'd be very impressed when they did.

Regardless of whether I'd made the right decision, the investigation certainly had a renewed sense of direction. I sat and watched in admiration as the plan unfolded. Shaun and Rob met and instantly bonded with Gary. Although they were already very accomplished at interviewing criminals, Gary taught them to treat the entire process of planning, preparing and conducting interviews, more as a kind of art form designed to give the criminal and their lawyer every opportunity to tell the truth with nowhere to hide. It was an approach the police service hadn't seen before, and it got me thinking about how far removed Gary's philosophy was from my early days as a constable, prior to PACE.

Back then, criminals were interviewed in their cells and notes of what was said were supposed to be summarised in pocket note books as soon after the conclusion of the interview as possible. In truth, that rarely happened. A bacon sandwich in the canteen always seemed to be a more attractive proposition than sat with your colleague trying to remember what questions had been asked and the foul-mouthed replies. Before PACE, a prisoner could be held indefinitely, there was no time limit, and I smiled to myself as I recalled arresting a man for shoplifting one Friday afternoon. I went off duty for the weekend and completely forgot about him until the Monday morning, when a bemused custody sergeant enquired as to what I intended doing with my prisoner. When I finally got around to dealing with him for theft of a Mars bar, I had some sympathy for his point of view,

"Bloody hell, I only stole a fucking Mars bar and I've been kept in this fucking cell all weekend without a smoke. What would have happened if I'd done something serious? Lock me up for ever and throw away the fucking key? For fuck's sake, it's not right, no fucking way."

I made out that his weekend break at the police station without being allowed to smoke was the norm and that he should be grateful that it wasn't longer. On the plus side, his admission of guilt made for a short interview and, after I'd charged and released him, I shouted in a wholly sarcastic way,

"And let that be a lesson to you in the future, not to steal

Mars bars."

He turned and looked at me and muttered something under his breath that sounded like,

"Go fuck yourself."

I judged it to be a fair comment in the circumstances.

TWENTY-TWO

'Brilliant, there was no other word to describe it'

As April loomed ever closer, the thought of leaving my beloved CID for the seaside made me more and more irritable and less patient by the minute. I felt an acute sense of humiliation, being the only SIO in the force ever to be moved from a live investigation. Whenever I came across another SIO, they invariably asked me how I felt about being posted. I duly gave a positive response, saying something about how I was looking forward to new challenges. They knew it was bollocks and so did I. It was obvious that my misfortune was a current favoured topic of conversation across the force. The police service could be a cruel and unforgiving organisation that loved nothing more than watching some poor unfortunate soul fall from grace. Whilst I was expected to be the next casualty, there was still a long way to go before I'd be strolling along the promenade at Bridlington, I thought.

I knew that to be able to hold my head up high and walk away from the investigation with my credibility and reputation intact, at the very least, those responsible for Natalie's murder and dismemberment needed to be charged. Time was against me and the evidence gathered to date, apart from TML/4, was purely circumstantial relying heavily on the accounts given by Pattison and Sunman, who was about as dishonest a human being who ever walked this earth. I held long meetings with Tony and the officers who'd be interviewing Adams, Larvin and Armstrong. Based on the assumption that they'd either make no comment or fail to tell the truth, on what we had so far, we knew there was no way a jury would be convinced beyond reasonable doubt of their guilt. If this case was to ever get to trial, I needed more, much more. We'd be up against smart-arse barristers, who'd tear Pattison and Sunman to shreds and probably argue, successfully, that the presence of TML/4 inside 119 St Johns Grove didn't prove that Adams murdered Natalie. I'd have to agree. If I were defending Adams, all I'd have to do was show that the house had been insecure and not been lived in for months. Reasonable doubt, without even trying.

The arrests and interviews were planned for Tuesday, 20 April. I reluctantly agreed to push the date back to give more time for the interview plans to be prepared. They had to be damn near perfect given our lack of tangible evidence. Although my posting was from 1 April, I put a strong, passionately argued case forward to DCS Jordan that it was vital I stay on the investigation to supervise the interviews. To his credit, he somehow got the ACC's approval. I never did ask him how he managed it, but it might have had something to do with me saying to DCS Jordan that, if they insisted, I'd simply refuse to go. It was a question of professional pride, and I could tell that he'd a great deal of sympathy for my position. However he managed to persuade the ACC, it didn't matter, I'd secured a temporary reprieve for now.

The pressure was on Shaun and Rob as the interviewing officers for Adams. When they finally came to my office to show me their interview plan, they were excited and clearly mentally exhausted. I scanned the thick file that ran to one hundred and twenty-six pages. I'd never seen such a comprehensive and thoroughly detailed plan. It was truly impressive, and I told them that they'd far exceeded my expectations. I'm not sure they understood the significance of their achievement. It was how they'd set the bar so high in terms of the quality of the plan they wanted to produce and then delivered it to such an exacting standard. Brilliant, there was no other word to describe it. I knew that Adams and his legal representative wouldn't be expecting to come up against such a formidable duo, and I took some comfort in the knowledge that the plan couldn't have been any better. If I was impressed with Shaun and Rob's plan, I was equally so with the interview plans for Larvin, produced by John Goddard and Boyd Walton, and Armstrong, by Kev Scarth and Andy Marshall. I recognised Gary's influence: staged disclosure to provide just enough information to the legal representatives so that it would be difficult for them to advise their clients to remain silent when interviewed. Juries desperately wanted to trust the police. Gone were the days of attempting to intimidate suspects by oppressive questioning and rightly so. Gary's approach was designed to intimidate them in a different way - by the sheer professionalism of the interviewing officers.

TWENTY-THREE

'Look, I know I'm no Leonardo Da Vinci'

As I drove into work, with the early morning blanket of mist shimmering above the vast open fields and the sun bursting through the windscreen, it was one of those days filled with promise when anything seemed possible. It was my favourite time of year and, with summer on the horizon, the thought of strolling along the promenade at Bridlington didn't seem so bad.

It was Tuesday, 20 April. The planned arrests had all taken place. I was on my way to Tower Grange where Adams would soon be arriving. Tony was already at Beverley with Larvin, and Mark Chapman was at Hessle with Armstrong. Tower Grange was a sixties-style building located to the east of the city. It had the appearance of a bloody great brick box with windows and a flat roof. The inside was just as uninspiring.

I'd started my CID career on the third floor of the station, and I remembered my first day as a detective walking into a big office full of people I didn't know. I was completely ignored and I wasn't sure if it was just the welcome everyone received on their first day, or because I was posted into the CID very young in service. I felt nervous but I tried not to show it. I looked around the room and I recognised a few faces I'd seen on major incidents before. They carried themselves with a 'we're on a murder case and more important than you', attitude. That's just the way it was and I knew it'd take a lot for them to accept me.

At the briefing, though, something totally unexpectedly happened that made me feel much better. The DS in charge for the day was a tall, slim character called Harold Wilkins. His hair was the first thing I noticed about him – it was a startling blend of ginger and red the like of which I'd never seen before. He wore a shiny mustard-coloured suit that had clearly seen better days, and with his reddened cheeks and nose, I could imagine him almost glowing in the dark. He spoke with a posh, public school accent that was not at all in keeping with his surroundings. I could've listened to his hypnotic delivery all day. He possessed a gift of being able to hold an audience in the palm of his hand. When he announced who'd be working together, my heart sank as my name was the only one not mentioned. Finally, he raised his voice and said,

"DC Davison, you'll be working with me today and I'd like to welcome you to our CID of which we are all very proud."

I took it as a friendly, kind gesture from the flame-haired DS and from that moment on, the day got better and better.

"Come on Paul, little job to do first and then we'll go visit my auntie. You'll like her."

I knew what he meant by 'auntie'. At the conclusion of my first day in the CID, I arrived home about two in the morning, having spent most of the day in various pubs with

Harold and his 'auntie'. Pulling into the station car park, I wondered what became of Harold, a true gentleman and unique character.

I went straight to the custody suite. It was still as gloomy as ever. There was a fresh smell of disinfectant as one of the cleaning ladies mopped the cell corridors. I knew her from when I'd started in the CID some ten years ago and she seemed pleased to see me. Shaun and Rob were stood next to Adams, who was still in handcuffs. He looked a picture of health compared to the last time I saw him just before his video statement back in August of last year. There was still a vacant expression on his face and his black eyes were as cold as I remembered. Gary was talking to Mike Waudby, who I assumed was Adams's legal representative. They were chatting together as if they were old friends.

It was time for the interviews to begin. Shaun and Rob sat opposite Adams and his brief across the familiar, wooden table with fixed tape machines. Gary and me were next door in a small room, not much bigger than a cupboard. We had a good view of Adams's face on the remote monitoring TV screen, and I was looking forward to seeing his reaction to Shaun and Rob's questioning. I was pleased Gary was with me. He'd done this a thousand times before and although it wasn't an exact science, if Adams decided to talk, Gary would be able to tell when Adams was lying and when he was telling the truth. His body language would give it away, just as it'd done during his video statement. I expected him to go no comment, given that he was free of heroin. When Adams began to answer the questions being put to him, Gary smiled.

"Bloody hell, Gary, he's talking. I didn't expect that."

"Aye well, I didn't leave Mike Waudby much of a choice. Had fair a natter with him and he came around to my way of thinking. Judges don't take kindly to legal reps advising their clients to say nothing when they've been given proper disclosure before an interview. Makes them look dodgy and their clients guilty."

"You're an absolute star."

"Aye, I know, I've been told before."

I was relieved. Over the next four long days, Adams freely admitted committing numerous crimes to feed his heroin addiction safe in the knowledge that he wouldn't be prosecuted. From the crime reports, this gave us his movements and whereabouts from when he'd reported Natalie missing on 14 May last year. To be honest, if he hadn't been given immunity, the interviews wouldn't have lasted long. Without Natalie to provide money for his heroin, Adams was forced to commit mostly burglaries and sneak in thefts with Larvin and sometimes, Armstrong. A picture emerged of Adams no longer living at 119 St Johns Grove and spending all of his time immediately after Natalie's disappearance staying at Larvin's house. This was exactly what we wanted him to say. A circumstantial case against Larvin for assisting Adams to dispose of Natalie's body, depended on putting them together after the event. And that's precisely what Adams did, in great detail. He even agreed that he was with Larvin when, following the sneak-in burglary in Beverley on 21 July, they disposed of a wallet in the drain upstream of where Natalie's mutilated body parts were found. He denied being violent towards Natalie and claimed that all of the numerous witnesses to the contrary were liars. When he was shown a pair of black ankle boots that we believed were removed from Natalie after she was killed by cutting each one with a sharp blade, he agreed that they could have been Natalie's but claimed not to have seen them in their present state.

As Adams was forced to lie, his entire demeanour changed from being calm and sure of himself, looking at both detectives in the eye, to a state of increasing anxiety - head bowed, hands sweaty and aggressive outbursts. And there was no respite for Adams as Shaun and Rob probed him over Natalie leaving him to pursue a lesbian relationship with Nini Thompson. When the detectives calmly asked him if that was the motive for killing Natalie, Adams literally hit the roof.

"Look I know I'm no Leonardo Da Vinci from that film Ti-fucking-tanic, but I've got my pride and it pissed me off. But I didn't kill her. I loved her."

Shaun realised that Adams had meant to say Leonardo Di Caprio,

"So, for the tape you're saying that you're no oil painting."

"Get fucked," came the reply.

It was a moment of light relief before Shaun and Rob introduced the contents of Sunman's statement, in which he claimed that Adams told him, 'five hacksaw blades man, five fucking hacksaw blades, it took me five hacksaw blades to cut her up 'cos they kept snapping'. Adams denied the conversation ever took place and argued that he doesn't say the word 'man', despite using it repeatedly during earlier interviews. He suggested that Sunman had come forward in an effort to facilitate an early release from prison. When he was told that Sunman had already been released from prison and was a free man when he gave his statement, Adams replied,

"I don't know what to say, gobsmacked me, I'm fucking gobsmacked."

Finally, Adams was presented with Pattison's evidence which, by now, had widened from the drain bank confession, to include a conversation with Armstrong whilst in prison. Pattison claimed that Armstrong told him that Adams had admitted 'doing her in' to him and that he'd helped move the body. Adams chose not to make any comment. In relation to the drain bank confession, Adams denied the conversation ever took place and claimed not to know the meaning of 'served her up'. He accused the police of 'forcing' witnesses to give statements against him because he's 'a junkie', and that he was 'stitched up' by corrupt police officers.

Just when Adams must have thought the interviews were coming to an end, Shaun calmly placed a photograph of Natalie's severed head on the table. I knew what was coming next. Shaun would create a long and awkward silence before asking the next question. It was a tactic that he used to unsettle suspects and it worked, most of the time. Adams didn't say a word. He pushed the photograph away from him as his brief retched at the sight of the badly decomposed skull. No eyes, no nose, no lips and no ears, just rotting flesh, maggots and a mass of matted hair. Eventually, Shaun broke the silence.

"Did you do this to Natalie, did you cut off her head with

hacksaw blades?"

"What you showing me this for. Fuck all to do with me. How many times do I have to tell you, it was fucking Amadi."

The sight of Natalie's severed head had no visible effect on Adams as he sat back in his chair and looked across at Shaun with a grin on his face.

"Why are you smiling? Do you think this is funny?"

"I know what you're doing, trying to shock me with gory photos. Won't work. How do I know it's her head anyway?"

Shaun didn't reply he just did the same thing again with a photograph of Natalie's torso. He placed it neatly next to the one of her head.

"Darren, look at the photograph. Can you tell me what it is?"

"'How do I know. You tell me, you're the fucking detective."

Gary hadn't said much as he'd watched Shaun meticulously cover every aspect of his mammoth interview plan.

"Shaun's done a brilliant job. Did you see Adams's body language change when he saw the photographs? Folded his arms. Classic reaction. He's under pressure. No doubt about it."

Although Adams was definitely under pressure, I knew there'd be no chance of him admitting what he'd done.

"It's Natalie's torso and those are markers to illustrate the number of stab wounds to her chest. You admitted to Pattison that you did this, didn't you?"

"Fuck off."

"How did he know that you'd stabbed her unless you told him?"

"Fuck off."

"Was Pattison there too. Is that how he knew. Did he help you to cut up her body?"

"Fuck off."

"Did you punch and kick Natalie in the chest before you stabbed her to death."

For a moment, Adams looked down at the photograph. It was as if he hadn't expected Shaun's question. Maybe he wondered how we knew about the assault on Natalie, given the degree of decomposition. Adams didn't reply. He didn't look at all comfortable as Shaun placed the last photograph on the table. It was of Natalie's severed right arm. Again, there was no cocky reply. He just looked away. Maybe it was because he was experiencing some kind of flash back as he recalled seeing the word CHAOS, just before he delivered the blow that severed her arm.

"You argued over Natalie preferring Nini to you and you lost your temper. You kicked and punched her before stabbing her over and over again. You then turned to Larvin for help to get rid of her body. Together, you set about cutting her body into pieces, put them in bin bags and threw them into the drain. The right thing to do would be for you to admit what you've done."

Adams looked straight at Shaun. I tried to imagine what would be running through his mind if that was exactly what happened, and how he'd be trying to come to terms with Pattison's and Sunman's betrayal of the bond of trust between villains never to grass. I just hoped that it would be preying heavily on his mind as Shaun held his gaze for the last time.

Larvin's approach was very different to that of Adams. Badly advised by his solicitor, Yvonne Hood, he chose to say nothing for the first twelve interviews. Their tactics were to receive written disclosure from John Goddard and Boyd Walton, and then proceed to conduct lengthy private discussions prior to each interview designed to significantly reduce the time available to the detectives for questioning. It was only when the discovery of his fingerprints on TML/4 was put to Larvin on Friday, 23 April that he, following legal advice, began to answer questions. By this time, he'd been in custody for three days and seven hours. Larvin strenuously denied any knowledge of the murder of Natalie, and denied helping Adams to dispose of her body. He could offer no explanation for the presence of his fingerprints on TML/4.

The circumstantial case against Armstrong was built around comments he'd made to a number of witnesses, including Pattison, indicating that he knew that Adams stabbed Natalie and how he'd helped dispose of her body. They were facts never released to the press, and it came as no surprise that he chose to make no comment during most of his fourteen interviews. Interview thirteen provoked an angry response though, when Pattison's evidence was introduced. He denied making any specific comments to Pattison. But then he unexpectedly admitted seeing Adams in a 'grafted' state covered in what he thought was blood on his clothing in the early hours of a day in mid-April. He believed this was after Adams had killed Natalie. Although Armstrong was clearly mistaken about the date – it must have been May, not April - every other detail supported Pattison's evidence. He denied any involvement in Natalie's murder or her dismemberment and said it was 'laughable' that he was a suspect, claiming it was 'too naughty' for him.

It was late Friday afternoon, and I knew I had to make a decision on what to do with Adams, Larvin and Armstrong. By tomorrow morning, they'd have been in custody for ninety-six hours, the maximum time PACE allowed the police to detain suspects for questioning without charge. I asked Tony, Gary and the six interviewing detectives to meet me back in my office. It was the logical thing to do. I wanted to get the views of everyone, although I'd already decided on whom I wanted to charge. In my mind, I had to make a decision that would withstand independent scrutiny.

The test applied by the CPS to any case was simple: is there a realistic chance of a successful prosecution, and so we set about the task of applying that test to each of the suspects. We imagined that we were unbiased members of the jury and began with Adams. I knew there was no way we'd be able to remain impartial but Gary's presence would help. I'd more to lose than anyone else in the room if we took the decision not to charge. The case would slip away from me, and I'd be resigned to following progress, someone else's progress, from Bridlington.

We began with Adams. Although there was a total lack of any tangible evidence against him, Andy Marshal and Kev Scarth believed that despite Pattison being a drug dealing, violent and dishonest criminal, he'd make a brilliant witness at Crown Court. I trusted them, and I trusted Shaun and Rob for their belief in Sunman's account. Whilst Andy and Kev felt that they could guarantee Pattison's cooperation to give evidence, Sunman was an altogether different matter. The view was that he'd probably end up being a hostile witness but that in no way diminished the weight of his contribution. Shaun and Rob helpfully and meticulously summarised the evidence of all the other witnesses against Adams, and by the time they'd finished, there was a strong circumstantial case that deserved to be put before a jury. We all agreed that Adams should be charged with Natalie's murder.

John Goddard and Boyd Walton repeated the process for Larvin, and they presented a compelling argument for charging Larvin with assisting Adams to dispose of Natalie's body. The most damning evidence against him would be his fingerprints on TML/4 discovered inside 119 St Johns Grove. Despite the recognition that a single fingerprint belonging to Dougie McKenzie (who'd been eliminated from suspicion) was also found on the bin liner, there was still a substantial case linking Adams with Larvin after 14 May. Again, I trusted John Goddard and he was sure of Larvin's involvement. That was good enough for me. Larvin would be charged with assisting offender.

Armstrong posed the biggest problem. Whilst Andy and Kev were sure that he'd played some part in helping Adams, they suggested that it might better to try and use Armstrong as a witness against him. There was some merit in their argument. Persuading Armstrong though to testify about seeing Adams in a 'grafted' state covered in blood, would be tricky to say the least. Finally, I turned to Gary for his view. He'd been unusually quiet and all he said was,

"You know you've got some canny lads on this

investigation. I agree with them. Adams is a cold-blooded killer but Larvin's the lad who sorted things out. Armstrong was probably involved somehow but I doubt you'll be able to prove it."

I called Mr Marshall, the head of CPS, at home. He was grateful for the call and agreed to sign my policy book to show that I'd consulted him over the charges. It was the right thing to do, but it also helped to cover my back against suggestions that I'd charged to satisfy my own agenda. Mr Marshall was very positive and agreed with my decision.

"We'll have to get on with instructing a top barrister. There's a chap called Francis Bernard based in Leeds. He's very good with complicated cases."

"You mean cases were there's no evidence."

He just laughed. But before he put the phone down, he was very complimentary about the whole team for getting this far. It meant a lot to me, given the circumstances.

DCS Jordan was pleased but more relieved than anything. This finally put to rest the theory of a serial killer on the loose and showed that his support for me to be the SIO wasn't misplaced, at least for the time being. The trial was yet to come. Adams and Larvin were charged and appeared at Hull Magistrates Court on Saturday, 24 April. They were both subsequently remanded to HMP Hull.

TWENTY-FOUR

'It was as if he was dead inside'

Detective Superintendent Taylor was now officially the SIO. I'd been replaced. It wasn't a great feeling if I'm honest. Although I'd beaten the deadline and that was some consolation, I felt lost. The investigation had been my life for almost a year and now it would go on without me. Others would leave and only a small team would be left to prepare for the trial that would be some months away.

I took a few days off to mentally prepare for my posting but it didn't work out as I'd planned. John Goddard called me at home on Thursday, 29 April. Larvin wanted to see him, and provided John stuck to the rules of PACE regarding post-charge interviews, we'd nothing to lose by listening to what he had to say.

Later the same evening, John rang me after his visit to see him in HMP Hull.

"Larvin's given Adams up. He admitted not telling the truth in interview. Basically, he's saying that Adams came to see him one morning and told him he'd woken up in the kitchen at 119 St Johns Grove on the floor next to Natalie. She'd a knife in her and he was covered in blood. They'd been arguing the night before, after taking a load of temazepam."

"Did he say what they'd been arguing about?"

"No. But I can guess. Anyway, Adams asked him for help and he refused suggesting that he should either burn the house down or report her missing. There's a load more to tell you. I think we should get him out of prison to interview him again on tape. I'm busy putting everything he said in my ONB. I'll get him to sign it when he's produced."

"What's he after, why the change of heart?"

"Clearly wants to help himself if he can. We've got a problem though. He's putting Pattison inside 119 St Johns Grove a few days later with Adams and Jodi Amadi. Says they looked to be covered in blood."

I was pleased that DS Goddard had called me even though I was no longer the SIO. I didn't ask him why, but as I'd come to know John over the months of working together, I liked to think that it was old school loyalty. Although we'd have to be extremely careful in dealing with Larvin after charge, his betrayal of Adams was significant even if it undermined Pattison as a potential witness. Arrangements were made for Larvin to be produced to Beverley Police Station. We had to get him on tape and I wanted to hear for myself what he had to say.

On Saturday, 1 May, I met Larvin's solicitor, Yvonne Hood, at the station. She was one of those people it wasn't hard to dislike. Clearly weighed down by a high opinion of herself, it was as if she was trying to annoy everyone she met, just for the hell of it. Without a moment's introduction, she waded in with, 'my client will only cooperate if there's a deal on the table'. She was obviously used to getting her own way. Adding an ounce of charm to go with her natural good looks would've made all the difference, I thought. I was doing it again, judging someone based on being in their company for about five seconds. Maybe she was insecure and her abrasive front was just that, a front to hide behind. That was something I could understand.

When I told her, firmly, that there'd be no 'deals on the table' and suggested that she'd watched too much police drama on TV, she stormed off demanding to see her client. This gave me time to read John's ONB entry for his meeting with Larvin in prison. It was thorough, detailed, impressive, and more to the point, believable.

In his first interview, he intimated that he hadn't expected to be charged and would be willing to give evidence against Adams in order to have his sentence reduced or case discontinued. He wanted to get out of prison to see his children. For the benefit of the tape, it was made clear to him that it would be the responsibility of the CPS to consider his position in due course and no promises could be made. This was obviously not the answer he was looking for and there was tension between him and his solicitor. I expected Larvin to change his mind and request a return to prison but instead, he talked freely and confirmed that John's ONB entry was a true and accurate record of their conversation.

It came as no surprise that he skillfully absolved himself of any part in the disposal of Natalie. He maintained that the only thing he was guilty of was lying to the police and that he did so out of loyalty to Adams. Larvin was an accomplished liar and it was harder than usual to know when he was telling the truth. His face remained without any kind of expression throughout both days of questioning. It was as if he was dead inside as he talked about his heroin addiction and how, when he could no longer find a vein to inject into, Adams would inject into his jugular and he'd do the same for Adams.

Larvin recalled in some detail when Adams arrived at his house banging on the door. One of Larvin's children woke him and he let Adams into the house. Larvin described Adams as looking 'frazzled' and unkempt, which was unusual. Adams then blurted out, 'Natalie's dead. I was temaze'd up last night, arguing, I woke up on the kitchen floor and she was dead next to me'. He continued to implicate Pattison and Amadi as being present a few days later inside 119 St Johns Grove, covered in what he thought was blood. When John challenged him on this part of his account, the part we believed to be mostly untrue, he remained unruffled and calm. I imagined that he'd pass any lie detector test put in front of him.

By the end of the second day, Ms. Hood demanded that the charges against Larvin be dropped given his protested innocence, but when I told her that her client might well be facing an additional charge of attempting to pervert the course of justice by lying to the police, she stormed out of the station like a spoilt child. My initial opinion of her was spot on.

I called Mr Marshall with Larvin's change of heart. We considered all the options and came to the same conclusion that, although it was a risky strategy, Larvin might be a better witness than co-accused, provided no more evidence came to light regarding his involvement in the dismemberment and disposal of Natalie's body. Mr Marshall was like a breath of fresh air with his no-nonsense approach to decision making. Before the call ended, he told me he'd managed to retain the services of Francis Bernard, the top barrister he'd mentioned before.

"They don't come any better than Mr Bernard. He has an outstanding reputation and the defence will have to go some to match him. Believe me. Can you arrange to see him at his chambers in Leeds?"

Although I hadn't met Mr Bernard, I knew that he'd be the difference at Crown Court. For us to win the jury would have to like him, trust him, believe him and given that the odds were heavily stacked against us, he'd have to be bloody brilliant and more.

Tony, Shaun and me travelled to Leeds to meet with him the following week. I knew that I should be at Bridlington but nothing was going to stop me. In my mind, I'd earned the right to meet the prosecuting barrister. I needed to know he cared and that he was a man of integrity with high principles. We parked the car in Park Square and walked the short distance to Zenith Chambers. There were some steps leading to an imposing, grand looking set of thick wooden doors. The world beyond was a million miles away from what I was used to. From the deeply impressive luxurious offices, to the feeling of being in the presence of people who immediately made you feel inferior with their public-school accents and razor-sharp pinstriped suits.

Mr Bernard's PA showed us into his office. It was

massive with wooden clad walls and furnished to a standard I hadn't seen before, anywhere. Mr Bernard sprang to his feet, hurried over from behind his desk, and shook our hands with a firm grip. It was a good start, I thought. Shaun had sent over a copy of all the statements and relevant documents, including transcripts of the interviews. I could see the file on his desk with a blue ribbon tied neatly around the bundle of papers. For some reason, all barristers and CPS lawyers used the tied-ribbon approach. It was as if they wouldn't accept delivery of a file without it. My heart sank a little because I assumed that he hadn't read the file. I couldn't have been more wrong. It was clear from his opening comments that he'd not only read everything, but knew the case almost better than me. So far, so good, I liked him from the beginning. He most definitely had the 'likeability' factor. There was a gentleness to his voice that made you want to listen and believe what he was saying, and he conducted himself with an air of reassuring confidence that fell just short of arrogance.

The introductions lasted for about three seconds as he peered over his half-moon glasses perched on the end of his long slender nose. Armed with an expensive looking Mont Blanc fountain pen in his right hand, he probed us in some detail over our opinions on Pattison, Sunman, Armstrong and Larvin, and how they'd come across giving evidence against Adams in front of a jury.

"In summary, Pattison might well turn out to be a credible witness, even though he's on remand charged with manslaughter and has an interesting list of previous convictions for violence and dishonesty. There is little chance of persuading either Sunman or Armstrong to give evidence and should they do so, they would probably do more harm than good to the prosecution case. You believe Larvin is lying about failing to assist Adams dispose of the body and has changed his story purely in the hope of furthering his own interests. No sign of a murder weapon…but there is TML/4. I admit that the case is not without its challenges and our chances of success, I suspect, will very much depend on Pattison's testimony. Very interesting case, if I may say so. Might there be more to come from Pattison? He seems to be a fascinating character."

We left the meeting pleased with the choice of Mr Bernard. I could see why he was so successful. He had charisma in spades and I knew that any reasonable jury would warm to him as a person. At least I hoped they would, I couldn't see any reason why they wouldn't. But as we travelled back to Hull, we recognised the significance of what he'd said about Pattison. How on earth would Mr Bernard be able to convince a jury to believe Pattison? The defence would destroy his character and show him to be a thoroughly evil, dishonest and violent drug dealer. And they'd be right. We talked endlessly about the missing parts of the story: what happened after Adams killed Natalie, how did the body parts get into Holderness Drain, where was the knife Adams used to stab her to death, and where was the instrument used to saw her into pieces. We needed more.

For the remainder of the journey though, my thoughts, inevitably, returned to why I'd been posted out of the CID. It was a restless, anxious feeling that had everything to do with starting over again in a world that I didn't have much of a passion for. I felt lost, and I'd no idea what the future had in store for me now.

TWENTY-FIVE

'I've served her up. We was temaze'd up with some Russian shit'

The following day, I was back in my office for the last time. I closed the door and sat for a while. A photograph of my family would have to be packed away for the journey to Bridlington and so would my Winnie the Pooh mug the boys had bought me for my birthday. It always served as a reminder not to take myself too seriously because his head was stuck inside a jar of honey.

I was going to miss the life of a DCI as I recalled the phone call from the ACC in late July of last year, and the subsequent months of high drama that followed. But there was nothing I could do about it now, chief officers wouldn't change their minds. Tony came in for a chat before I left. We'd become really close and I was going to miss him.

"Now I know you wouldn't want a leaving do but I'm afraid the team have arranged one anyway. So, you'll have to come. No excuses. It's in the Old Town. Come on, let's have an early finish."

Although I wasn't a leaving do type of person, the thought of sinking a few pints with my trusted colleagues was exactly what I needed right now. Just as we were about to leave, the unexpected happened again. Andy Marshall burst into my office.

"Boss, Pattison wants to talk to us again. He wants us to get him out of prison to a police station. He says he's got a lot more to tell us and it'll be worth our while. What do you think?"

"Andy, absolutely. We've nothing to lose. Why now?"

"He didn't say but my guess is he knows we interviewed Larvin again, might be worried about what he's said."

Again, I was glad that Andy had come to me with the news. Whilst I'd no idea what Pattison would say, Andy had been convinced all along that he'd far more information to give and that it was just a question of when, and not if, he'd tell us.

I managed to pull some strings to get Pattison out of prison and by mid-afternoon of the following day, he was sat facing Andy Marshall and Kev Scarth in an interview room at Beverley Police Station. I was in the next room with Shaun, Gary, Tony and John. It was bigger than the one at Tower Grange, where I'd watched Adams being interviewed by Shaun, but it was still a squeeze to fit us all in. Nobody cared though, we were all too nervous to notice. We could see and hear what was happening via the TV screen. When Andy explained that the interview was being monitored, Pattison stared at the camera and held his gaze for what seemed like forever. He knew he'd the upper hand with not only Andy and Kev hanging on his every word, but now the SIO, deputy SIO, a detective sergeant and a national expert in investigative interviewing.

"You two have treated me like a human being from the start. Never happened with coppers before. Always been made to feel like scum. I loved Natalie. What Adams did to her was wrong. I'm going to tell you what happened. It'll take some time."

Pattison wasn't wrong. He kept us all spellbound for the next two days, and the tapes of his evidence amounted to a lengthy sixty-page statement. As soon as a tape was complete, Shaun set about transcribing its content onto paper. It was a mammoth task.

He began by reliving the early morning meeting with Adams on the drain bank near to Flinton Grove. It took place on Wednesday, 13 May 1998, sometime shortly after eight. He was precise about the time and date because he always kept a diary. It was something he'd done since he was a kid. Andy and Kev didn't need to ask any questions as Pattison proceeded to tell his story of what happened that day. The depth of his recall was astonishing; it was as if we were there watching.

It was a bright, crisp morning. A man and a couple of kids were throwing an old carpet into the drain. The grass was wet as he sat down next to Adams. He'd never seen Adams in such a state before: head bowed between his knees, rattling, disheveled, filthy hands with dirt under his fingernails. At first, he just thought that it was because he needed to score, but then the words came tumbling out, 'I've served her up. We was temaze'd up with some Russian shit. We was arguing over her leaving me for that fucking lesbian cunt Nini. I just woke up next to her in the kitchen. She had a knife sticking out of her stomach. Blood all over the fucking place'.

Pattison made it clear that although there wasn't much to

like about Adams, his natural instinct was to put his arm around him and offer a rare moment of friendship. He formed a mental picture of poor Natalie presumably still lying on a filthy kitchen floor, alone, cold and dead. Any sympathy he might have had for his longtime associate, evaporated as he felt an overwhelming sadness for her. He'd always liked Natalie and remembered when he first saw her with her children in the company of Adams. They became good friends, and he admitted having a soft spot for her. He'd watched her decline into drug addiction and prostitution because of Adams. Within a few months of arriving in Hull full of hope and ready to start a new life, she'd lost her children into care, she'd lost about half her body weight, she'd lost pretty much everything. Adams just used her to fund his own habit so he didn't have to commit crime.

With a 'fuck that's bad man', they parted, and Pattison watched as Adams shuffled along in the direction of Leven Grove where Larvin lived. Pattison didn't give Adams the chance to ask for his help. He believed that Adams had killed Natalie and wanted to get away from him so he could 'get his head around' what had just happened. He felt sure that Adams would turn to Larvin. He guessed that Adams and Larvin would need a fix before they'd be able to stop rattling, never mind get rid of a body. He wandered the streets wondering what to do and deep down, he knew that there was only one thing to do - go to 119 St Johns Grove and see for himself. Part of it was natural curiosity but mostly, he just wanted to see Natalie. Maybe Adams was wrong, maybe she was in bed asleep, maybe she was still alive and he'd be able to save her. Whatever the motivation, he knew he had to go, and go before Adams returned, presumably with Larvin.

You could hear a pin drop. Pattison had us all utterly spellbound. For most of the time he talked, I almost forgot I was monitoring an interview with a criminal, who the system judged to be just that, a criminal, the enemy, me included. I was witnessing something I hadn't seen before in police custody: hidden beneath the dreadlocks, was a mind of an intelligent man, blessed with a razor-sharp intellect and the ability to recall in precise detail what he'd seen and felt that day. In a different life he'd have made a brilliant policeman, I thought. His statements would have been first-class. The mutual respect between Pattison and the two detectives was obvious. It'd taken months and months to build such a rapport with him to get to this place.

The next part of Pattison's account, even though it was after charge, was worth waiting for. He took a sip of water and seemed to purposely slow his speech. It was perhaps his way of heightening the drama of the occasion. He knew the significance of what he was about to say.

He recalled entering 119 St Johns Grove through the backdoor that was partly ajar. He stepped into the kitchen expecting to see Natalie on the floor as Adams had described, but she wasn't there. He looked for blood but he couldn't see the floor for the carpet of rubbish. If Adams had been truthful, he expected there to be obvious signs of a struggle with blood everywhere. His heart was pounding. He shouted, 'Natalie, Natalie are you OK?' There was no reply. Maybe she was asleep. He made his way carefully from the kitchen into the hallway intending to make his way upstairs.

It was partially lit with natural light, and he saw what looked like smears of blood on the linoleum floor leading to the bathroom. He took a closer look trying to convince himself that it could be something other than blood. The bathroom door was half-open and, as he pushed against it, Natalie's body lay motionless in the filthy bath. She was partially covered with a blue-coloured blanket. The light from the window gave him a clear view. It was Natalie with her bleached hair and long dark roots, layer upon layer of cheap makeup and lipstick. Her right arm covered with track marks lay on top of the blanket. Her CHAOS tattoo stared back at him. He sat on the edge of the bath for a few moments. Although he'd seen some bad things in his violent life, nothing came close to this. Touching her face made him flinch because he hadn't realised it'd be so cold.

He left via the backdoor knowing that he couldn't do anything for Natalie now. When he was asked why he hadn't called the police, he looked at Andy and Kev with a look of absolute contempt. He didn't bother to answer the question. I wondered why he'd chosen to cooperate now. Had he been there all along to help Adams? Is that why he could recall everything in so much detail? If so, then he'd be worried that Larvin could've implicated him during his recent interview after charge. Larvin had already put Pattison and Amadi in 119 St Johns Grove covered in blood. If I'd to choose whom to believe between Larvin and Pattison though, I'd choose Pattison every time.

Pattison told nobody what he'd seen. He went home and just sat wondering what to do. He felt sure that Adams would seek help from Larvin. But how would they get rid of her body? It was a simple question he asked himself, and he'd never know the answer unless he returned to 119 St Johns Grove. He couldn't bear the thought of Adams just leaving her there to rot in the bath. What would he do if that proved to be the case? He convinced himself that he'd no option but to go back.

By mid-afternoon, Pattison returned. As he approached the rear of the house intending to go in via the back door again, he could hear voices. It was Adams and Larvin. They were sweating, out of breath and washing what appeared to be blood off themselves at the kitchen sink. Larvin didn't look pleased to see him but he stepped into the kitchen anyway. The first thing he noticed was the smell. He tried to describe it but he didn't know how to. All he said was,

"It was the smell of death."

There were a number of black bin bags that were tightly knotted. They looked full and heavy. There was no sign of Natalie. He noticed broken hacksaw blades on the window sill. Adams broke the eerie silence with,

"That took some fucking doing. The bitch was hard man, hard to cut. I'm knackered now."

The gruesome realisation that the bags contained Natalie's body hit him as if he'd been kicked in the stomach. The bastards had cut her up and they acted as if it was no big deal. He tried to remain cool and calm as if he condoned what they'd just done to someone he very much cared for. He wanted to do something, but he couldn't move, paralysed with nausea. They just carried on despite Pattison's arrival. He believed that Adams had told Larvin that Pattison already knew he'd killed Natalie and that he was coming around to give them a hand.

Larvin brought bleach and a change of clothes from his car parked at the front of the house. They discussed the best way to Bransholme, where they planned to dump her body in an isolated part of Holderness Drain. If he hadn't known that they'd just dismembered poor Natalie, they could be discussing a day trip to the seaside. It wasn't long before they were carrying the bags to Larvin's car. It was broad daylight and they calmly walked out from the back of the house with the bags as if they were full of household rubbish for the bin-men to collect. Adams and Larvin looked at each other and Larvin told him to carry a bag to the car. Adams swore him to secrecy. He agreed and managed to pull his coat sleeve over his hand to prevent his fingerprints being found on the bag. They didn't ask him to come with them. He wouldn't have gone anyway, even if they'd insisted. They drove off in Larvin's blue Sierra and that's the last time he'd been inside 119 St Johns Grove.

By now, it was getting towards the end of the second day. Even though Pattison had done pretty much all of the talking, listening to his evidence over two long days had clearly drained Andy and Kev. Their final question to Pattison was - why had he decided to come forward now and implicate himself by admitting to carrying a bag that he believed contained parts of Natalie's body to the car.

"I know what you're thinking. I want a deal over me manslaughter charge. I don't. I'll take what's coming. What they did to Nat was out of order."

After Pattison had gone back to his cell, Andy and Kev joined us. It was one of those 'bloody hell, did that just happen', moments when we all knew we'd finally discovered how Natalie died, and how parts of her mutilated body came to be buried in a rubbish heap at the pumping station. Although convincing a jury beyond reasonable doubt would be an altogether different challenge for a different day, I believed Pattison's account. It was authentic, precisely detailed and added considerable weight to the circumstantial case against Adams. We all agreed that Larvin's position had changed again. He'd be stood shoulder to shoulder with Adams at Crown Court. A decision had to be made regarding Pattison. We'd need him to give evidence against Adams and Larvin, despite being implicated by his own admission.

I called Mr Marshall at home and he agreed to offer immunity to Pattison, in return for his testimony at Crown Court. Larvin would be charged with assisting Adams to dispose of Natalie's body. As I'd come to know him during the course of the investigation, Mr Marshall possessed a dry sense of humour, and I believe that his closing remark was his way of saying, 'well done'.

"Detective Chief Inspector, will there be any more revelations in this case?"

I resisted the temptation to go for a pint to celebrate what had just happened over the last couple of days. They'd been remarkable, extraordinary and almost beyond belief. I wanted to get home. I was absolutely shattered and I needed to mentally prepare myself for the anti-climax of knowing that I was no longer the SIO and wouldn't be there to witness Adams's and Larvin's reaction to Pattison's evidence.

It was a lonely journey home. I knew that it would be.

But it was of some consolation to know that, provided Pattison cooperated, we now had the best chance I could've hoped for to secure justice for Natalie.

TWENTY-SIX

'So be it heart; bid farewell without end'

There was one thing left to do before going to Bridlington and that was to attend Natalie's funeral in London. The coroner had released her body, or what was left of it, now that charges had been brought and a defence post-mortem carried out on behalf of Adams and Larvin. I travelled down with Sam, the FLO, on the train to Kings Cross and then we made our way on the underground to Kingsbury.

The funeral was held in a small church not far from the tube station. The REM song, 'Everybody Hurts', was playing as we entered. I caught the words 'when you're sure you've had enough of this life, well hang on, don't let yourself go 'cause everybody cries and everybody hurts sometimes'. Hearing the song again took me back to the last time I'd heard it. It was in the White Harte pub in Alfred Gelder Street at the beginning of the inquiry, when I'd thought that the song could've been written for Natalie. Maybe her mother did too, or maybe it'd been Natalie's favourite song. I wondered what the pre-drug-addicted, wide-eyed and chaotic Natalie, would have thought about the life she'd made with Adams. Perhaps she might have got clean in the future, got her children back and built a new life away from him. A naive view of the world, probably, given that I was a policeman, but sat in the tranquility of the church, anything seemed possible.

Even though we were afforded a cool reception, I was glad that I came. In death, Natalie had been a big part of my life for so long, and I wondered what she'd have thought about the investigation and the extraordinary commitment and professionalism of my officers. I hoped that she'd have been proud. I liked to think that maybe Natalie was in a better place now, released from the living hell caused by Adams, and would finally be able to rest in peace. I left a card for Natalie's mother. I couldn't think of the right words and so I wrote down a verse from 'The Glass Bead Game' by Hermann Hesse.

'Even the hour of our death
May send us speeding on to fresh and newer spaces,
And life may summon us to newer races,
So be it, heart: bid farewell without end'

TWENTY-SEVEN

'Everything passes, everything changes just do what you think you should do'

I arrived in Bridlington towards the end of May, nearly two months later than planned by chief officers. The trial was set for 22 February 2000. Adams was still to be interviewed again so that the post-charge evidence of Pattison and Larvin could be put to him. I wouldn't be there. Detective Superintendent Taylor would be making the decisions now and, to begin with, I found it hard to let go. Really hard. Being back in uniform was like stepping into a different world. In one of his songs Dylan captures perfectly just the way life is, 'Everything passes, everything changes, just do what you think you should do'. This was the beginning of the next part of my life, and I'd no option but to try and make a success of my time by the seaside.

Although being back in uniform was a massive culture shock, I soon discovered an unlikely appetite for having my own small command. I was ably supported by two Inspectors, Robin Cross and Mark Davidson. Robin proved to be one of the most likeable individuals I'd come across in the force blessed with an easy going, laid back attitude to life that gave the impression he didn't have a care in the world.

Mark was the exact opposite. Solidly built with close-shaven hair, it wasn't difficult to see why he was a good rugby player in his younger days. He liked to give the impression that he was an abrasive character, angry all the time about nothing in particular. But he wasn't like that. He'd boundless energy and enthusiasm and he just wanted to take the fight to the criminals.

The outgoing Chief Inspector had done a first-class job in tackling the high level of crime in Bridlington's deprived neighbourhoods, and so I simply continued his approach with a relentless crackdown on the top-ten villains in the popular seaside resort. Detectives would be outside their houses in a morning to greet them with a friendly wave, before hounding their every move, 24/7. The aim was to get them off the streets and into prison, so that they'd be unable to steal or burgle in order to fund their heroin addiction. It worked better than I could've hoped for. To begin with, they'd no option but to stop their criminal behaviour but, inevitably, their craving for heroin led to their arrests and return to prison.

The bigger problem, though, was that parts of Bridlington were, apparently, no-go areas for the police. I took a drive through one of the worst housing estates, Gypsy Road, late one evening accompanied by the FSG, in one of their reinforced riot vehicles. The FSG had been formed around the time of the miner's strike, just after I'd joined the force, to deal with serious outbreaks of public disorder. I knew that I was amongst battle-hardened, no-nonsense officers with bags of experience and so I felt re-assured as we made our way into the estate. But it wasn't long before the first firebomb smashed against the side of the van. Hordes of locals surrounded us hellbent on causing as much damage as possible. Heavily outnumbered, we had no option but to make good our escape to the obvious delight of the baying crowd.

Back at the station, my instinct was to see this from a SIO's perspective as just another problem to solve. I didn't know what else to do. With a huge smile on his face, Mark volunteered to lead a nightly show of force, supported by the entire FSG, to send a strong message to local residents that our gang would always be bigger than theirs. But I knew that it would only be short-term fix. A different approach was needed, one that provided long-term solutions to local problems.

And so, Robin and Mark came up with the idea of dividing Bridlington into geographic areas. Each shift of officers, led by two sergeants, was allocated a specific area with responsibility for reducing the level of crime and anti-social behaviour, accordingly. I gave Gypsy Road Estate to two enthusiastic, competent and intelligent sergeants, Dave and Chris. I had some sympathy for their reaction to the news that they'd been given one of the most deprived areas in the entire force,

"With all due respect, Sir, how do you expect us to sort out Gypsy Road Estate when nobody else has been able to. It's virtually a no-go area."

"I don't care how you solve the problem. Come up with a plan. Start with those bloody vandals stealing motorbikes and treating the estate as their own private racetrack. Can't get near them."

Within a week they came to see me in high spirits beaming from ear to ear as they told me how their plan had worked. They'd posed as rugby players, training with a local team near to where the TWOC merchants congregated. It gave them the opportunity to arrest the gang and confiscate their high-powered motorbikes. It solved the problem, and as they basked in every detail of how they'd pulled it off, I knew it was the way to go. Their enthusiasm proved to be the catalyst that inspired numerous other cunning plans to solve similar problems in other areas of Bridlington. We seemed to gain control of the streets again. Levels of crime and anti-social behaviour tumbled, calls from the public fell dramatically, and we received positive coverage in the local press.

Chief Superintendent Bland, who'd recently been promoted, was over the moon at what we'd achieved and he often came to visit. Whenever he did, he insisted on going for a walk along the promenade. On one occasion, we'd called into the local cobbler to collect my police boots that had been repaired, when he asked a question that stopped me dead in my tracks,

"Do you sell second hand shoes by any chance?"

The cobbler looked at me clearly surprised by the question posed by a Chief Superintendent in full uniform. He didn't know what to say other than,

"Not really, no. Not much of a market for second hand shoes these days."

Most of my spare time was spent reading Pattison's mammoth statement looking for ways to corroborate what he'd told us in elaborate detail over two long days. Even if the jury believed Pattison, I was pretty sure they'd want to some form of corroboration to verify his version of events. I set about retracing his steps. The drain bank confession revealed the true cause of death, which he couldn't have learned from any other source but the killer, Adams. The defence would attempt to show that it was in the public domain. They'd be wasting their time though, because Lisa had kept a careful eye on precisely this issue and she assured me we'd be OK.

In relation to Pattison's claim to have seen Natalie dead in the bath partially covered with a blue blanket or sheet, the bath was clean compared to the rest of the house. Tony and me both thought it unusual when we'd entered the house, way back in August of last year. Mr Bernard would be able to reasonably argue that Adams and Larvin used bleach to get rid of Natalie's blood and that was the reason for its absence of it in any of the drains. Bleach would destroy traces of any body fluids.

It was when I looked again at the pathologist's report from the post-mortem on Natalie's right arm, that I realised the significance of Pattison's reference to the blue blanket. It was there in black and white: the presence of about thirty blue-coloured fibres on tapings taken from her forearm. Although we hadn't recovered a blue blanket or sheet, it added considerable weight to Pattison's story. And then there was TML/4. The pathologist had finally given an opinion that the piece of Natalie's scalp stuck to the bin bag was shed as a result of trauma. It'd been pulled out with a fair degree of force. This was, perhaps, the most compelling piece of evidence, given Pattison's claim to have seen Adams and Larvin washing blood of themselves, surrounded by bin bags containing Natalie's dismembered body.

The trial loomed closer and closer, and Tony's phone calls providing me with valuable updates became more frequent. With only a few months to go before the trial was due to begin, Tony came to see me at Bridlington. He'd called to say that he was coming but wouldn't tell me why. When he arrived, he burst into my office with a big scouse grin on his face.

"We've got Craig Walker and Shaun Adams. Walker's evidence is bloody sound."

He was really excited. I asked him to slow down so that I could take in every detail of what he was about to tell me. I knew that they'd had Craig Walker out of prison a few times after he'd asked to speak to us about Adams. And I knew that John Goddard was spending a load of time with Shaun Adams. John had moved him to Scarborough, where he could keep an eye on him so that he'd be in a fit state should he agree to give evidence.

"Walker finally came good. He shared a cell with Adams and one day Adams said, 'if I tell you something, you won't tell anyone, it was me who did her in. It was me who killed Natalie. We'd been arguing I just flipped and I killed her'. Walker asked him why he'd chopped her up. Adams replied, 'it was the only way of getting rid the bitch. It worked better than I could've hoped for. Mick was involved'."

Tony assured me that he'd met Walker and would be a credible witness, even though he had, in the past, given cell confession evidence in another trial. The magnitude of Walker's testimony couldn't be underestimated. It would be massive, provided the jury believed him. Pattison would no longer be stood alone. It was what we'd been waiting for, to fill the hole left by Sunman's hostility. Work was ongoing to prove that Pattison and Walker couldn't have conspired together over their evidence.

Tony talked at length over the outstanding job John Goddard was doing with Shaun Adams. John had finally persuaded him to give a statement and when its contents were put to Adams, it was as if he'd been punched in the stomach. It was a body blow for his own brother to be helping the police. It captured the period just after news of Natalie's remains being found hit the newspapers. He was with his brother outside Dr. Hussain's surgery when he told him that he thought she'd been, 'chopped up and killed. Stabbed'. Adams told his brother that he'd need his help in the future but Shaun Adams 'didn't want any part of it'. Tony went on to describe what Shaun referred to as the 'sick joke episode'. He'd shared a cell with a man called Sanderson when Adams came to the cell door and said, 'how did Natalie get identified? She had dandruff because she didn't use Head and Shoulders'. Shaun felt sick at his brother's joke at Natalie's expense and thought it was, 'totally out of order'. I was pretty sure that the jury would think so too. It got better still when Shaun was in prison and present when other inmates were accusing Larvin of killing Natalie. Larvin's response was, 'you know it was Darren who stabbed her, not me'. I was overjoyed at the breakthrough with Walker and Shaun Adams. I wished I could've been there to experience the incredible highs the team must be feeling.

Before Tony left, he asked me if I was OK. We'd become close over the course of the lengthy investigation. He'd seen me at my lowest ebb, and he must have guessed that I was finding it hard sitting here miles from HQ, miles from where I really wanted to be. I felt like telling him that I wasn't OK, that I'd no idea what the future had in store for me, and that I still hadn't come to terms with the humiliation of being taken off the case. I didn't, because it wouldn't have made any difference. We went for a pint instead.

TWENTY-EIGHT

'Tears of relief streamed down my face'

Bridlington was a small station. Some might describe it as cosy, with the cells, CID and uniform, all under one roof. Being miles from HQ definitely had its advantages. Nobody ever ventured this far to see me unless there was a good reason. So, when Stephen Hodgson breezed into my office one day, I knew it wasn't a social call.

"Stephen, really good to see you. Let me guess this must be something to do with PC Lee I interviewed. Am I right?"

"You are as a matter of fact. How did you know?"

"Just a wild guess. You once said you'd come and see me with good news for a change. But today's not the day judging by your surprise visit."

"Sorry to have to tell you that the CPS have deliberated for some months over the file you submitted following your investigation into constable Lee's conduct, and I am afraid they have decided not to charge him with either perverting the course of justice or, indeed, attempting to do so."

"No point in asking why, I suppose."

"I don't know I'm afraid. But there is some other news you may judge to be more positive. The DCC has set a date, the 17th of November, for his discipline hearing to be chaired by a Chief Constable from another force. Oh, and I almost forgot to tell you, that it looks almost certain that the industrial tribunal will not be proceeding after all. It seems as though the federation is unwilling to fund the ongoing disputes between PC Lee and a number of other officers he's making accusations against."

It was almost a throwaway comment and yet if the tribunal had gone ahead, then it'd have been the mother of all industrial tribunals, with countless innocent police officers being falsely accused of racism. I'm not sure that he realised the implications of what he'd just said. I'd have been his main target, together with DI Wilson, and even if I was successful in defending my reputation, the ordeal of doing so would have almost killed me. Whilst I was naturally disappointed with the CPS decision, at least the officer would surely be kicked out of the force for discipline offences, or so I thought.

The discipline panel consisted of three chief officers from outside forces to ensure that the entire process would be as independent and transparent as possible. PC Lee was found guilty of numerous serious breaches of discipline, with a recommendation that the officer be dismissed from the force. Our Chief, however, had other ideas and decided to go against that recommendation and allowed PC Lee to keep his job.

Stephen Hodgson came to see me again to tell me what happened. He seemed nervous, which was unlike him. I remained quiet throughout as I tried to make sense of our Chief's decision. Before I was able to think about the implications, Stephen, in his impeccably precise and softly spoken voice, said,

"I'm sorry to have to tell you that as soon as the Chief delivered his verdict, which the officer and his team were clearly not expecting, his barrister jumped to his feet and demanded that you be investigated for being 'overbearingly racist' towards his client. He went on to suggest that it must be you who should be dismissed from the force."

It only took a moment for my veins to fill with adrenalin, heart beating as if it was about to explode and my stomach told me that I was about to be violently sick. But he hadn't finished. There was some good news. It's just that with his measured delivery of the spoken word, it took him forever to tell me,

"The Chief considered the barrister's demands for only a few minutes and then told everyone present, 'DCI Davison is not a racist officer. On the contrary, he is a man of the highest integrity and I believe that he's conducted a very thorough and fair investigation. Therefore, there will be no investigation into DCI Davison and that is the end of the matter'."

Tears of relief streamed down my face. I'd been one decision away from suffering a lengthy life-changing and career-ending investigation conducted by an outside force. The criminal justice system wasn't just there to put the deserving behind bars, it could just as easily be used to target the innocent who are there to uphold the law. I was grateful to the Chief for standing by me, more grateful than he'd ever know. For, although I knew I'd be completely vindicated by any inquiry, it would take maybe two to three years to complete. It would be an exhausting and cruel punishment in itself, and something that I wouldn't be strong enough to endure. I'd seen it happen to other officers and it never ended well. They were never the same again. I thanked Stephen for taking the time to come and see me to deliver the news in person. It meant a great deal. He must have been slightly embarrassed at my tears of relief. I would've been.

After he'd had gone, I sat gazing out of my office window at the rooftops of Bridlington. It was raining heavily, and the seagulls seemed to be crying louder than usual. Perhaps they were complaining about the rain, or lack of fish and chip scraps to eat, now that the tourists had all gone home.

I reflected long and hard over Stephen's visit. There was much to think about. It was demoralising to have conducted a bloody first-class investigation, only to come a whisker away from being investigated myself. On what basis did the officer's barrister consider me to be racist? There was no objective reasoning. I'm sure that if I'd the opportunity to ask him though, he'd say that he was just doing his job and tell me not to be so sensitive, before moving on to the next case - prosecution or defence - it didn't matter to them. The officer received a reprimand (slap on the wrist) and a fine. Ridiculous. And when I'd calmed down, the irony of having to rely on a barrister to secure a conviction against Adams wasn't lost on me. At that moment, I hoped more than anything that my faith in Mr Bernard wouldn't be misplaced.

TWENTY-NINE

'News of the almighty cock-up would travel across the force like lightning'

In early December, Tony arranged a meeting with the forensic scientist in the case, Martin Eddows and his boss, Amanda Hudson. When I arrived at the conference room at HQ, most of the investigation team were there and it was good to see everyone again, even though it felt awkward for a while. Mr Taylor, apparently, was unable to attend and neither was DC Long, the SOCO supervisor.

Tony seemed anxious. He took me to one side. I could tell something was wrong. In his usual no-nonsense manner, he told me that there was a problem with TML/4. According to Amanda Hudson, the piece of Natalie's scalp had been 'tested to destruction', and they'd failed to take a control sample. There was nothing left as if it hadn't existed in the first place.

"Tony, how the fuck can there be nothing left. I was there when we found it. It was a piece of her scalp. It had hair coming out of it."

I realised the implications of what Tony had just told me: there'd be no likelihood of presenting it in evidence. It was a crushing blow. The very basis of the entire case had vanished. The only piece of tangible evidence for us to argue that Natalie was killed and dismembered in 119 St Johns

Grove, was gone. How on earth would any jury be convinced of Adams's guilt based mainly on the testimony of Pattison?

"How long have you known?"

"For a while. I didn't want to tell you. I knew you'd hit the roof. Trying to find out how it's happened. But they're saying it's an honest mistake."

I glanced over towards Martin Eddows, who'd responsibility for TML/4 as the lead scientist on the case. He looked nervous. I'd have been nervous in his position, because he'd yet to face the wrath of the investigation team. When Amanda revealed what'd happened during her presentation, there was almost a riot in the conference room. Tony and me stepped in to calm the situation. They were justifiably angry and they directed it mostly towards Martin. Amanda tried her best to answer what seemed like a thousand questions from the floor, but the result was the same - they just couldn't understand how it'd been allowed to occur. They'd invested over a year of their lives to this investigation and it was about the worst thing you could have told them. To make matters worse, they weren't convinced that TML/4 had been 'tested to destruction', and came to the conclusion that it'd been lost. It was the only logical explanation. Failing to take a control sample was a serious mistake but, ultimately, I knew it was my responsibility as the SIO. It came with the job. I assumed that it would have been looked after as if it were the crown jewels. I assumed wrongly, I should have known better.

News of this almighty cock-up would travel across the force like lightning. This was the lowest point of the investigation to date. The remainder of the meeting was understandably downbeat, despite Tony's and my best efforts, and it didn't get any better when the implications of losing TML/4 as evidence became clearer. The presence of Larvin's fingerprints would be inadmissible.

As expected, Natalie's and Adams's fingerprints were all over the inside 119 St Johns Grove, but so were those of numerous known associates, together with a sizeable number of unidentified fingerprints that probably originated from punters ripped off by Adams. The defence would be smiling when they received full disclosure of the prosecution case minus TML/4. They'd also be delighted to learn that blood and semen belonging to other people, apart from Natalie and Adams, were found. Even though we'd eliminated those we could identify, the defence would surely steer the jury towards the idea that an angry punter could have been responsible. I would. Motive - being set up by Natalie and robbed by Adams. Reasonable doubt? Absolutely.

But as the discussion hovered around the weaker areas of the circumstantial case against Adams and Larvin, Amanda was right to remind us all that we still had the pale-blue fibres from Natalie's arm from the first post-mortem. She told us that she'd done some further testing, and the good news was that eight of the fibres matched in colour and composition and probably came from the same source, such as a sheet or blanket. Her evidence at the trial would be that in her opinion, Natalie's arm had been in contact with a surface shedding pale-blue fibres. The jury would have to be convinced that they came from the blanket that partially covered Natalie's dead body as described by Pattison.

I met with Tony after the meeting to find out what really happened to TML/4. He told me that both DI Chambers and Amanda Hudson, were sticking to the 'tested to destruction' story as if it was just one of those things. It didn't make any sense to me. Why was no control sample taken? Once DNA testing confirmed that it was Natalie, then why continue to test further? There were about a million more questions I wanted answers to. But as Tony rightly pointed out, we needed to somehow deal with the fact that TML/4 would be inadmissible at the trial. Detective Superintendent Taylor had, apparently, already discussed it with Mr Bernard.

"Fucking hell, Tony, is there anything else I don't know. I know I'm at Bridlington but you could always pick up the bloody phone."

I apologised to Tony for my outburst. I knew that I was behaving as if I was still the SIO, and whatever the reason for the issue over TML/4, it wasn't Tony's fault. We both knew that without it, for the prosecution case to stand any chance of success, it was essential that all the witnesses stayed healthy and were willing and able to attend Crown Court in Sheffield, only a few months away. We tried to remain positive but it was going to be a logistical nightmare.

Sunman's testimony would have been dynamite, but there was no way we'd get him to the court, never mind persuade him to give evidence. I thought back to when I'd called to see Nini Thompson with Kev and Andy. What would the jury think of the pale, ghost-like, gaunt figure of Nini, stood trembling before them? Would they judge her by her appearance and lifestyle, or would they keep an open mind?

Would she stay alive until the trial? Or would she overdose and die like so many heroin-addicted prostitutes? I knew that much could go wrong between now and the trial. I trusted Tony though, and I knew that he'd move heaven and earth to limit the damage caused by the mysterious loss of our only tangible piece of forensic evidence.

Driving home after the meeting, alone with my thoughts, I was still fuming. I'd lived for over a year safe in the knowledge that at least we had TML/4 to support Pattison's story, but not now. And without it, I'd a strong feeling that the chance of a jury finding Adams and Larvin guilty, had probably all but disappeared.

PART 3

THE FIGHT

FOR JUSTICE

THIRTY

'Cruel and unforgiving world of prostitution'

Sheffield Crown Court, Tuesday, 22 February 2000. Regina v Darren Adams and Michael Larvin. We all met in the court canteen. Everyone seemed nervous. Detective Superintendent Taylor was there with his team for the Samantha Class trial, which was into its third week already. I hoped that the accused, Gary Allen, would be found guilty, everybody did. The verdict would come long before the end of our trial, and there was little doubt that we were the underdogs, with only an outside chance of getting justice for Natalie. Now that the trial was about to begin, it didn't really matter who was the SIO. Nothing mattered other than the twelve members of the jury, the judge, prosecution and defence teams and witnesses.

The tannoy gave fair warning that the trial was about to begin and we all took our places in the gallery, except for those police officers who were due to give evidence. The Honourable Mr Justice Klevan entered the courtroom magnificently clothed in red, his head buried beneath a wig that sat a little too far forward and gave the impression that it might slide down his forehead at any moment. In keeping with the gravity of the circumstances, he showed no emotion as he nodded acknowledging Mr Bernard, acting on behalf of the Crown, Mr Logan, representing Adams, and Mr Stanford, for Larvin. Although he'd a kind face, without saying a word, this was his territory and the barristers, no matter how important they believed themselves to be, knew that he was in charge. Peering over his half-rimmed glasses and looking down from his elevated grand position, he asked for the jury to be called and sworn in. They marched in single file from the jury room, which would be their home for the next few weeks. I counted six men and six women. They looked like frightened rabbits in headlights and they'd every right to be. They'd have absolutely no idea of the nature of the case until the opening arguments. I felt sorry for them in a way because the gruesome details of Natalie's dismemberment would shock anyone with a heart. They were going to be introduced to the cruel and unforgiving world of prostitution, driven by the need for some of the girls to simply cloth and feed their kids, but for the majority, to satisfy their drug addiction. At the close of proceedings today, I wouldn't blame any of them if they failed to turn up for day two.

The sense that this case was going to test the criminal justice system to its limits was overwhelming. This was real life with Adams and Larvin stood handcuffed as the charges were read out. They both pleaded not guilty. Mr Logan and Mr Stanford asked for the jury to be excused so they could submit legal arguments to the judge. Once the jury had left the courtroom, Mr Logan opened by asking the judge to exclude the evidence of Neil Pattison and Craig Walker, for the reasons outlined in a written document he'd prepared for

Judge Klevan's consideration. Mr Stanford supported the request. The trial was duly adjourned until Thursday 24 February.

I was used to delays in trials but this was an anti-climax to say the least after waiting so long for this day to arrive. Mr Bernard didn't seem concerned though and gave me the impression we'd be OK. But, as I sat nursing a cup of coffee in the court canteen, I knew that if the judge agreed, the trial would probably collapse. With the prosecution case built around Pattison and Walker, without their evidence, I was pretty sure there'd be no trial. We braced ourselves for a long and nervous wait to hear Judge Klevan's ruling on the matter. It was going to be a long couple of days.

At last the waiting was over as Judge Klevan announced his decision. The courtroom fell silent.

"In this application both Mr Logan and Mr Stanford, invite me to consider, essentially, the evidence of Neil Pattison and also the evidence of the witness Craig Walker, and to consider the evidence in this way. That, as Mr Logan puts it, I should invite the Crown to consider its position in regard to the calling of Neil Pattison. And, in Mr Stanford's case, that under Section 78, of the Police and Criminal Evidence Act, I should exclude the evidence of Pattison and Walker because it would lead to unfairness in the trial."

The judge sipped water from a glass.

"Mr Logan has argued that a view was taken to call Pattison, and the same view has been maintained to this day that Pattison should be called without a review of all that is known about Pattison. Mr Bernard, for the Crown, answers in this way. That a decision was made at an early stage to call Pattison. That serious consideration was given to that decision. That over the last two days all information that could be gleaned about Pattison has been considered by Mr Bernard. And he confirms that having considered all the matters, acting as an independent member of the bar, as a minister of the justice, that he puts forward Pattison as a credible witness."

Judge Klevan's delivery was slow, measured and precise.

"Mr Bernard is realistic enough to know that witnesses who are called in criminal trials cannot always be of perfect character. But, having considered the matters fully, he is content to allow the jury to make the decision about Pattison's credibility. He, having satisfied himself, with those that advise him, that Pattison, in this matter, can be put forward as a witness worthy of belief on the material matters. Therefore, in that light, I am perfectly satisfied, insofar as Mr Logan's application is concerned, that there is nothing in the conduct of Mr Bernard, or those that advise him, to show that discretion has either not been exercised or exercised inadequately, frivolously or indifferently. I am, therefore, against Mr Logan's application."

It took a while for Judge Klevan's words to sink in. So far so good, but the judge hadn't finished, he had to deal with Mr Stanford's submission.

"The way Mr Stanford puts it, gently but firmly, is that the prosecution's judgment is now blurred in this case. And, if that is the case, if I were to come to the view that Pattison's evidence would lead to unfairness, then I should exclude it. There is nothing I have heard to indicate that Mr

Bernard's judgment is in any way blurred. I repeat he would, no doubt, prefer to present to the jury for their consideration witnesses of unblemished character, of moral rectitude of such a state that all would say there is a repository of truth in that witness. In a case of this kind I must be realistic. What I have to be satisfied of is firstly, has Mr Bernard exercised the necessary care required? I have already dealt with that. And next I must look at Section 78. If Pattison's evidence and Walker's evidence is heard by the jury would that lead to unfairness? I am afraid I cannot say that. This is essentially a matter for the jury to determine in such a serious case as this, and there is nothing on the face of any statement, which could cause me to exclude the evidence of the two witnesses named under Section 78, and I will not exclude that evidence. It is evidence to be put before a jury and for them to determine. That is the end of my ruling. The trial begins at 2pm. I trust that you will be ready Mr Bernard."

There was going to be a trial. Pattison and Walker would be allowed to give evidence. It took a while for the judge's words to sink in again. To say that I was relieved would be a bloody understatement. I glanced across at Mr Logan and Mr Stanford and they definitely both looked crestfallen; the judge's ruling was a major body blow. Judge Klevan didn't give Mr Logan or Mr Stanford the opportunity to respond and they made no effort to do so. They busied themselves by consulting with their juniors as the courtroom gradually emptied for lunch.

Whilst I realised there was still a long way to go, we'd clearly won the first round. All we had to do now was trust the jury to make the right decision. I managed to catch up with Mr Bernard in the corridor outside the courtroom and he was delighted with the judge's ruling. He'd fully expected both defence teams to attempt to have the evidence of Pattison and Walker excluded under Section 78, because that's exactly what he'd have done. It'd give them grounds for appeal at a later date, should Adams and Larvin be found guilty.

"The learned judge's ruling means that the trial will go ahead. He's delivered a serious blow to both defence teams. It's a good job that Pattison's evidence in particular was gathered quite properly and fairly, otherwise the judge's ruling might well have gone against us. Pattison is the key to winning this case and they know it."

At two o'clock, Judge Klevan invited Mr Bernard to open the case for the prosecution. I wondered just how he got to be so bloody good, with his brilliant mind, articulate delivery of the spoken word, clarity of thought, and the ability to grasp in an instant complex issues that would take me forever to understand. I was glad he was on our side because, after all the months of hard work, it all came down to who would win the battle of wits between Mr Bernard, Mr Logan and Mr Stanford. They'd all know each other and there would surely be a kind of league table. They were silverbacks in the criminal justice world blessed with massive egos. I just hoped that our man was the dominant one of the three.

The jury looked towards Mr Bernard.

"Members of the jury, I am Mr Bernard representing the Crown. I'm sorry that you have been called to hear this case. Sorry, because you will have to listen to the evidence I must lay before you of how Natalie Clubb, a mother of three, was lured into drug addiction and prostitution by the defendant Darren Adams. How he used the rewards gained by Natalie's nightly visits to the red-light area of Hull to feed his own heroin addiction. You will hear evidence of how, when Darren Adams argued with Natalie over her affair with Nini Thompson, he viciously kicked and punched her before brutally stabbing her to death in the kitchen of 119 St Johns Grove, which is a semi-detached council house in Hull. And, instead of calling the police, you will hear of how he enlisted the help of Michael Larvin to dispose of Natalie by dismembering her body, putting her body parts in refuse bags and throwing them in a local drain."

Some members of the jury fixed their gaze on Mr Bernard, others stared at Adams and Larvin.

"The world that you are about to become familiar comes with a warning, because it is bleak, unforgiving, cruel and desolate. It will not be your world. You will hear from a number of witnesses and I would invite you to please keep an open mind when they appear before you. Many – indeed the majority - will be under the influence of drugs as they give evidence. It will be up to you whether or not you believe what they are telling you. And this is an important point because, as the defence will point out, the evidence in this case is purely circumstantial. There is no murder weapon. There are no witnesses to the murder. There is no admission of guilt. The evidence to show that Darren Adams murdered Natalie and that Michael Larvin helped him dispose of her body, will come from a few key witnesses. I believe them to be credible witnesses. The police officers who painstakingly spent months building a rapport with these witnesses to gain their trust, believe them to be credible. And, members of the jury, there is one witness above all whose credibility will most certainly be tested by these proceedings, and that is Neil Pattison. You must decide whether you judge him to be credible. His testimony is central to the prosecution case because Adams confided in him to the effect that he murdered Natalie by stabbing her to death. Pattison could not have known the cause of death from any other source than the killer. The police were very careful not to make public how Natalie died. In fact, the Senior Investigating Officer made an unusual and, in many ways, controversial decision to keep this information from his colleagues within the police, apart from his small team of detectives. It is indeed an important matter and goes to the very heart of Pattison's credibility."

Mr Bernard skillfully counterbalanced the complete lack of direct evidence, with a plea for the jury to consider carefully the credibility of key witnesses. It was delivered with subtlety and if I were a member of the jury, I'd be warming to him. He possessed the 'likeability' factor in spades. He was one of those people that seemed almost too good to be true but not in an arrogant or high-handed way. I hoped that the jury, over the coming weeks, would come to trust him and trust in the integrity of the investigation. The jury would only be able to make a decision based on what Judge Klevan allowed them to see and hear. They wouldn't have the benefit of the investigators perspective with time to consider whether or not to believe a witness. The prosecution witnesses were dishonest and untrustworthy with a deep hatred of the police. Why should anyone believe a word they said, particularly when told to the police without any apparent inducements, is a question I'd be asking if I were a member of the jury. I knew the answer to that question, but how would Mr Bernard persuade a jury that it was down to the extraordinary skill and commitment of my officers. Nothing else.

"So, who was Natalie Clubb? Well, she was in every sense of the word a victim. Her formative years were heavily influenced by being placed into the care of Wiltshire Social Services by her mother Linda Purdy. As a consequence, Natalie was a very frightened little girl with a big chip on her shoulder and her way of coping was to be disruptive. It is believed that she tattooed the word CHAOS on her arm because that is what she caused wherever she went. Natalie craved love and attention and found it briefly with James McAlister. They set up home in Salisbury and they had three children between 1992 and 1994. But the relationship broke down and by 1997, Natalie had moved to Hull. She telephoned Christine Morgan, one of her mother's sisters, and told her that she had a drug problem and wished that she'd never met her current boyfriend Darren Adams. Natalie was easily led. She was not addicted to drugs prior to meeting Mr Adams, nor was she a prostitute. You will hear evidence of how Natalie became a victim of Darren Adams's violence towards her, how he orchestrated this violence to force her into heroin addiction and then into a degrading life of prostitution. By the time Darren Adams murdered Natalie, she was barely recognisable from the person she used to be. Weighing less than six stone, she would perform any sexual act for just a few pounds. She did not wash herself or her clothing. She had no veins left to inject heroin into her body."

I looked at the jury once again. Six men and six women with a broad mix of ages and I began to wonder about where they came from, what their lives were like, what kind of people were they. Each one of them would have their own unique story to tell, each one influenced by their past, and there was no way of knowing whether they were kind or cruel, open-minded or prejudiced, thoughtful or selfish, humble or arrogant. If I was anything to go by, I reasoned, they'd probably be emotionally fucked-up with zero confidence and an inability to escape the past. But then I gave up thinking too deeply about the jury system. It's all we had, and I could do nothing about how they'd react to the many aspects of this case that they'd likely never forget. In the meantime, Mr Bernard pressed ahead. He'd more to say.

"You will hear evidence of how on Thursday, the 30th of July 1998, the police were called to a pumping station on Bransholme on the outskirts of Hull. It is a facility to ensure that local drains flow freely into the River Humber. A dog belonging to the caretaker discovered Natalie's severed right arm within the grounds of the station. The arm was severely decomposed and the police made a preliminary identification from the word CHAOS tattooed on the forearm. Two post-mortem examinations were carried out on body parts recovered following a thorough search of the grounds. The pathologist discovered at least eight stab wounds to the chest area of Natalie's butchered torso, together with four areas of soft tissue bruising probably caused by kicks or punches. Some of the stab wounds were so forceful they pierced through bone. Natalie would have been alive when she was kicked or punched and when all eight stab wounds were inflicted on her body, because they were all ante-mortem injuries. The weapon used was a knife with a serrated blade about one centimetre wide. Natalie was dismembered using a thin bladed saw. Her head was severed from her body, so were her arms and legs. Parts of her body are still missing. Her left arm, both legs from above the knee caps and fingers of the right hand from above the knuckle bones."

There was sadness in Mr Bernard's voice as he delivered the horrifying details of how Natalie died and how her body parts were discovered in such grim surroundings. If he'd wanted to paint an unforgettable, vivid and degrading picture for the jury, then he'd succeeded. They hung on his every word. What he said next, almost brought a tear to my eye.

"In her short life, Natalie Clubb was let down time and again by people who were supposed to care for her. If Natalie were able to tell you, members of the jury, exactly what happened, your task would be a simple one. But she is not I am afraid as you are now all well aware. The fact that she fell into a life of drug addiction and earned a living through prostitution does not, in any way, make her less of a human being. In some ways, it is because Natalie was so little cared for in life that this case demands the utmost degree of scrutiny, due consideration, and fairness to ensure that justice is done, so that she can finally rest in peace. Ladies and gentlemen, your task may seem a daunting one after what you have just heard and I will not pretend otherwise. But it may be of some comfort and reassurance for me to repeat the words of Lord Devlin. 'Trial by jury is more than an instrument of justice and more than a wheel of the constitution. It is the lamp that shows that freedom lives'."

When Mr Bernard sat down, an eerie silence fell over the courtroom. He'd delivered a brilliant and moving opening speech that, for a moment, seemed to catch Mr Logan off guard as he failed to acknowledge Judge Klevan's invitation to respond on behalf of Adams. Perhaps he was pondering how to match the empathy of Mr Bernard's words so as not to seem heartless in the eyes of the jury. I didn't envy him though because as it stood, Darren Adams was definitely the villain, Natalie the easily led victim used and abused and finally tossed aside by her pimp boyfriend. Mr Logan did his best in difficult circumstances.

"Ladies and gentlemen of the jury, I am Mr Logan here to represent Mr Adams, who stands before you charged with the murder of Natalie Clubb. The task of upholding the highest traditions of trial by jury in this case is going to be a challenging one for you. It is a complex case, and Mr Bernard is right to point out that the evidence you will be presented with will be purely circumstantial in nature. There is no direct evidence. It is indeed an important point, a crucial point, and one that I would urge you, with respect, to keep upper most in your minds throughout the trial. That means that you will hear from a number of witnesses whom I believe to be totally untrustworthy, and your task will be to decide whether they are telling the truth or whether they are not telling the truth. And, furthermore, you must be sure beyond reasonable doubt that they are indeed being truthful. But, members of the jury, how are you to decide whether they are being truthful? The future of my client depends upon your ability to seek out the truth in this case and, if you are able to do so, then I am sure that the only fair and just conclusion should be that Mr Adams is not guilty of the murder of Natalie Clubb. Whatever you may think of Mr Adams following my learned colleagues opening address, there is not one shred of evidence to prove that Mr Adams murdered Natalie Clubb. There is not one shred of evidence to show that my client had a motive for murdering Natalie Clubb. Please bear in mind that it is for the prosecution to prove beyond reasonable doubt the case against Mr Adams. He does not have to prove his innocence. It is the one golden thread that is the very foundation of English common law. May I also remind you, members of the jury, that under Article 6 of the European Convention on Human Rights, 'Everyone is entitled to a fair and public hearing and everyone charged with a criminal offence shall be presumed innocent until proved guilty according to law'."

Short and to the point and, to be fair to him, he was right to concentrate on whether or not they were going to believe the broken, drug-addicted and untrustworthy witnesses we were going to parade before them. I would have. All he had to do was sow the seed of reasonable doubt and use this as a basis for his defence of Darren Adams. Mr Stanford followed Mr Logan.

"I am here today to represent Mr Larvin. My client should not be stood here before you charged with assisting Mr Adams to dispose of Natalie Clubbs body. Why? Well as you have already heard, members of the jury, it is for the prosecution to prove the case against Mr Larvin, and it is a very high standard of proof that is required in order for you to be sure of his guilt. As my learned colleague, Mr Bernard, has already told you, the prosecution case will rely heavily on the word of Neil Pattison, who I believe to be wholly untrustworthy, because there is no direct evidence to link Mr Larvin with the dismemberment of Natalie Clubb. My client's misfortune was to be associated with Mr Adams. That is all. I accept that it was a close association following the disappearance of Natalie Clubb. They did commit crime together to fund their addiction to heroin. They did spend much time together. And, members of the jury, when the police were convinced that they had their man in Mr Adams, you may think that because of their friendship, it might follow that my client assisted in the disposal of Natalie Clubb's body. It does not. If Mr Larvin is guilty of anything, it is lying to the police in an attempt to be free to see his children. Members of the jury, I would invite you to consider carefully the circumstantial nature of the prosecution case."

I couldn't disagree with anything that Mr Stanford had said, particularly his closing comment. There was no tangible evidence against Larvin without TML/4. Judge Klevan brought an end to the day's proceedings. I knew I'd miss much of the prosecution case due to commitments back in Bridlington and would have to rely on others to keep me updated. Whatever happened though, I wasn't going to miss Pattison's evidence. I had to be there.

Just as we were all preparing to leave the court, there was an announcement over the tannoy asking for all interested parties to attend court 2. That was the court where Gary Allen was on trial for the murder of Samantha Class. I made my way to the public gallery. People were whispering in anticipation that a verdict was imminent. I saw Detective Superintendent Taylor and his team waiting for the jury to be called in. I kept my fingers crossed for him because, whilst we'd had our differences, I had a great deal of respect for him. I'll never forget how he developed me as a constable when he arrived as the new Inspector. He was blessed with an ability to make you feel good about yourself. He'd heap praise on the deserving, and his approach to policing at the start of each shift was to arrest as many criminals as possible.

The verdict came. Not Guilty. There was a general air of panic and disbelief. I left the court. I didn't want to stay and witness the inevitable fallout. A not guilty verdict just wasn't something the police were ever prepared for. It posed so many questions. Should the case be reopened? Is the real killer on the loose free to kill again? Will the official line be that the police are not looking for anyone else? And then there was the family of the murdered victim. How would Samantha Class's family come to terms with the verdict? I didn't see Mr Taylor before I left. I wouldn't have known what to say to him. On the way home, I thought about my chances of a guilty verdict with nowhere near as much evidence. They seemed about as bright as the darkening sky over Sheffield.

THIRTY-ONE

'I couldn't help thinking that everything was going too well'

It was frustrating not to be there every day in court, because I still thought of myself as the SIO. I knew I'd get no peace until the trial was over, and I looked forward to Tony's daily telephone calls to update me on progress.

During the first week, Mr Bernard concentrated on producing witnesses to show examples of Adams's violence towards other women before he met Natalie. One such witness, Sarah Grindell, told a story that was chillingly reminiscent of how Adams had groomed Natalie into drugs and prostitution. She told the court how Adams's mother and his sister, Stacey, were prostitutes back in 1993, when they'd met. Her description of how she'd become a prostitute and heroin addict because of Adams, caused her to break down in the witness box. With tears streaming down her face, she'd said, 'Adams is a fucking bastard. It could've happened to me what happened to Natalie. I'm a fucking addict because of him, he got me into going on the game'.

Judge Klevan warned her about her language and asked her if she needed a moment to compose herself. When questioned about Adams's violent nature she described an occasion when, during an argument, Adams placed a pillow over her head and tried to suffocate her by sitting astride the pillow. When she managed to break free, he tried to stab her in the head but missed. Adams, apparently, completely lost control. When Mr Logan, during cross-examination, asked whether she'd reported this to the police, Tony said that her reply was worth repeating. 'Your fucking joking, he'd have bloody well killed me. Are you for real? What the police going to fucking do'.

Apparently, Judge Klevan just shook his head in despair. I asked about the jury. I don't know why. How would Tony know what they were thinking? All he said was they should get used to listening to prostitutes give evidence because Mr Bernard had only just warmed up, he was about to introduce evidence of Adams's violence towards Natalie.

Veronica Dunlin spoke of Adams viciously kicking Natalie in the face causing her nose to explode. Donna Palframan witnessed Adams pin Natalie against the wall, his hand pushed tightly against her throat in an attempt to choke her and he'd a six-inch bladed knife with him at the time. And Nini Thompson saw Adams hit Natalie in the face with a coat hanger causing cuts to both eyes.

"Boss, you'd have been proud of each and every one. They stood up to cross-examination better than some detectives I've seen. Must be the drugs giving them confidence. Nini in particular was brilliant. She had a real soft spot for Natalie. Mr Bernard kept ramming home the fact they'd all had their statements taken on video. Logan and Stanford had no answers and couldn't attack the way we'd obtained the evidence from them. They didn't do themselves any favours either. They'd a way of looking down to them and it didn't work. Mr Logan tried to suggest that the only reason they'd come to give evidence is because they disliked Adams and their evidence was made up accordingly, to which Nini had replied, 'Too fucking right we hate that bastard but I'm here for Natalie. She was one of us and we all look out for each other. Nobody else will. Pimps just kick you to fuck if you don't earn enough. You can think what you like but I'm telling the truth'.

The next phase of the prosecution case concentrated on Adams's behaviour after he reported her missing. I realised that I was asking a lot of Tony to keep ringing me with lengthy updates and so I told him just to give me the highlights, both good and bad.

Shaun Adams told the court how his brother knew about the relationship with Nini Thompson and wasn't happy. He also said that Adams told him that he thought Natalie had been stabbed and chopped up. He'd said much more but the inference was that he thought his brother had killed Natalie. In cross examination, Mr Stanford accused him of lying over his claim that Larvin, whilst in prison together, told him that Adams killed Natalie. Given the amount of time and effort that had gone into making sure that Shaun would actually give evidence against his brother, Tony was relieved that it was over. It was done. He'd not only conducted himself well in the box, but he was adamant that the police didn't offer him any inducements to give evidence, despite forceful questioning from both Mr Logan and Mr Stanford to the contrary.

I couldn't help thinking that everything was going too well. Tony called late one day to tell me that during cross-examination, Steven Brewster told the court that Neil Pattison was a compulsive liar, and that he'd heard him say that he expected to get a reward for helping the police. It wasn't what we'd expected from a prosecution witness given that Pattison's appearance in the box was only a few days away. Brewster was present with Neil and his brother Jeff, when they'd come across Adams as they were waiting to use a public phone box to call a drug dealer. Jeff told Adams that he'd just seen Natalie getting into a punter's car and Adams 'freaked out, he was white as a ghost and said you couldn't have done, that's impossible'.

Mr Bernard though, had done a first-class job in carefully painting Adams to be prone to outbursts of extreme violence towards women, and for being cruel and uncaring towards Natalie in particular. Shaun Adams had done well, and there'd been a number of other witnesses who evidenced Adams making inappropriate comments to different people about what he thought had happened to Natalie.

Tony and his team had pulled off a masterstroke in successfully managing the logistics of ferrying drug-addicted witnesses to and from court, so that they were in a fit state to give evidence. It'd been, without question, the most challenging aspect of presenting a circumstantial case to the jury. I'd no idea how they'd achieved it, but it was done. We just had to hope that Walker and Pattison wouldn't let us down.

THIRTY-TWO

'But everyone tells lies, don't they?'

The scene was now set for Craig Walker and Neil Pattison to enter into proceedings. I made sure that I was there in person and not stuck on the end of a phone receiving, admittedly, colourful insights from Tony. I cancelled some meetings to be able to go to Sheffield but I couldn't have cared less. It seemed as though promotion in the police meant abandoning the streets and the public, in favour of endless meetings that had bugger all to do with actual police work. It didn't make any sense to me and it made even less sense as I sat in the courtroom - one day chairing a meeting about shift patterns for officers at Bridlington, the next waiting for Craig Walker to be called. I really missed being a SIO. I really did.

It was the first time I'd seen Craig Walker and I wasn't surprised by his appearance, with his hollow, gaunt face reminiscent of so many Hull drug addicts. It was hard to describe but if there were such a thing as the colour of cold and damp, then it would be the colour of his skin. Mr Bernard began his questioning with,

"Can you tell the court about an occasion when you shared a prison cell with Darren Adams."

When Walker told the court that Adams had freely admitted to him that he'd killed Natalie following an argument and that Larvin was involved, he had to withstand fierce cross-examination from Mr Logan and Mr Stanford. Both seized on the fact that he'd given evidence in the Gary Allen trial that ended only a few weeks earlier. Unfortunately for us, he was shown to have lied under oath. They were also keen to know why, when he'd given his assurance to Adams that he wouldn't reveal details of their conversation, he changed his mind. They were also keen to know whether the police offered any inducements in return for his evidence. But to be fair to Walker, he came back at them in a way that took me by surprise and the rest of those present in the court, I should imagine.

"When Darren said to me if I tell you something, you won't tell no one. I agreed because I wanted him to tell me what it was. Human nature isn't it? How was I to know that he'd tell me something so fucking bad? I kept quiet for ages but I couldn't. What would you have done?"

Walker looked at Mr Logan and waited for an answer. When Mr Logan realised what was happening, he cleared his throat and reminded Walker that he was asking the questions. Judge Klevan warned him about his language. He'd had to do the same thing about a thousand times since the start of the trial already.

"It's alright stood there judging me when you don't know nothing about me. Just 'cos I've been in prison don't make me a liar. The police never offered me nothing for me statement. I asked to see them. And I'll tell you this Adams was out of order for what he did to Natalie."

Would the jury believe Walker? I tried to imagine what I would make of Walker if I were a member of the jury, with his colourful and lengthy criminal record that included theft, burglary, shoplifting, robbery, and assault, to name a few. He was a career criminal with a hard drug addiction and we were putting him forward as a credible witness to be believed. The jury must have been hoping for a trustworthy witness to appear before long, so they'd be on more familiar territory. The more I thought about it the more depressed I became. Wouldn't the jury look for reasonable doubt when judging the evidence of Walker? And justify doing so because of his bad character and propensity for committing offences of dishonesty? Nobody would blame them if they did. It was his word against Adams, who was yet to give evidence, and there was no corroboration to say that it'd ever taken place.

Pattison was up next and the jury would soon realise that he was our star witness. I was relieved that Andy Marshall and Kev Scarth had done such a professional job with Pattison. If I were defending Adams or Larvin, I'd absolutely concentrate on how we obtained the evidence from him and whether or not it'd been done within the rules of PACE.

Judge Klevan, probably sensing that Pattison would be in the box for some time, ordered an early lunch. Maybe he just wanted to put his feet up for a while. After all, he was only human, despite being a Crown Court judge. I wondered how he spent his spare time: did he do ordinary things like watching football on the TV, or did he have weird hobbies that nobody could understand? I'd have to admit that of all the so-called experts I came across in my job as a SIO, I'd the most admiration for Crown Court judges. In my eyes, they were experts in the field of criminal justice, nobody more so. Their ability to listen for weeks on end to complex evidence and then summarise it into plain English was nothing short of astonishing.

In the court canteen I sat alone because the police officers were yet to give their evidence. It was awkward with both Detective Superintendent Taylor and me present at the same time. He was officially their boss, but there was a bond between us formed over months and months of hard work, from the very first days when we were struggling to make sense of what we were dealing with to this point, waiting to hear Pattison give his evidence. In our wildest dreams we could never have predicted this. I overheard DC Marshall, who'd deservedly grown in confidence in his own abilities during the investigation, try to reassure his colleagues.

"Pattison will come good. Trust me he won't let us down. I've never been more certain of anything. I know him and he wants justice for Natalie. I think he'll be more than a match for the defence."

It was time for Pattison. He strode into court handcuffed, flanked by two burly prison officers. His dreadlocks were tied back to show his bearded face and he looked around the courtroom as if it was his first time. In one sense it was, because usually he'd be stood in the dock charged with a serious crime, not about to give evidence for the prosecution. I caught a glint of determination in his eyes as he walked past me to the witness box. The jury looked puzzled at the handcuffs. He looked much stronger somehow than when I'd seen him before in the interview room. Truth really was stranger than fiction. What was about to happen had to be true. If it was put forward as a work of fiction, I'm pretty sure that it wouldn't be taken seriously.

Adams and Larvin glowered at Pattison. This was high drama, with Pattison about to stand tall in front of both defendants and deliver damning testimony against them. The tension was electric. I wondered what Adams and Larvin were thinking. They couldn't have imagined this scenario, not for one second.

Mr Bernard opened his questioning in a way that must have caused confusion amongst the jurors, and everyone else in the courtroom.

"Can you tell the court about your criminal past so that we may better understand the person you are before hearing your evidence."

Pattison paused for a moment, more than likely wondering what lay behind the loaded question from our barrister. He'd be expecting a hard time from the defence, but not from the prosecution.

"Armed robbery, assault, aggravated burglary, drug dealing. My life has been dedicated to crime. It's all I've ever known since I was a kid."

The jury looked horrified. I couldn't blame them because he'd just given them a brutal insight into his world, a world they'd know nothing about. Mr Bernard hadn't finished with his character assassination of Pattison.

"Mr Pattison can you tell the jury why you stand before the court in handcuffs."

"I'm on remand charged with manslaughter of an old lady who fell and died after being robbed. I'm waiting to go to trial."

I knew that Mr Bernard wouldn't ask Pattison about the case because it hadn't come to trial, but the jury would surely be wondering whether he was guilty, given that he'd been already charged. And if they did, then I'd no idea what they thought about someone who could commit such a cowardly crime. Mr Bernard pressed on.

"We have heard from Mr Brewster who says that he knows you to be a compulsive liar. Is he right?"

"On balance, I'd say I am. But everyone tells lies, don't they? Telling lies is more of a game to me than anything. I've lied to just about everyone I've ever known."

"Now that we've established that you are a liar, and a violent career criminal, I want to ask you why the jury should believe a word you say when you give your evidence before this court."

Mr Bernard was playing a dangerous game. He was clearly giving the defence nowhere to go in terms of digging up Pattison's cruel and villainous past, without them lifting a finger.

"The jury has seen me telling the truth about who I am and what I've done. They should be able to tell if I'm lying. But why would I lie? I've nothing to gain by coming here today and telling a pack of lies. If I'm found guilty, I'm going down for a long time. I know that. But I liked Nat and she didn't deserve to be chopped up man and tossed away as if she was rubbish. No way. I've read a lot in prison. There isn't much else to do. And the books I've read made me think about how I want to be remembered. I want to be remembered for doing something good for once. That's all. So, the jury will have to decide whether or not to believe me.

All I can do is tell the truth. I'll know I've told the truth and that's all that matters to me now."

Pattison's delivery was measured and precise. It was as if he was stripping away his human instinct to hide what he'd been all his life and what he'd done to others, in a way that kind of set him free. If Pattison wanted to be the centre of attention then he'd succeeded. It was extraordinary. There was silence in the courtroom.

"Did the police offer you any kind of reward or inducement in return for your cooperation?"

"Definitely not. The two detectives have been brilliant with me. I trust them, which is saying a lot for me. I don't know what else to say."

Mr Bernard's approach would prove to be either a masterstroke or a huge mistake. Only time would tell. At least the jury would know by now that there was a great deal more to Pattison than his criminal past. Although I hated criminals in general for what they did to victims, if he'd had a different start in life, then maybe he'd have made something of himself. As a police officer, I saw at first hand the squalor and deprivation forced upon most kids on run down housing estates. Entering houses that were disgustingly filthy, with dog mess all over the place, came with the job, an occupational hazard, when you wiped your feet on the way out, not the other way around. Kids were brought up not knowing anything other than to live that way. A ready-made future generation of burglars. If I'd been one of them would my life have turned out differently, I wondered. The council estate I was brought up in was just as bad, but the difference was that I'd great parents. Thank God.

Pattison gave his evidence over the next day and a half. He stood motionless throughout and fixed his gaze on the jury as if he was having a conversation with them. He definitely loved the attention. I'd wondered how he'd come across in Crown Court. It was one thing recalling what happened to two friendly detectives in a small interview room, but it was quite another to do so in such grand surroundings, with Adams and Larvin sat listening to every word he said. I needn't have worried. If anything, his account was more detailed, more descriptive, more of everything, delivered in a slow and precise way.

He often paused for effect, but I didn't expect him to break down as he recalled seeing Natalie dead in the bath. There were tears streaming down his face as he described what he saw,

"I touched her to see if she really was dead. Nat was so cold and stiff. She was covered with a blue blanket. I pulled back the blanket. It was laid across her chest. What he'd told me was right there was like puncture wounds close together around her chest. I don't know how many but there was loads."

I looked at Adams and Larvin. They were shaking their heads as if in disbelief. They turned to look at each other and said something like, 'you must be fucking joking'. I'm no good at lip reading but it was along those lines. Judge Klevan raised his eyebrows and asked Pattison if he needed a moment. I'm sure the learned judge had seen just about everything there was to see in a trial but I imagine this was a first, even for him. If Pattison planned this then he was a brilliant actor, but his degree of distress seemed very real to me. From my perspective, the impact of his evidence was heightened considerably by the occasion in open court, compared to watching him on a video screen in a tiny room at Beverley Police Station with my trusted colleagues. I just hoped that the jury would be convinced by his forensic attention to detail. The jury gave nothing away.

Pattison composed himself and continued but it wasn't long before he wobbled again. This time it was when he went back to 119 St Johns Grove and realised that Natalie's body had been butchered and put into black rubbish bags. He'd tried to make it look like he was there to help them, but he never imagined for a second that they'd done such an unforgivable thing to someone he very much cared for. He was almost sick as they calmly washed Natalie's blood off their arms and bodies, but the heavy smell of bleach stopped him from retching. He described the complete lack of emotion shown by both Adams and Larvin. They were angry at the inconvenience of dismembering Natalie. When he recalled what Adams had said, his voice trembled, his body stiffened.

"It took us fucking ages to cut the bitch up. The blades kept snapping."

He readily admitted carrying one of the bags to Larvin's blue Sierra but claimed that Adams told him to do it so that he'd be involved too. He'd agreed only because he didn't know what else to do. He was careful not to leave any of his fingerprints on the bag.

Mr Logan stood ready to cross-examine him. Although Mr Bernard had cleverly revealed Pattison's bad character as part of the prosecution case, Mr Logan was not to be outdone and he began with,

"Mr Pattison it is correct, is it not, that you are a criminal with numerous convictions for dishonesty and you have been described by a friend of yours, Mr Brewster, as a compulsive liar."

"Yes, it's true. I've told the court already."

"We have heard from a number of witnesses addicted to hard drugs and the one thing they all had in common was difficulty in remembering times and dates. The police assisted witnesses to remember by events that could be corroborated independently, such as crimes they had committed. So, my question is this, why is it that you are able to recall so much detail? Was it given to you by the police?"

"I'm not sure what you mean."

"Let me be more specific, you are addicted to hard drugs are you not?"

"No, I'm not. I said earlier that I was a drug dealer, but I'm not and never have been a drug addict. Never. There's a big difference between being a dealer and being an addict. And no, the police didn't tell me anything much other than their support for Manchester United. Became a bit boring in the end if I'm honest."

Mr Logan had made a big mistake to assume that Pattison was an addict. You could see where he was going with the line of questioning. There'd be no way an addict could remember so vividly the events of 13 May 1998, given that it was now early March 2000. Pattison stood waiting for the next question knowing that he'd already gained the upper hand. Mr Logan struggled to regain his composure.

"If you maintain that you are not a drug addict then we

must accept that you are not a drug addict. But what I am not clear about is why it took so long for you to finally cooperate with the police. Indeed, your information was given in stages, is that correct?"

"Yes, that's correct."

"Can you please tell the court why?"

"I needed to trust the detectives. It was a big deal was for me to talk to the police. Never grassed in my life so I needed to be sure they were genuine."

"Is it not more likely that it took so long because the police told you what to say. After all, there is nobody to corroborate your story."

"No. I agree it did take some time for me to give everything I knew. I was betraying a friend. Never something I've done before. He murdered Nat though and cut her up like a piece of meat. Out of order. Had to tell what I knew for Nat's sake. That's all."

Mr Logan laboured with this approach for what seemed like forever. He was trying to put reasonable doubt in the minds of the jurors based on the premise that Pattison could have been fed information by the police over a period of time. But to infer the police were in some way corrupt, particularly when there were hours and hours of taped interviews, was an approach that might well backfire on him, I thought. His team clearly hadn't taken the time to listen to them all because if they had, they'd have surely concluded that Andy and Kev had conducted themselves with a great deal of professionalism throughout their many conversations with Pattison. With a healthy measure of indignation and a fair degree of frustration, Pattison responded with,

"You can believe what you like. It took me a long time to get to know the two detectives. After I'd given them when I met Darren on the drain bank and he'd told me he'd stabbed her, I felt bad for a long time for grassing as I've already said. But then I wanted the detectives to earn the rest. If I'd given everything, they'd have stopped getting me out of prison, stopped coming to see me."

Mr Logan moved away from this line of questioning. Perhaps he realised that Pattison had, on balance, gained the upper hand with his raw but authentic sounding delivery and needed to regain some lost ground.

"Mr Pattison, if we are, for a moment, to accept that you were not given details of how Natalie Clubb died by the police, can you please tell the court how you knew about the stab wounds to her chest?"

Pattison looked surprised at the question and so was I, because up to now, neither Mr Logan or Mr Stanford had raised this directly as an issue.

"I've already said. How many times do I have to say, it was when I saw Darren on the drain bank and he told me he'd served her up."

"Is it not more likely that you read about how she died in the local newspapers or heard it on the radio or saw it on the news on television? The investigation did receive a great deal of exposure at the time."

"No. Definitely not. I don't read the news in newspapers, I just do the crosswords. Don't watch tele much. Don't listen to the radio."

"Do you seriously want the court to believe that the considerable amount of press coverage during the investigation did not give you the circumstances of how she died, so that you were then able to concoct the pack of lies you have told the court?"

Pattison took some time before replying, but he remained calm at the direct challenge to his integrity.

"You can think what you like. So, what you're saying is I found out how Nat died from the press and then made the whole thing up to get Darren convicted of something he didn't do. Laughable. Insulting."

Mr Bernard leapt to his feet and told the court, yet again, that the cause of death had never been made public, at any time, and hammered home the reasons for that decision. Did Mr Logan know something we didn't? Had there been something in the news about the stab wounds that we'd not seen? Could there have been a leak the press we weren't aware of? These were all questions racing through my mind. If Mr Logan had found something at this late stage in the trial, then it might well cast doubt on the very basis of Pattison's evidence-in-chief. I'd no idea what was coming next.

Mr Logan approached Judge Klevan. What was he up to? Mr Bernard looked puzzled and so did Mr Stanford. Following a brief conversation, the judge told the court that Mr Logan had requested an adjournment until tomorrow morning. He asked to see all three barristers in his chambers. I started to panic. I knew that Mr Logan would be trying everything to undermine Pattison's credibility, and my mind went into overdrive wondering whether they'd found something.

I decided to wait for Mr Bernard. It transpired that Mr

Logan was confident that the cause of death had been made public and they needed more time to produce the evidence. Mr Bernard though wasn't concerned, probably because I'd been able to convince him from the beginning that we'd be OK. Lisa was certain that it hadn't been and that was good enough for me. Nevertheless, it was a sleepless night because I'd no idea what 'needed more time to produce the evidence' meant. Could it be that they'd found a witness able to testify that somehow Pattison could have discovered how Natalie died from another source? Anything was possible when it came to the drama of Crown Court, when the stakes were about as high as you could get for the accused.

The next morning, Pattison was recalled to the witness box. Judge Klevan invited Mr Logan to begin. My heart was beating fast, pulse racing, adrenalin filled my veins.

"Your Honour, thank you."

Mr Logan proceeded to do exactly the opposite of what I'd expected him to do. There was no reference to the cause of death having been in the public domain. They must have endured a frustrating night searching, without success, for something to produce that might cast doubt on Pattison's credibility. Instead, Mr Logan launched a venomous attack on Pattison's credibility as a witness.

"I do not know why you have come to this court and attempted to convince the jury that you are telling the truth. Some might say that your degree of distress when giving your testimony was real. Members of the jury do not be fooled by this witness because he is a consummate liar, a skilled liar, and he has had many months to perfect his performance. Your evidence has been shameful. I have no further questions."

I breathed a massive sigh of relief. All I could think of was that Mr Logan had been convinced that they would find something in the public domain about how Natalie died. Most SIOs did routinely give out the cause of death, and I couldn't blame them for assuming that this case would be any different. But Mr Bernard had given due warning in his opening speech that it'd been kept a closely guarded secret. Why had they left it so late in the day to challenge the success of that policy? The jury looked puzzled.

Mr Stanford tried to suggest that being produced from prison on such a regular basis was a form of inducement in return for his cooperation. Pattison made it clear that those were his terms so that his fellow prisoners would have no idea that he was helping the police. To be fair to Mr Stanford, his cross-examination was brief. He probably realised that there'd be little point in going over the same ground already covered by Mr Stanford, at great length.

Judge Klevan thanked Pattison for his attendance at court and that was the end of our star witness. He walked out of the courtroom slowly and purposefully flanked by his two prison guards. It must have taken courage for him to do what he'd just done. There'd be nowhere to hide in prison, everyone would know that he'd grassed and yet he seemed at peace with the world as he turned to take one last look at the scene of his extraordinary performance. I was sure that he'd told the truth, but had he been involved more than he'd led us to believe. Probably. Pattison knew though, that neither Adams nor Larvin would dare to say otherwise, for obvious reasons.

On the way home, my thoughts, inevitably, turned to Pattison. I wondered what would be going through his mind as he contemplated his return to prison to face the inevitable and brutal fallout for giving evidence at Crown Court. In all my time as a SIO, I'd never witnessed anything remotely similar to what had just happened. It was astonishing.

It'd been a good couple of days for the prosecution. Pattison had withstood fierce cross-examination, with raw but authentic sounding responses. Mr Logan had made an error of judgement by assuming that Pattison was a drug addict, and he'd been unable to find any evidence to show that details of how Natalie died, were in the public domain. What would the jury be thinking? I'd no idea.

THIRTY-THREE

'I couldn't blame him after the brutal attack on his honesty'

Mr. Marshall, the head of CPS, was called to give evidence and asked why he took the decision to grant Pattison immunity given that he'd helped dispose of Natalie's body. Despite being nervous, he soon hit his stride and set out the reasons for his decision with authority. He was given a much harder time over the decision to grant blanket immunity for crimes admitted by prosecution witnesses, in return for cooperating with the police. It was the first time Mr Marshall had given evidence in Crown Court and he told me later that he hoped it would be the last. I felt a little guilty because I'd intentionally made an entry in my policy book, stating that he was consulted over the decision knowing full well that by doing so, he'd be called to give evidence and not me. Better to have someone independent of the police, I always thought.

I had to miss the evidence of DC Long, Russell Walker and Amanda Hudson, but Tony kept me updated with regular phone calls. On a positive note, DC Long was able to introduce the pair of ankle boots discovered in 119 St Johns Grove belonging to Nini Thompson but borrowed by

Natalie. And, according to Tony, the jury seemed impressed by how he'd managed to obtain the words behind the paint on the living room wall referring to Lynda Le Plante's TV Series. Just imagine if he'd been able to produce TML/4. I still thought about how it'd happened. It still didn't make any sense. It would have provided some much-needed corroboration to support Pattison's evidence. I'd heard that since the issue over TML/4 had come to light, DC Long had faced fierce criticism from his colleagues in SOCO. They, apparently, held him to be just as responsible as Marin Eddows for the cock-up. I wondered whether that was the reason for his absence at the meeting held in December, when Tony had first dropped the bombshell. The prosecution had to accept that the bin bags used to dump Natalie's body didn't match those found in 119 St Johns Grove or Larvin's address.

The pathologist's evidence was largely uncontested. Even the defence acknowledged that, although Natalie's internal organs were completely decomposed, the eight or nine forceful stab wounds to her chest would certainly have led to her death. But they dwelt for some time over the blue fibres he discovered on tapings taken from Natalie's arm. They wanted to know whether they could have been there as a result of her arm being laid on a blue cotton sheet in the mortuary. Amanda Hudson was called to answer the question, and she was adamant that the blue fibres recovered from Natalie's arm couldn't have originated from a blue sheet used in the mortuary. When Mr Bernard asked Amanda to give her view on the possible source of fibres, Tony told me that her evidence had been clear and delivered with confidence.

"There is no doubt in my mind that eight of the fibres matched in colour and composition and probably came from the same source, such as a blanket of some kind."

Mr Bernard was quick to remind the jury of Pattison's evidence in relation to the blue blanket covering Natalie.

I was able to be there for the next phase of the prosecution case. I was looking forward to it because it would give the jury the opportunity to see and listen to Shaun Weir, John Goddard, Kev Scarth and Andy Marshall. They'd be first-class ambassadors to show that the investigation was conducted to the very highest ethical standard. It mattered, because I believed that juries wanted police officers to be credible, dependable and trustworthy, and to know that their evidence wasn't tainted in any way.

I watched Shaun take the stand. I knew that the jury wouldn't be anything but impressed with him. Tall and immaculately dressed, he looked impressive before he'd said a word. It took a full day for Shaun to give his evidence. There were nineteen interviews before Adams was charged and five after charge. If the jury were expecting a TV detective-style interview lasting about two minutes before the villain admitted the crime, then they couldn't have failed to be impressed with the shear breadth and depth of Shaun's questioning of Adams. Although there was no admission of guilt, every question had been put to Adams in a very professional manner, and from the way the questions were asked, it was crystal clear that Adams had been treated fairly and properly given the circumstances. The jury would have been left in no doubt that, following Natalie's disappearance, Adams and Larvin were inseparable and that they'd committed crime together to fund their very expensive heroin addiction. I was proud of Shaun as he stepped down from the stand. He was so impressive that neither Mr Logan nor Mr Stanford bothered to cross-examine him.

John Goddard wasn't in the box as long as Shaun, mainly because Larvin had made no comment responses in most of the interviews before he was charged. Mr Bernard concentrated on what Larvin told John Goddard when he asked to see him in prison after he was charged and remanded back into custody. John read word for word from his notebook entry made after his visit to see Larvin. It was remarkable in that it was almost as good as if the conversation had been recorded on tape. It accurately captured the way Larvin spoke, the length of their time together, and Larvin's desperation to get out of prison to see his children. It was, above all else, authentic. Larvin signed John's book to say that it was an accurate account of what he'd said - Adams killed Natalie but he wasn't involved. The fact that neither Mr Logan nor Mr Stanford challenged John's notebook entry, was an indirect acknowledgement of his forensic attention to detail. John projected the same kind of image to the court as Shaun had done: humble and honest, highly skilled and dedicated, trustworthy and believable.

Kev Scarth was called to the stand on the morning of Friday, 10 March. I knew, and he knew, that he could expect to be cross-examined with a fair degree of determination by Mr

Logan and Mr Stanford. He walked slowly to the stand. Bespectacled, with close-cropped sandy to ginger-coloured hair, he spoke with a slight tremble in his voice. You couldn't blame him for being nervous and apprehensive though, because the manner in which Pattison's evidence was obtained was about to be rigorously challenged. I'd always liked Kev. He was quiet and unassuming - two qualities I always found to be endearing in a police officer - but on occasions, it meant that he could be overshadowed by his more outspoken colleagues. I just hoped that today would be his chance to step into the limelight.

Kev told the court that, together with DC Marshall, they persevered with Pattison because they had a 'gut feeling' that he knew a great deal about the murder of Natalie, nothing more. When Pattison finally gave them Adams's drain bank confession, they believed him because the cause of Natalie's death was never made public. Kev was in the box the whole day as Mr Bernard painstakingly asked him to read from transcripts of their taped their conversations. There were more than forty. It wasn't designed to bore the jurors, but a means of demonstrating the extraordinary relationship they'd formed with Pattison over many months that culminated in his dramatic appearance at Beverley Police Station, when he'd finally told us everything. Although I'd listened to the tapes before, hearing the words spoken by Kev in open court seemed to add a further dimension of authenticity to Pattison's testimony.

Cross-examination had to wait until Monday. Judge Klevan warned DS Scarth to have no contact with DC Marshall over the weekend, and pointed out that it was possible that they might be followed to make sure that they complied with his request. Judge Klevan's warning came as a surprise to everyone in the courtroom judging by the looks of bewilderment. I'd heard of this kind of thing happening in other cases and so it wasn't unexpected.

Monday morning came, and as soon as Kev took the stand and was sworn in, Mr Logan sprang to his feet ready to browbeat the poor detective and call him a liar. And that's what he did, or at least that's what he tried to do, but Kev was more than a match for him. The problem for both Mr Logan and Mr Stanford, was that Kev came across as honest a person you'd ever wish to meet, in any walk of life. Naturally calm under repeated accusations that he'd conspired with Andy to make the whole thing up from start to finish, he simply made them both look like bullies. I wouldn't have been surprised if the jury demanded that the nice detective be left alone and offered a cup of tea. When his ordeal was over, I could see that he was agitated. I couldn't blame him after the brutal attack on his honesty that had seemed to go on forever.

Mr Bernard responded by asking the troubled detective if there was anything he'd like to say before leaving the stand. I wondered why. I'd no idea whether he was going to accept Mr Bernard's invitation to say something. Kev cleared his throat, wiped his brow with a handkerchief, took a sip of water and turned to address Judge Klevan.

"Your Honour. It seems to me that I'm being accused of what amounts to attempting to pervert the course of justice, by feeding information to Mr Pattison to get Mr Adams sent down for a crime he didn't commit."

Gone was the nervous delivery of his evidence, he was now speaking with a degree of confidence I'd not seen before. I'd a good idea what was coming next.

"I wish to place on record that I've never ever done anything in my police career to undermine the oath I took as a police officer on the first day I joined the force. To serve the Queen in the office of constable with fairness, integrity and impartiality. That's all I've ever tried to do. Thank you."

There was an eerie silence as he stepped down from the witness box. Well done, Kev, I thought. It was a brave thing to do in such grand surroundings, and I hoped that it would somehow help him to find a measure of peace in the days to come.

 Andy was next to give his evidence and it didn't take long for both Mr Logan and Mr Stanford to treat him in the same way they'd done with Kev. I'd often thought that if you could describe someone you'd want to be your friend, Andy would be that person. He had a presence that was everything to do with all that is good in life. But I knew that he wouldn't respond well to the sustained and relentless attack on his integrity, and at one point, he became distressed and needed a moment to compose himself, before delivering a heartfelt and credible response.

"What you're suggesting is that DS Scarth and I colluded with Pattison over a period of about ten months to make the whole thing up just to get Adams convicted of something he didn't do. Ridiculous. You're attacking my integrity. You're attacking everything I believe in. You're attacking the reason why I became a copper in the first place."

That brought to an end the case for the prosecution. I was proud of the way all of the detectives had conducted themselves when giving evidence. They couldn't have done any more to convince the jury that they'd every right to put their trust in the investigation.

Time for a belated lunch, time for a walk into Sheffield to collect my thoughts. I headed out of the court building and made my way along Bridge Street towards the River Don. It was bitterly cold, but it was one of those brilliantly sunny days that often come towards the end of winter as if to announce the impending arrival of spring.

I stopped at the Blonk Street Bridge and walked halfway across. Looking down at the water brought back memories of the pumping station where Natalie's butchered remains were found. And just like bloody clockwork came the inevitable wave of questions: why had I been taken off the case? Was it for career development, or payback time for being seen as a smart-arse? I knew that I'd never find the answers staring at the water as it tumbled over a small weir beneath the bridge. The frustration and humiliation brought a bleak and unfriendly feeling of desolation because I knew that this wasn't some kind of bad dream, I really had been posted out of the CID. I was no longer a SIO. As my thoughts turned to the afternoon session and how Adams would come across to the jury, I heard someone say in a broad South Yorkshire accent,

"Hope thas not thinking of ending it all. Waaters not deep enuff."

I turned around and saw a man peering over the bridge wall. His weather-beaten face smiled at me with a toothless grin. He'd clearly fallen on hard times judging by his shabby clothes and the battered old suitcase he was carrying that appeared to be on the verge of bursting open.

"No, no just doing some thinking that's all."

"Aye well tha knows what they say, too much thinking's bad for thee. Betta off doing something rather than thinking, I allus say."

He ambled across the bridge, muttering something to himself that I didn't understand. The words of a complete a stranger, who was clearly living rough on the streets, made more sense to me in a moment than all my soul searching looking for answers. He was right of course, but over thinking was a weakness of mine. Although his words of wisdom made me feel better as I made my way back to court, I knew that it would take me a long time to shake off this empty feeling, this sense of loss, this reality of maybe never returning to my beloved CID.

THIRTY-FOUR

'Stitch up by them coppers'

Adams stood between his prison guards, looking stronger and fitter than when I'd watched him being interviewed before he was charged. He was agitated and anxious. Beads of sweat were visible on his forehead as he gazed around the courtroom. I wondered if he'd a plan to convince the jury of his innocence. He was going to have to lie consistently and with a high degree of skill, to cope with Mr Bernard's cross-examination, I thought, as Mr Logan opened with,

"Mr Adams this is your chance to tell the court what really happened. Do you promise to tell the truth today?"

"Yes."

"Why should the jury believe you?"

Adams didn't look at all happy with this line of questioning. It was probably a question that he hadn't ever been asked before. I could see that he was thinking hard about how to reply. Judge Klevan reminded him that he must answer the question. He looked at the jurors,

"Don't know what to say. Not good with words. All I can do is tell it like it was. Didn't kill Nat I loved her. Why would I kill her? We was happy."

"Mr Adams, the point I am trying to make is that we have

heard evidence of your criminal history in relation acts of theft, burglary and robbery. They are all crimes of dishonesty. Are you a dishonest person, Mr Adams?"

Mr Logan's approach looked like an attempt to mirror Mr Bernard's tactic that he'd employed with Pattison.

"If you're asking have I always told the truth. No, I haven't. Where I was brought up nobody did. Thieving's just what everybody did. But I'm telling the truth now. I didn't kill Nat."

"Mr Adams, did Natalie support your heroin addiction with her earnings from prostitution?"

I could see where he was going with Adams and if I was right, then Mr Logan would be counting on raising the one thing that we'd never understood: why kill your ready-made source of heroin. It was a point first introduced by John Goddard during the early days of the investigation, and if I were in Adams's position, that's exactly what my defence would be. But to do so successfully, Mr Logan would need Adams to openly admit to his reliance on Natalie for her earnings as a prostitute to fund his addiction and committing countless crimes to pay for his heroin, when she was gone. The problem was that he'd told us a very different story when interviewed.

"Yes, but I didn't like her going with punters. I loved her but she needed smack as well as me. She had a bad habit."

"For the benefit of the jury, is smack a slang expression for heroin?"

"Yes."

"So, what did you do when Natalie left you to go and live with Nini Thompson? What did you do for money?"

Adams paused again. For his - why would I kill my source of heroin - defence to work, he had to somehow elicit sympathy from the jury by appearing to be the victim having to go out and steal, burgle and rob for a living, instead of doing nothing but doze all day in a drug induced stupor.

"Yes, I did have to go robbing. I had a bad habit. Coppers know I did. They said something about immunity."

"And is it fair to say that your chance of being arrested and put back into prison significantly increased with this criminal behaviour, and indeed led to your subsequent arrest for burglary."

"Yes, there was nothing else for me to do but rob. I had to score."

"Can you tell members of the jury what it is like if you are not able to administer heroin when needed."

"Real bad. Pain in your stomach, bones ache like fuck. Shivering, sweating, feel like killing yourself, you just want to die. You'll do anything to get a hit."

I looked at the jury, and their faces were showing anything but sympathy for Adams. Even though they'd listened to days of evidence that painted a depressing landscape of violence, prostitution and drug addiction, how could they begin to understand Adams's perspective?

"Would it be fair to say that your life was much worse after Natalie disappeared?"

"Yeah. Definitely. I missed her. I loved her. It wasn't all about feeding me habit. We was happy together."

"The prosecution will press you on an argument that you allegedly had with Natalie over her lesbian relationship with Nini Thompson. Their position, helped by Mr Pattison, will be that it led to you stabbing Natalie to death. What have you to say about that? Did you have an argument that led to you killing Natalie?"

"No way man, no way. Pattison's fucking lying. Never met him on the drain bank. Never told him nothing."

Judge Klevan shook his head and pounded his gavel.

"Mr Adams, it would assist us all if you could refrain from using bad language. Please try not to swear anymore."

Adams looked ready to explode. I felt sorry for the jury because what they were hearing would certainly leave a lasting and dark impression on them for a long time to come. They still had to face the most difficult part: how to decide who's lying and who's telling the truth. I had a feeling that they'd have to rely heavily on Judge Klevan's summing up to point them in the right direction.

Mr Logan did his best to convince the court that all the witnesses who'd testified as to his violent nature, particularly towards Natalie, were lying, that both Pattison and Walker were lying and were persuaded to do so by the police, and so on. But I wasn't sure whether his plan had worked. Branding all the witnesses who'd given evidence about his propensity for violence as liars, to my mind, lacked reality. Mr Logan should have encouraged Adams to accept their evidence whilst forcefully raising the only two relevant issues for the jury to consider: Adams's so-called love for Natalie, and lack of motive based on why would he kill his only source of heroin. The problem was that Adams had no redeeming features to make you believe that he could love anyone or anything. Then again, I wasn't on the jury and I'd no way of knowing what they were thinking.

It was time for Mr Bernard to cross-examine Adams. He looked more than ready to tackle the defendant.

"Mr Adams, you and you alone were responsible for making Natalie a heroin addict. Are you not?"

"No."

"But when she arrived in Hull, she was not an addict and she was not a prostitute. You are solely responsible for Natalie's desperate decline into the degrading life that she led before you finally and cold bloodedly, murdered her. You should be ashamed of yourself. Tell the truth. It is the very least that you can do for poor Natalie."

Mr Bernard's words were spat out with venomous contempt, each one carefully chosen to provoke a reaction from Adams and he succeeded. He kicked out at the prison guards and ranted,

"This is a fucking stitch up by them coppers. Why won't no fucker listen to me. Didn't kill no one."

Some members of the jury flinched at his outburst towards Mr Bernard. The judge pounded his gavel over and over again.

"Order, order, order. I will not warn you again Mr Adams. Any more of this conduct and I will hold you in contempt of court."

Adams wisely kept his mouth shut but the damage was already done. Adams had shown something of his violent nature to the jury, and I imagined that it might well be enough to make them believe the evidence they'd heard at the beginning of the trial about Adams's violence towards women.

"Mr Adams, you say that the whole thing has been in

some way an elaborate 'stitch up' as you put it by the police in an attempt to send you to prison for a crime that you claim not to have committed. Is that your position? Is that what you want the jury to believe?"

"How many more times do I have to keep on saying it. It was Amadi who killed her over some money we owed."

"You keep referring to Mr Amadi as the person responsible. Do you have any proof?"

Adams didn't reply.

"You have lied to the police over and over again. I believe that you argued with Natalie over her relationship with Nini Thompson, an argument that brought out the very worst side of your brutal and violent nature. You flew into a rage, kicked and punched her before picking up a knife and stabbing Natalie to death with lethal force. You showed no mercy to the person you were supposed to love and care for. And then you enlisted the help of Mr Larvin to dispose of her body in a way that is hard to imagine. Butchered and tossed into the drain."

Adams didn't wait for the eloquent barrister to finish, he did exactly what Mr Bernard hoped he'd do: lose control of his temper but much worse than before as he threatened Mr Bernard with,

"I'll fucking have you, clever twat."

Judge Klevan had no option but to have him removed from the court. Mr Bernard finished with,

"I have no further questions for Mr Adams."

He said it in a 'there you have it members of the jury an open display of threats and intimidation', kind of way. It was subtle and clever. Mr Logan looked forlorn and if I wasn't mistaken, I was pretty sure that I detected a worried slight shake of the head.

Larvin took the stand and before he said a word, it was clear that his performance would be far more accomplished than Adams's. He was the one who'd taken control of what to do with Natalie's dead body. Adams had done as he was told. Mr Stanford opened with,

"Can you tell the court why you told the police after you were charged that Mr Adams came to your house, and admitted stabbing Natalie Clubb following an argument whilst under the influence of temazepam?"

"Did it so they'd let me out. I thought they'd let me out. I needed to see me kids. I needed to score badly. Driving me crazy being locked up."

"Did Mr Adams ever admit to stabbing Natalie?"

"No. I just told what I thought they wanted to hear so I could get out to score and see me kids."

"But Mr Pattison puts you in 119 St Johns Grove with Mr Adams dismembering her body."

"He's lying. About everything. No truth in anything he's said."

"So, you took no part in helping to dispose of Natalie Clubb's body."

"No way."

"Do you know who killed Natalie Clubb?"

"No."

It was a simple defence for the jury to consider: he'd lied in an attempt to secure his release from prison. Would the jury believe him, I wondered? His answers were delivered with calm assurance from someone with years of experience of lying as a way of life and he was good at it. There were no outbursts, no ranting, just authentic sounding replies.

Mr Bernard couldn't wait to get started on Larvin.

"Mr Larvin, I am at a loss to understand what you have just told the court. It is a pack of lies from beginning to end. When Detective Sergeant Goddard visited you in prison, you told him in elaborate detail how the defendant came to your house asking for your help to dispose of Natalie's body. You signed the officer's notebook saying that it was a true and accurate record of the conversation. Are you saying you were lying?"

"Yes, already said before."

"I put it to you that it was the truth and you did help your friend dismember Natalie's body, but you were hoping to trade your freedom for giving evidence against the defendant. Is that not the case?"

"No."

"The problem was that your plan might well have worked. The police were indeed considering that course of action until Mr Pattison came forward with his evidence that put you in the kitchen of 119 St Johns Grove with Adams."

Larvin thought for a while before answering.

"Look, I admit I was lying to the police the whole time. But I'm an addict. Didn't know what I was saying. All I know is Darren never came to my house and he didn't kill Natalie. Why would he? They was together and she fed his habit for him."

"You have lied to the police and you are now lying to this court. I will not bother to ask you about the occasions when you told other people that Mr Adams was responsible for killing Natalie because I know what your answer will be. I have no more questions for Mr Larvin."

That was the end of Larvin's appearance in the box. To be fair to him, he'd kept his composure as he blamed his heroin addiction for making him lie about everything. As he walked past me, he looked directly at me and spoke the words 'you're dead', so I could just hear them. I mimed the words 'fuck off' right back at him. His threat didn't bother me. Should he be found not guilty, maybe he'd come after me but his main priority would be to score, so he probably wouldn't have the time, I thought. All that was left now were the closing arguments and Judge Klevan's summing up. They'd have to wait until the morning.

The drive back from Sheffield gave me time to think. Kev and Andy couldn't have done any more to convince the jury that they'd acted quite properly and honestly in their dealings with Pattison. Would it be enough to make them sure they could trust his evidence? I didn't underestimate for one moment just how difficult it was going to be for them to be sure beyond reasonable doubt of Adams's guilt.

My thoughts turned to the stranger on the bridge and his words of wisdom - less thinking, more doing. And so I put on Dylan's 'Desolation Row' and wondered what it would've been like to meet the famous people mentioned in his masterpiece. From Ezra Pound to T. S. Eliot, Cinderella to Bette Davis, Einstein to Robin Hood, and Ophelia to the Phantom of the Opera. It was a damn fine way of taking my mind off the adrenalin-fuelled atmosphere of Crown Court.

THIRTY-FIVE

'The voice of negativity raised its ugly head again'

The next morning arrived in the blink of an eye. The case was all that I could think about on my journey to Sheffield and, try as I might to look on the bright side, I just couldn't see how the jury would be sure beyond reasonable doubt that Adams murdered Natalie. I found myself listing all the reasons why they wouldn't and there were many. But I was looking forward to Mr Bernard's closing speech. Perhaps he'd be able to convince the jury to put aside the fact that there was no direct evidence to prove that Natalie was killed and dismembered inside 119 St Johns Grove. Perhaps he'd be able to pull the strands of the circumstantial elements of the prosecution case together to provide a compelling argument for guilty verdicts on both Adams and Larvin.

Mr Bernard was ready to begin. Thankfully, he looked to be in a confident mood.

"Members of the jury you will be relieved to know that I'm not going to deliver a long-winded closing argument. It has already been a protracted and complex trial. When you do retire to consider your verdict, I believe that your task will be a daunting one. Do you believe Neil Pattison to be a credible witness who has told the truth? It is a question that I am sure will be occupying your minds with some degree of deliberation and rightly so. By his own admission, he is a compulsive liar with a history of dishonesty from being a child. Would you normally take the word of someone like Mr Pattison to be truthful outside of this courtroom in everyday life? I think not because, with respect, you would never be in the position that you are in today, having to decide the fate of the two defendants stood before you with no direct evidence to corroborate what he has told the court. Accordingly, I must now, members of the jury, set before you the reasons why I urge you to reach the conclusion that Mr Pattison has told you the truth. The most obvious place to begin is this. Why would he put himself forward as a credible witness in the first place? What has he to gain by coming to this court and giving evidence, if his evidence is a pack of lies from beginning to end? What motive would he have for doing such a thing? There was no bad blood between Mr Pattison and the two defendants, and Mr Pattison knows that his life may well be in danger upon his return to prison for giving evidence at Crown Court for the prosecution."

Mr Bernard paused for a moment. Maybe he was just collecting his thoughts before continuing, or maybe it was to allow the jury time to imagine what life would be like for Pattison after the trial and back in a prison cell.

"And now, if I may, I would like to shine a light on the way the evidence was obtained from Mr Pattison. You have already heard, members of the jury, from the two detectives who spent much time with him so that he felt able to recall, in elaborate detail, the events of the 13th of May 1998. If you choose to trust in the integrity of the two officers, then I submit that it would lack reality to consider the possibility of a complete fabrication of the evidence. My learned colleagues challenged the officers to this effect, and you heard DS Scarth's heartfelt address to the court about never having done anything to undermine the oath he took as a constable. You also heard what DC Marshall said in his defence and I quote: 'what you're suggesting is that DS Scarth and I colluded with Pattison over a period of about ten months to make the whole thing up just to get Adams convicted of something he didn't do. Ridiculous. You're attacking my integrity. You're attacking everything I believe in. You're attacking the reason why I became a copper in the first place'. You may remember that the officer became distressed at the accusations and needed a moment to regain his composure. I consider the evidence to have been obtained from Mr Pattison in a way that was in keeping with the highest traditions of the police service and that is why Mr Pattison was put forward as a credible witness, despite all that you have heard about him that would make you want to believe otherwise."

Mr Bernard paused to take a sip of water. He'd a gift for making you want to listen. I'd describe it as a gentle kind of hypnosis, the kind that made you want to believe every word that he said.

"Think back if you will to what he told the police. How could he have known how Natalie died if he was not told by Adams that morning on the drain bank? It is indeed and important point and, in many ways, the most important point of the entire trial. You will remember that the police went to extraordinary lengths to keep the cause of death a secret known only to the investigation team. The stab wounds inflicted by Mr Adams were never in the public domain. How could he have known about the blue blanket that covered Natalie as she lay dead in the bath, if he had not visited 119 St Johns Grove to see for himself? How could he have known about the position of the wounds if he had not seen them for himself as he pulled aside the blanket covering Natalie? You may remember what Mr Pattison said and I quote: 'I pulled back the blanket. It was laid across her chest. What he'd told me was right there was like puncture wounds close together around her chest. I don't know how many but there was loads'. And there is corroboration to support what Mr Pattison told you from Larvin himself. You will recall that Larvin asked to see DS Goddard whilst he was on remand and he told the officer and I quote: 'Adams came to see me on the morning of 13th May and told me that he'd woken up in the kitchen of 119 St Johns Grove on the floor next to Natalie. She'd a knife in her and she was covered in blood'. Even though he later retracted this statement, how did he know that Natalie had been stabbed unless that is what Adams told him? He could not have known that fact from any other source but Natalie's killer, Adams. If you do believe Pattison, then everything else you have heard will fit into place. Craig Walker's testimony, the account of the brother Shaun Adams, the blue fibres recovered from Natalie's arm, the cut ankle boots, the unusually clean bath in the bathroom of 119 St Johns Grove, the writing on the wall at that address, Rebecca Carroll's observations and so on. If that is the case and you do find Neil Pattison to be telling the truth beyond reasonable doubt, then Darren Adams is guilty of the murder of Natalie Clubb, and Michael Larvin is guilty of helping to dismember and dispose of her body."

Mr Bernard paused again. He was on top form, on a different level to anything I'd seen before from a barrister. It was impressive but he hadn't finished. He'd more to say.

"Members of the jury, the Crown's position is this. On the evening of the 12th of May 1998, the defendant Adams and Natalie Clubb were present inside 119 St Johns Grove when an argument took place. It is likely that the cause of the argument was over Natalie's lesbian relationship with Nini Thompson. It is also likely that they were both under the influence of temazepam. You have heard, members of the jury, the defendant's propensity for violence towards Natalie from a number of key witnesses and I submit that during the argument, Adams flew into a violent rage, a rage that caused him to kick and punch Natalie with forceful blows that knocked her to the ground. He then picked up a knife, sat astride her, and brutally stabbed Natalie repeatedly until she was dead. The defendant then turned to his good friend Larvin and together they set about butchering her body, cutting it into pieces so that they would fit into bin bags. They then calmly placed the bags inside Larvin's blue Ford Sierra motorcar in broad daylight, and transported them to a location somewhere upstream of the Bransholme pumping station, where they tossed them into the Holderness drain. Adams tried to cover his tracks by calling the police and reporting her missing on the 14th of May. They carried on with their lives as if nothing had happened. Members of the jury, there are no words to describe the horror, the unbelievable cruelty that lay behind the actions of the two defendants stood before you."

Mr Bernard's oratory reached fever pitch as he delivered the words 'horror' and 'unbelievable cruelty'. I guessed that a long pause would follow and I was right. I felt sorry for the jury because his sense of outrage at what they did to Natalie, would surely leave a lasting impression long after the end of the trial. They would have no option but to picture in their minds the brutal nature of Natalie's death. It was a picture I'd not been able to erase from my waking thoughts, either.

"Members of the jury, I began by saying that your task will be a daunting one but, on reflection, after listening to everything I have said, you must be thinking that the task that lay before you is much more than daunting, it is overwhelming. This is a case that has tested the criminal justice system to the very limits, from the lack of any direct evidence to the prosecution witnesses, the majority of whom come from a background of drug dealing, drug addiction and prostitution. Returning, if I may, to the testimony of Mr Pattison once again. Are you sure he has told the truth? If you are sure, and sure of all the supporting evidence that corroborates his narrative, then I submit that the prosecution has proved beyond reasonable doubt that Adams is guilty of the murder of Natalie Clubb, and Larvin is guilty of assisting to dispose of her body. Members of the jury, thank you for listening."

Mr Bernard's closing speech was all that I'd hoped it would be – articulate, persuasive, and filled with just the right level of emotion. It was brilliant. I was pleased with the way he'd reminded the jury of how Pattison's evidence had been obtained with such patience and professionalism by DC Marshall and DS Scarth.

Mr Logan rose to his feet. I wondered how he was going to follow Mr Bernard's understated eloquence.

"Members of the jury, I agree with my learned colleague in that Neil Pattison's evidence is the key to this case and to convict my client for the murder of Natalie Clubb, you must be sure beyond reasonable doubt that he is telling the truth. But how can you be sure that he is telling the truth when the evidence is purely circumstantial? There is no evidence to even prove that Natalie Clubb was killed inside 119 St Johns Grove. We have only the word of Neil Pattison. The instrument used to stab her has not been recovered. The bin bags used to conceal Natalie Clubb's body do not match those found in 119 St Johns Grove. Michael Larvin's blue Ford Sierra motorcar was forensically examined and no incriminating evidence was found. The prosecution has placed much importance on the clean bath. Members of the jury, we know that the house was insecure for some time, is it not possible that someone else used the bath for another purpose? And great emphasis has been placed on the blue fibres recovered from Natalie Clubb's arm and how that fits with Neil Pattison's story. Could they not have been shed by contact with something else prior to its discovery? Surely that must be possible."

Mr Logan paused for a moment to take a sip of water. It was all part of the performance to heighten the sense of drama. That's what they got paid to do and I had to admit that they were bloody good at it.

"But perhaps the issue that must not be overlooked and is of central importance to this case, is that the police have failed to establish a motive for the murder of Natalie Clubb. The defendant has time and again pleaded his innocence and offered the name of Jodi Amadi as the person responsible because they owed him money. That would be a motive. Mr Pattison would have us believe that the defendant committed the crime during an argument whilst they were under the influence of temazepam. But, even if some of the witnesses who have given evidence describing Mr Adams's less than favourable treatment of his girlfriend are to be believed, none of those episodes, as far as I am aware, led to serious injury, let alone murder. So why should we believe that this argument was different, if indeed an argument did take place? Members of the jury, you may think that there is not much to like about Mr Adams. He was, by his own admission, heavily dependent on heroin at that time and none of us can begin to imagine what that must be like. Drug addicts will do anything to support their habit just as Natalie did as a working prostitute. And so, my point is this, regardless of whether you believe that he had a loving relationship with Natalie, why would he kill the person who provided his daily fix of heroin? It may seem a heartless thing to say but the defendant is fighting for his liberty and I want to be sure, members of the jury, that you understand the impact that the disappearance of Natalie had on the defendant. It was catastrophic and you have heard how it led to his arrest for burglary. It is not my intention in any way to portray Mr Adams as a victim in this case because that would be highly inappropriate given the circumstances, but I believe that the lack of motive and the questionable testimony of Mr Pattison, are two issues that I would respectfully suggest undermine the prosecution case. They must surely, you may think, give just cause for reasonable doubt and therefore to convict Darren Adams of murder would be a grave injustice. Thank you."

Mr Logan did his best to undermine the prosecution case by doing exactly what I would've done, concentrate on the fundamental weaknesses of the circumstantial elements of the evidence. Adams didn't have to prove his innocence, and Mr Logan would be well aware that the standard required for a jury to convict was a very high standard to achieve.

Mr Stanford would be the last closing statement. The jury didn't look at all comfortable and I couldn't blame them. I wondered what his approach would be, given Larvin's authentic admission to John Goddard after charge implicating the person he was now stood next to in the dock.

"Members of the jury, Michael Larvin is innocent. But before I would ask you to come to that conclusion let me, if I may, briefly set out the evidence, or more to the point, lack of evidence against him. Craig Walker told you that Darren Adams implicated my client during a prison cell conversation. Mr Adams denied that meeting ever took place. Can Mr Walker be believed given that he has been exposed as a liar when giving cell confession evidence in another trial? I think not. Neil Pattison told you how he witnessed Mr Larvin assisting Darren Adams to dispose of Natalie Clubb's body in the kitchen of 119 St Johns Grove, again the word of a compulsive liar. There is no independent evidence, not one bit, to help corroborate his story. There is no independent evidence to prove that Natalie Clubb was killed and dismembered inside 119 St Johns Grove. We have heard that my client's car was forensically examined and no incriminating evidence was found. You were told that a listening device was placed secretly inside Mr Larvin's home, and the police told you that they listened for a significant period of time to his conversations with different people, and nothing was said by him that would suggest he had any involvement in the disposal of the body. And yes, he did tell the police that Darren Adams was responsible for killing Natalie Clubb. You will recall that he was sorry for misleading the police. He just wanted to be free to see his children again. I submit that, based on the argument I have just laid out before you, the evidence against my client is purely circumstantial, and is, I believe, certainly not sufficient for you to be sure beyond reasonable doubt of his guilt. Thank you, members of the jury."

On the journey home, after listening to Mr Bernard, it made me realise that we couldn't have done any more. It made me realise that it was a miracle that we'd got to this position in the first place, from the discovery of a severely decomposed arm, to a prosecution case that I still believed in. And, if the jury didn't share my belief and found them not guilty, maybe there was a chance that I could come to terms with their decision. I'd no idea if Mr Bernard had done enough to sway the jury. The voice of negativity reared its ugly head: 'so you're pinning your hopes on the jury believing Pattison and Walker without a shred of evidence to corroborate their stories. Good luck with that'. For once, the voice chattering away in my head had a point, and if I were an independent person having listened throughout the trial, what would reasonable doubt look like, I wondered. I couldn't help thinking, yet again, that TML/4 would've made all the difference.

THIRTY-SIX

'Criminals are just as capable of telling the truth'

Judge Klevan began his summing up of the evidence on Wednesday, 15 March 2000. It was always fascinating to hear Crown Court judges and their unique perspective on the evidence. Judge Klevan certainly had a difficult task ahead of him: should they be found guilty, there would be every likelihood that Adams and Larvin would appeal. They'd already given notice of their intentions at the very beginning of the trial by attempting to get Pattison's and Walker's evidence excluded. Mr Logan and Mr Stanford would both be listening to every word the judge said looking for grounds to appeal. Accordingly, at a guess, I'd put money on his summing up to be ever so slightly biased in favour of the defence.

The atmosphere in the courtroom was different to any of the previous days. Maybe it was because, over the past three weeks, the jury had been exposed to the graphic testimony of witnesses who'd described in vivid detail, unimaginable depths of degradation, cruelty, deceit, and brutality. And now, the end was in sight. Judge Klevan would be taking back control of his domain, and his voice, with its gentle eloquence, would be the only one allowed to be heard.

Judge Klevan spent some time on what Shaun Adams told the court.

"Members of the jury, I pause to remind you, now just moving away from the evidence to observations for your assistance. This is the first defendant's brother giving evidence. Has he got it right? Is he for some reason telling lies in order to gain advantage, or is he telling you the truth, and do you, and can you, rely on it? He said that although he had seen police officers, he has made no pact with them. He did not ask for bail and was sure that he had not been pressurised by the police. 'I wanted to help my brother and my freedom didn't take priority', is what he also told you."

Judge Klevan clearly viewed Shaun Adams as a key witness, a brother giving evidence against his own brother. It'd been a crushing blow to Adams when first put to him in interview. He definitely hadn't seen it coming and couldn't understand why his brother had betrayed him.

"Shaun Adams then turned to the matter in relation to Larvin. He said he was in prison with Larvin, and Larvin was being accused by other inmates of the killing of Natalie Clubb. Larvin responded, he said, by saying, 'you know it was Darren who stabbed her, not me'."

I wanted Judge Klevan to emphasise the importance of Larvin's reference to stabbing. It would have gone a long way to show that Shaun Adams was a credible witness and wasn't lying.

The next time Judge Klevan moved away from the evidence to assist the jury, was the conversation outside the telephone box, when Adams spoke to Neil Pattison, Jeffrey Pattison and Stephen Brewster, who were sat in a car waiting to phone their drug dealer.

"Again, pausing there, because it touches upon the telephone box conversation. That you now know is not disputed as a conversation. At one time, as we will see in a moment, in interview Adams said it had not taken place. It might have been a lack of recollection, confusion. Now the defendant concedes and accepts that that phone call did take place. It is in many ways, you may feel, an important conversation. Great emphasis is put on this conversation by the prosecution. You will, I am sure, consider that evidence carefully, as Counsel have asked you to do."

Did the jury understand the significance of this conversation, I wondered? Neil Pattison clearly hadn't disclosed to either his brother or Brewster, anything about Adams's drain bank confession and what he saw at 119 St Johns Grove on 13 May. It was a wind-up but it'd unnerved Adams. With reference to Brewster's evidence,

"He agreed with Mr Stanford that he had heard Neil Pattison say that he thought he was going to get a reward in this case. He said he did not know whether to believe that, because he knew Neil Pattison to be a compulsive liar."

Hearing the words come from Judge Klevan somehow seemed to add weight to the defence argument that Neil Pattison was lying throughout. The jury would certainly remember that phrase, 'Neil Pattison to be a compulsive liar', because Judge Klevan's voice cut through the air with clinical authority. My heart sank because if the jury didn't believe Pattison, then they'd certainly bring not guilty verdicts. The tension in the courtroom was definitely building.

"I will return to a witness that Mr Stanford called to

indicate that Walker is a liar because Walker said certain things in the inquiry in the other murder, and Mr Stanford brought forth a witness who spoke of that."

Whilst I knew that Judge Klevan had no choice but to be fair and balanced when he summarised Craig Walker's evidence, unfortunately, the words 'Walker' and 'liar' had been spoken together in the same sentence. My heart sank even further if that were possible. Within the space of five minutes, the jury had heard both Pattison and Walker referred to as liars. But then the judge moved onto the evidence of the pathologist and Amanda Hudson and the source of the eight pale-blue fibres.

"The Crown's point here, and great emphasis was placed on it in their closing speech, was that those blue fibres came from the sheet that was seen to be covering the body of Natalie Clubb when she was in the bath, as seen by Neil Pattison."

Now that sounded a whole lot better from my perspective - the judge spoke as if he believed that's what happened. The presence of the blue fibres was the one thing that caused me to believe Pattison's story. If he'd made the whole thing up, how had he chosen the colour blue for the blanket? Or why mention a blanket in the first place? I hoped these were the kind of questions running through the minds of the jurors.

Judge Klevan moved on to summarise the evidence of Neil Pattison and towards the end, he said this,

"The Crown have placed much importance on the evidence of Neil Pattison: the drain bank confession, visiting 119 St Johns Grove alone and seeing Natalie Clubb in the bath covered with a blue sheet or blanket, and returning later to see Adams and Larvin with black refuse bags containing parts of Natalie Clubb's body. Neil Pattison made no secret of the fact that he has a long and varied criminal past. You may or may not feel that this has any relevance to whether or not he is telling the truth. You will have to decide that matter for yourselves. I'm afraid I'm not able to assist you in that regard. However, my observation in relation to Mr Pattison, is this - just as law-abiding citizens are capable of lying and often do tell lies, criminals are just as capable of telling the truth."

If I didn't know better, I'd say that Judge Klevan had just given the prosecution case a much-needed boost. But then, on reflection, he'd stated the obvious, and I suppose he was merely pointing out to the jury that they shouldn't assume that just because he was, according to Brewster, a compulsive liar, that he wouldn't be capable of giving an honest testimony. I couldn't help thinking that it was a small victory, nevertheless.

Turning to what Adams said when interviewed, for all the hard work Shaun Weir put into the interview plan for Adams, Judge Klevan only highlighted two areas for mention: the conversation by the telephone box and the cut shoes found in 119 St Johns Grove.

"So that interview reveals on two separate occasions, it would appear, this conversation I will refer to as the telephone box conversation was brought up with Adams. Adams denied it took place. He now said he could not remember and he was confused, and that is why he denied it. The Crown's position is at that stage he was denying it. Now he is admitting it. You have to decide where the truth lies, and if it helps at all. The only other area also that you will wish to consider, the Crown invite you to consider, is with regard to the cut shoes. At the interview he was conceding that they appeared to be Natalie's. He is now saying they are not, and as you will remember why that is the case, he said they were shown to him in a bag. Again, you must decide whether he is telling the truth. Those are the only two areas I refer you to."

Judge Klevan made no observations to assist the jury when he moved on from the interviews with Adams, to what he said in court. The jury sat and listened as the judge repeated that Adams denied pretty much everything any of the witnesses had said. In my opinion, it cried out for the judge to pose the question: is he telling the truth, or has he been lying from start to finish. Is it likely that all of the witnesses could be mistaken or lying? I'd a feeling Judge Klevan would focus much more on Larvin and I wasn't wrong.

"Larvin's position is a little different. His interviews, again you will remember, are relevant only in his case to his state of knowledge and belief of matters. When first seen by the police really nothing was said of substance it is put, but then he made a request to see the police. He was acting without knowledge then of his solicitors and he said to the police, 'you've fucked me about for a year now. My head's gone. I've swallowed razor blades, tried to hang myself, lost my wife, and I've been suicidal'. He added: 'I've some information I want to tell you, sooner rather than later. I'm worried about my kids. I can confirm some of what Neil

Pattison told you. Darren did it all. He stabbed her after an argument after they'd taken a load of temazepam'."

Judge Klevan was referring to what Larvin told John Goddard when he visited him in prison at Larvin's request after charge. The fact that Larvin later changed his story didn't escape Judge Klevan's attention.

"The Crown is saying that Larvin's first account is a narrative of truth. The defence of Larvin say, 'not a bit of it. It gives the appearance no doubt of truth, but it was a lie from beginning to end. It was a belief that Larvin had that if he would say things of this kind against Adams, bail may be his'."

I expected Judge Klevan to highlight the fact that Larvin told John that Adams stabbed Natalie. Again, because the cause of death wasn't made public, he must have been told by Adams. How could he then turn around in court and say that it was all a lie? It was a crucial point, and it'd also put into context Pattison's testimony and Walker's prison cell conversation. All he said was,

"You will reflect on this and these interviews, and decide have the prosecution made you sure that Larvin was telling the truth on the first occasion. He did not go the whole way, but that what he said in so far as it did go, is the truth. You are going to have to assess has he told the truth here? Is the way these interviews continue, the language used, what was said, evidence of the truth, or is this a man with consummate skill, lying and making up a false story for his own advantage?"

Judge Klevan paused for a moment, maybe to give the jury time to think about what he'd just said before concluding with an indirect acknowledgment that the evidence against Larvin was purely circumstantial.

"You have before you two issues raised by Mr Stanford: Larvin's home was the subject of surveillance, that nothing was revealed of anything said or done that was in any way incriminating by Larvin in that period when he did not know he was being watched or listened to. And that the Ford Sierra, Larvin's car, has been examined by scientists, and nothing has been found of an incriminating nature that would connect him to the offence he has been charged with. Members of the jury, that brings me to the end of this summing up."

Mr Stanford must have been pleased with Judge Klevan's last comments before closing. I expected and hoped for a kind of mini-synopsis of the relevant points again, but instead he chose to leave the jury with a boost for Larvin's defence. It was an anti-climax from my perspective.

"Members of the jury, that brings me to the end of this summing up. When you retire in a few moments, you may find it easier to elect a foreman to chair your deliberations. When I ask you to retire now you must reach, if you can, a unanimous verdict, a verdict with which you are all agreed. You may know that the law allows me in certain circumstances to accept a verdict, which is not the verdict of you all. Those circumstances have not arisen, so when I ask you to retire now, I would like you to reach a verdict on which each one of you is agreed."

The jury retired at eleven-thirty on Thursday, 16 March. How long would the jury take to reach a verdict, I wondered? Sometimes it could be a matter of hours, sometimes days. By four-thirty, they'd not reached a decision and so the judge sent them home.

THIRTY-SEVEN

'Deep in thought, I nearly fell off my chair when the phone rang'

At ten forty-five the next morning, the jury began their deliberations again. There was nothing else to do but hang around in the court canteen. I didn't want to go for a walk, in case the verdict came, and towards the end of the afternoon, it looked like the jury would be sent home again. But then the tannoy burst into life.

"Will all interested parties in the Adams and Larvin case please proceed to court three."

This could be the moment I'd been waiting for since July 1998. But would it be the verdict or the jury asking for direction on a particular issue? With the courtroom assembled, Judge Klevan asked for the jury to be brought back into court.

"Members of the jury, have you reached verdicts on the two defendants upon which you are all agreed?"

The elected foreman of the jury stood and replied.

"Yes, we have your Honour."

"Very well. Mr Adams and Mr Larvin, would you please stand. In relation to Darren Adams, do you find the defendant guilty or not guilty of the murder of Natalie Clubb?"

I closed my eyes, held my breath and did something that I'd not done since I was a kid. I prayed.

"GUILTY."

Adams's knees crumbled beneath him. The two prison guards held him upright as he struggled to regain his composure.

"Fucking stitch up by them coppers. I've been fucking set up by that bastard Pattison."

"Order, order. Mr Adams, you will refrain from making any further comment otherwise, I will have no option but to find you in contempt of court."

Judge Klevan repeatedly hammered down his gavel to show that he was in charge and it was his courtroom.

"Fuck off. Do you think I'm bothered, I've just been found fucking guilty of fucking murder."

I could see his point, in a way. Out came the gavel again. Bang, bang, bang.

"Mr Adams, I find you in contempt of court. Please take him down."

Adams continued to shout, 'fucking set up, fucking coppers', but thankfully, his cries became less audible as he was led further away to the obvious relief of the jury.

"Foreman of the jury, I'm sorry for that. I will continue. Do you find Michael Larvin guilty or not guilty of assisting Darren Adams to dispose of the body of Natalie Clubb?"

"GUILTY."

Larvin just stood and turned his gaze on the jury. I could see him look at them one by one as if to say, you haven't seen the last of me, I'll be coming for you. It was a stare filled with hatred – cold, unforgiving and in many ways, probably unforgettable for most of the jurors. They'd just condemned two people to many years in prison. It wasn't what the average person did every day.

"Please bring back Darren Adams for sentencing."

Adams reappeared with a kind of 'fuck the lot of you', attitude as if he couldn't care less about what Judge Klevan was about to say. I'd a feeling, though, that he should have.

"Darren Adams, you have been found guilty of the murder of Natalie Clubb and the only sentence I am allowed pass by law is that of life imprisonment, of which you will serve a minimum of twenty-five years. Yours was a terrible and despicable crime. You lured Natalie Clubb into a life of drug addiction and prostitution, so that she provided an income for you to sustain your own heroin addiction. You were often violent towards her. Leaving you for Nini Thompson caused you to become jealous and I believe this led to the fateful argument on the evening of the 12th of May 1998. You lost control and stabbed her repeatedly in the chest. The blows were so forceful they pierced bone and passed the whole way through her body. Did you do the right thing and call the police? No, you did not. You enlisted the help of your closest friend Michael Larvin and you both set about butchering the dead body of Natalie Clubb. Together, I believe that you tossed her body parts into the Holderness drain intending that they would never be discovered. The police gave you every opportunity to admit your guilt. Did you admit your guilt? No, you lied repeatedly. I find you to be an evil man. Take him down."

Adams looked as though he'd just been delivered a knockout blow by Mike Tyson. There were no words of defiance, it was as if it'd finally sunk in that there really was no way out for him. The jury's verdict was unanimous.

"Michael Larvin, you have been found guilty of assisting Darren Adams to dispose of Natalie Clubb's dead body. You will serve a minimum of six years in prison. When Darren Adams asked you for help you had a choice to make. I believe you were the one who took control and came up with the idea of dismembering her body, you were the driving force and Adams was grateful for your help. The gruesome nature of your unspeakable crime says much about you – cold, callous, cowardly and without remorse. You had every opportunity to admit what you had done to the police. When you did, it was a partial truth to assist you and you alone. You implicated Adams, not yourself, and then you later told this court that it was all lies. Again, I find you to be an evil man. Take him down."

As he was led away, Larvin made a point of looking straight at me and made a slashing motion across his neck with his hand. I took it to mean that he'd get me too, when he got out. But this was no time to worry about Adams or Larvin. The moment had come that I'd hoped and prayed for - unanimous guilty verdicts. The judge thanked the jury for, 'enduring the difficult challenges associated with a complex trial of this nature'. He specifically referred to the upsetting details of the case and hoped that they hadn't suffered too much distress by what they'd heard throughout the trial.

"Before I dismiss you all from this courtroom, there is one last task for me to do and that is to commend the actions of Detective Sergeant Kevin Scarth and Detective

Constable Andrew Marshall. The evidence of Neil Pattison was crucial to outcome of this case. The professional manner in which both detectives formed a trusting relationship with him over many months was, in my opinion, the reason why Pattison was put forward by the prosecution as a credible witness worthy of belief. The detectives struck the right balance between the requirement to obtain potentially vital information, and the expectations of the public for the police to be trusted and believed. They did so with a high degree of skill and honesty and they should be justifiably proud of their achievement."

Outside the courtroom, I saw Detective Superintendent Taylor being swamped by an eagerly awaiting press. That should have been me, I thought, but somehow it didn't really matter. I knew he'd do a good job. Mr Bernard came across and spoke to us all. I could tell that he was pleased with himself, and he'd every right to be given the unanimous verdicts against all the odds. I thanked him for believing in the case and for a moment, he was lost for words. He politely declined the invitation to go for a celebratory pint and with a firm handshake he was gone. We, on the other hand, had no intention of going home without a well-deserved visit to the closest pub we could find. I walked with Tony, my trusted colleague who'd been with me every step of the way, and all he could say was,

"Bloody hell, Davo, we did it, fucking hell we did it."

He kept repeating the words over and over again as if he couldn't believe what had just happened. It was one of those occasions when you wished you could bottle the moment to enjoy sometime later, to remember just what an astonishing result this was.

The pub was busy filled with teatime drinkers. Detective Superintendent Taylor arrived a few minutes later and, to his credit, bought everyone a drink. There was an awkward moment between us, maybe because the presence of two SIOs celebrating the same guilty verdicts just wasn't something either of us had ever experienced before. Even though he was officially the SIO on this case, in reality, the Samantha Class case was his investigation in every sense, from the beginning to the end, the one he'd invested months of his time to solving, in the same way I'd done. If I was in his shoes though, I'd have felt awkward too. It should have been guilty verdicts in both cases.

I thought about the jury and what made them come to their decision. I noticed some of them sat at a corner table. They looked across at us and we looked at them, and just for a moment, I felt on overwhelming urge to go across and ask them how they'd arrived at their unanimous decision. But deep down, I knew it would be ethically wrong to do so, and if someone from one of the defence teams saw us, it would almost certainly lead to accusations of collusion and provide grounds for an appeal. It didn't stop me wondering though. I'd have loved to be a fly on the wall in the jury room when they must have surely wrestled over whether to believe Pattison. What made them believe him? What did they think of Craig Walker? Was there anything we missed? What did they think of the investigation? I'd so many questions. It felt like my head was about to explode.

I congratulated Andy and Kev on receiving Crown Court Commendations from Judge Klevan,

"You should both be proud of what Judge Klevan said about you both."

I didn't say anymore, it would have embarrassed them. They just smiled and sank another pint. Nothing else was discussed about the case, and in an instant we all seemed to be heading back home after a lot of firm handshakes.

It was an emotional journey back for me. If my Dad were alive, he'd be the first person I'd have called. He'd have been so proud of me, and at times like these when you put your heart and soul into a challenge in life and come out the other side, win or lose, it was human instinct to want a kind word from your Dad. It would've meant the world to me. I knew it wouldn't come from chief officers. In any case, it wasn't my place to break the news of the verdict, it would be Detective Superintendent Taylor calling his boss, DCS Jordan, who'd then inform the ACC. The rank structure had to be obeyed.

Instead of going straight home, I decided to go back to my old SIO's office at HQ. When I arrived, the incident room was empty and in darkness. I made myself a coffee and sat for a while. Memories came flooding back, so many, so vivid. They'd stay with me forever, because they were made at a time when my senses were heightened by the complexities of trying to solve the case. Each day brought a new challenge, a new decision to make without knowing what I was doing in the first place. Investigation by instinct would be the way I'd describe those early days. Deep in thought, I nearly fell off my chair when the phone rang and shattered the gloomy silence.

"It's Neil Pattison. Is DC Marshall or DS Scarth there?"

Of all the people that could have called, Neil Pattison was

the last person I expected.

"No, sorry. They've gone home."

Before I could say anything more, Pattison put down the phone. I tried to imagine how he'd be feeling right now facing years behind bars, and how he'd deal with the consequences of his performance in Crown Court. His fellow inmates would be unforgiving and brutal. I wondered why he'd wanted to speak to Andy or Kev.

My mind turned to the moment the foreman delivered the guilty verdicts. I knew then that I'd be able to hold my head up high whatever the future might hold. DCS Jordan's faith in me hadn't been misplaced and the difficult decision's I'd made, proved to be the right ones. Withholding the cause of death, video recording witnesses, and the forensic search of 119 St Johns Grove, were all tough decisions. And in a way, I was glad that I was given a hard time over those decisions, because it taught me a great deal about myself and how to be a better SIO. It also made me realise that I wanted, badly, to be a SIO again. This result wouldn't have done my prospects any harm, even though I wasn't the official SIO, I told myself. Surely, chief officers would recognise and give credit for my role in progressing the investigation to the point of charging Adams and Larvin. But would they? I wasn't convinced.

I felt an overwhelming sense of loneliness. Looking around the incident room, it was as if it'd never happened. The pulse of the investigation team that was once so vibrant and full of life, would fade forever now as the remaining few returned to their normal duties. I'd so many memories that would stay with me: the moment Andy and Kev had burst into my office brimming with excitement with news of Adams's drain bank confession, and when Shaun had done the same thing shortly afterwards, with his graphic recall of Sunman's astonishing admission. Looking back, they were moments that couldn't be experienced by doing any other job, and they made me realise why I'd wanted to be a policeman in the first place.

THIRTY-EIGHT

'The wounds we inflict on our souls when we look the other way'

The next day, I was back at Bridlington feeling empty and mentally exhausted. I knew it'd be a challenge to get myself motivated again after the emotional rollercoaster of the last couple of weeks. All I had to look forward to now was to do the best job I could for the people of Bridlington and I knew that I would. But then there was a knock at the door. It was Tony Burke.

"Boss, hope you don't mind me coming but I've got some news about Pattison. I wanted to tell you in person."

His face was pale and he looked like he'd just seen a ghost. Something was wrong. This wasn't the confident, upbeat Tony I knew.

"What is it you've got to tell me? Are you OK?"

"I've just come from the prison. Pattison committed suicide overnight."

I didn't know what to say other to ask him how it'd happened.

"Apparently, he threaded his boot laces through the tiny ventilation holes in the cell door. They don't know how he did it. He must've put the laces round his neck and lifted himself into a fetal position so his arse was clear of the cell floor. That's how they found him, hanging from the back of the cell door."

"I didn't see that coming. I spoke to him only last night. He called the station asking for Andy or Kev. When I told him they'd gone home, he just put the phone down."

I made us both a coffee and we just sat in silence. My mind went into overdrive trying to make sense of Tony's news. I'd spoken to Pattison only last night and now he was gone. My thoughts turned to Andy and Kev and I asked Tony whether they knew.

"Yes, I called in to see them both before coming here. There's something else, boss. Pattison left Andy and Kev an envelope. He left one for his family and one for the prison guard who found him. They won't release it because of the ongoing investigation into his death. Is there anything you could do? It'd mean a lot to them both to find out what's inside."

That was something I could understand. I'd witnessed the bond between the two detectives and Pattison grow during the long months of the investigation. The journey to get to this place had been an extraordinary one for them both. Unlocking Pattison's evidence was a remarkable achievement, one that led directly to the convictions of Adams and Larvin. Accordingly, I'd have been surprised if there hadn't been a bond of some kind. Perhaps Andy and Kev had been able to see beyond Pattison's villainous past, and caught a glimpse of an ordinary, intelligent human being beneath his outward swagger and violent reputation. Or maybe it was simply because Pattison had been such a big part of their lives for so long, and a kind of mutual respect was an inevitable consequence of spending so much time together. Whatever the reason, I knew that I had to try and find out what was in the envelope. Tony didn't stay long. We both knew that it'd take us all a long time to come to terms with Pattison taking his own life.

It was a strange, empty feeling, to be high on adrenalin at the guilty verdicts one day, to contemplating the ultimate demise of someone, who it seemed to me, had given their life to secure justice for Natalie, the next. I put a call in to the governor at Hull prison. I didn't hold out much hope of them changing their minds though, and I was right. It was prison policy, and I was pretty sure that Pattison's family wouldn't agree, either.

Sat alone in my office, it all started to make sense. If he'd planned his suicide months ago, then he'd been in control all along as if he was playing an elaborate game of chess. He knew that the drain bank confession would be just enough to make us focus the investigation on Adams. You couldn't blame him for withholding the rest of his story because he obviously enjoyed the time spent with Andy and Kev, when they'd produced him from prison for his mini-breaks, courtesy of the force. And maybe he'd really not wanted to 'meddle' or interfere any further by deepening his betrayal of Adams and Larvin. But, in the end, he'd eventually given us the whole story. When he'd said in court that he wanted to be remembered for doing something good, perhaps he'd meant it. Was it because he felt a great deal more for Natalie than he'd led everyone to believe and was sickened by what they did to her? If that was the case, then he'd used his intelligence to convince us that he was telling the truth and to make sure that he was a credible witness in front of the jury.

I decided to go for a walk down by the harbour to clear my head. It was bloody freezing and the grey, darkening clouds threatened rain. The waves crashed hard against the boats that seemed to be huddled together for comfort and safety. It was a bleak outlook, but seen through a different pair of eyes than mine right now, it would probably be viewed very differently. Beautiful almost. I tried to put myself in Pattison's shoes, to see things from his perspective, and for some reason, I recalled a quote I'd read by Martin Luther King Jnr.

> 'Never, never be afraid to do what's right,
> Especially if the well-being of a person is at stake.
> Society's punishments are small compared to
> The wounds we inflict on our soul when
> We look the other way.'

He must have judged the giving of evidence to be the right thing to do. But it was the last words of the quote that played on my mind, 'The wounds we inflict on our soul when we look the other way'. Did he feel as though he should have saved Natalie from Adams and the escalation of violence that eventually led to her death? After all, he wasn't an addict, and so he would have observed their heroin-dependent relationship spiral out of control with a clear head. Maybe he couldn't cope with knowing that he'd looked the other way.

I thought about the envelope Pattison left for Andy and

Kev again. I knew they'd have a burning desire to know what it contained, and I knew they'd be disappointed at my failure to have it released. Pattison enjoyed being one step ahead, and maybe the envelope was his final act in letting us know that even at the end, he was the one in control. Perhaps it was simply a note to say goodbye, and thank them for treating him as an equal and not some scumbag criminal. That would've meant a great deal to the two unassuming detectives. Or perhaps it was to confess to other crimes he'd committed in some grand gesture to say sorry to his many victims. That would've meant a great deal to all those he'd terrorised throughout his long criminal career. Maybe we were better off not knowing, I thought. It wouldn't change anything. It wouldn't make any difference to Natalie now. All that mattered was that Adams and Larvin were where they belonged and would be for a very long time to come.

Some would, I'm sure, judge Pattison to be as evil as Adams and Larvin for the cruel acts of violence he'd inflicted on many throughout his life. And some might take the view that he was a coward for committing suicide to escape justice. But the giving of evidence against Adams and Larvin in the grand setting of Crown Court, was a courageous thing to do and, given his background, it would surely have been the hardest thing he'd ever done, apart from taking his own life.

Now that the trial was over, life would go back to normal for me in uniform, in charge of Bridlington, and my thoughts turned to what the future might hold as the waves battered the promenade. Miles from HQ, would I be forgotten by chief officers? I hadn't given up hope of promotion but somehow, I just didn't seem to fit the kind of person they were looking for. For now, all that self-interest didn't seem to matter. What did matter was that I'd built and led an outstanding team of detectives who'd found their true potential. They were the real heroes who all had one thing in common: they lived by a code of conduct that was difficult to put into words. If I were asked to describe it though, it would be their approach to whatever task they were given. Their starting point was always to go beyond expectation, to do more than could be reasonably asked of them. Shaun's mammoth interview plan, or the way Andy and Kev dealt with Pattison, were perfect examples. They did everything with a refreshing degree of humility, based on a strong foundation of honesty, and it was an absolute privilege to have worked alongside them. Natalie was lucky to have had them on her case, I thought, and I hoped that now she'd find a measure of peace with Adams and Larvin behind bars.

On the way back to the station, a woman approached me walking her dog. She looked at me in a way that suggested she was about to say something and I wasn't wrong. I was in full uniform and used to having abuse hurled at me. I braced myself in readiness to take what was coming, but I couldn't have been more wrong.

"Excuse me. Sorry to bother you but are you the officer in charge of Bridlington?"

"Yes, I am. How can help you?"

"I'm a member of a local residents association and I just wanted to thank you for making us all feel safe again."

"Sorry, what did you say?"

It'd been so unexpected I was lost for words.

"For tackling those bloody drug dealers and bringing crime down. We all read your weekly article in the Brid. Free Press and very impressive it is too. Keep up the good work Chief Inspector."

I watched her struggle against the howling wind with her chocolate Labrador by her side, and I realised - probably for the first time - that effective policing was simply about listening and talking to the public and making a difference to their lives. Her compliment gave me a well-needed boost on a dark day, when my thoughts were with Natalie and all those who missed her.

THIRTY-NINE

'We can find no evidence of police corruption in this case'

Tony and me travelled down to the Court of Appeal on 29 June, 2001. Detective Superintendent Taylor had retired and so it was down to me to attend. We both stood in awe. You couldn't fail to be impressed by the architectural magnificence of the mother of all courts: it was both majestic and intimidating at the same time.

Mr Bernard was already in the courtroom looking over some papers. He seemed genuinely pleased to see us both as we exchanged firm handshakes. It was as if there was a bond between us based on the madness of the trial and the unlikely outcome - unanimous guilty verdicts against all the odds. It was good to see him again and he was brimming with confidence.

"Don't worry, we'll win. I've seen their outline arguments and they don't have a leg to stand on. Full of hot air. Good to see you both again. Have to go and prepare now. See you when it's over."

We looked around the court in wonder more than anything. It was a sight to behold.

"This is a bit smart. Look at where the judges'll be sitting, so high up they'll be dizzy looking down at Adams and

Larvin."

Tony was right. It looked to me as though the judge's seats perched high above everyone else, next to the grandest and biggest table I'd ever seen, were positioned there for a reason: to take your breath away the moment you entered. It'd worked on Tony and me. Crown Court was a significant step up from Magistrates' Court, but this was most definitely in a different league. And if to prove my point, I noticed the absence of both Mr Logan and Mr Stanford. There was another barrister chatting to Mr Bernard, and he didn't look at all comfortable. We assumed that he was representing Adams and Larvin. It turned out that he was and his name was Mr Kendall.

Adams and Larvin walked into the courtroom handcuffed. They caught sight of Tony and me; they both stared with an intensity I'd rarely witnessed before. It was pure hatred. There was no show of emotion from either of them as if they knew this was their very last chance for freedom and they had to behave. The three judges entered like a mini-parade, all dressed in robes of velvet red. I wondered how Adams and Larvin would be feeling seeing such a spectacle. I'd have been trembling with fear and I hoped they would be too.

From the moment Mr Kendall opened his mouth, I knew that he'd be no match for Mr Bernard. It was obvious from his lack of confidence and the way he conducted himself, that he wasn't a major league barrister. It almost seemed as though he was overwhelmed by the grandness of the occasion before he'd begun to present his arguments. As expected, they centered on Pattison and how he shouldn't have been allowed to give evidence.

"My Lords, the evidence of Pattison should have been excluded as the prosecution were in breach of the Criminal Procedure and Investigations Act 1996 and the Codes of Practice issued under that Act for police officers. This is set out in Archbold 12-101. Paragraph 4 of the code, in particular 4.4, requires information to be recorded. Yet the officers who spoke to Pattison failed to make records of what occurred and what was said on several occasions."

Mr Bernard was invited to respond and he did so with a dismissive and slightly irritated tone to his voice.

"My Lords, this matter was dealt with by Judge Klevan at the original trial, quite properly in my view. The officers who spoke to Pattison were commended by the learned judge for their honesty. They recorded conversations when they were relevant to the case so that information would not be missed. That is all the Codes of Practice require of police officers. They do not require, as far as I am aware, police officers to record conversations that have nothing to do with the investigation, and could be classed as a means of building a rapport by discussing football, for example."

It took about five seconds for the three judges to side with Mr Bernard. Although clearly surprised by the swiftness of their decision, Mr Kendall battled on.

"My Lords, whilst I must accept your direction on this matter in relation to Pattison, there is another matter of the gravest nature I wish to raise. It is a challenge to the police evidence and goes to the very heart of Pattison's evidence-in-chief. It is my submission that Pattison was groomed into being a cogent witness against Adams. I say this because despite the number of times he made statements which did not fit in with the alleged facts, they persevered with him until he got it about right. During these meetings, the police officers provided material on which he could make his statement."

Mr Bernard leapt to his feet clearly outraged at the suggestion that the police officers were corrupt in the way they had obtained Pattison's evidence.

"My Lords, forgive me for exhibiting a degree of frustration over this, if I may say so, quite ridiculous accusation. Apart from the fact that, and I am repeating myself, Judge Klevan found no such evidence to support the original challenge to the police evidence at the trial. Quite the contrary. There was abundant other material in the possession of the police that confirmed Pattison's story. My Lords, I believe you have details of that material before you."

They conferred for a few minutes and then asked Mr Bernard to explain his reference to, 'several potential witnesses who might have given incriminating evidence and who had provided statements but were not relied upon by the prosecution, because it was considered they were unreliable and potentially unworthy of belief'.

"My Lords, one potential witness in particular is worthy of mentioning at this point. Trevor Sunman was, at the time, a drug addict with a long criminal record. His evidence was given freely to the police. He was at the time a free man in no need of bail as a means of reward. He was also clear that the police offered him no reward for his testimony. If the police advised me that he would have been a reliable witness, then I believe I would have called him to give his evidence.

His evidence was graphic in nature and described how, when he shared a prison cell with Adams, Adams complained about the number of hacksaw blades it had taken to dismember Natalie Clubb because they kept snapping. That would have been highly incriminating evidence to support Pattison's testimony and yet the police chose to argue against calling him as a witness. Why? Because the police investigation from the very beginning was based on transparency, so that every aspect would be open to the closest scrutiny, from the decision to video record every witness to the exemplary manner with which Pattison was dealt with. My Lords, may I respectfully suggest that should you find in favour of the prosecution on this matter, due to the seriousness of the allegations against the police, that you may see fit to make comment, in order to set the record straight."

A brilliant response from Mr Bernard. I couldn't help thinking though that Mr Kendall had taken a big risk in alleging police corruption when a Crown Court judge, a colleague of the Appeal Court judges and probable friend of theirs, had taken the opposite view at the original trial. And it backfired spectacularly as Lord Chief Justice Rose responded.

"We can find no evidence of police corruption in this case. It seems to us that the police investigation was, as Mr Bernard puts it, transparent at all times and therefore it would seem highly unlikely that the police would enter into an elaborate relationship with the witness Pattison over many months in order to secure a false conviction. We think the idea fanciful at best, and at worst, an error of judgment on your part Mr Kendall for bringing the matter to our attention in the first place. We find that there was other evidence to support Pattison's testimony. Craig Walker, Shaun Adams, Rebecca Carroll, the pale-blue fibres recovered from Natalie Clubb's arm, the clean bath, the cut boots, the writing on the wall of 119 St Johns Grove, and Michael Larvin's partial admission after charge. Accordingly, we support the comments made by Judge Klevan at the original trial commending the two detectives who dealt with Pattison. Mr Kendall, your appeal has been unsuccessful. Take them back down."

It was finally over. There'd be no more appeals, and after thanking Mr Bernard for being a bloody star, we left the court with our heads held high and a youthful spring in our step. We headed for the nearest pub and it gave us time to reflect on what'd happened to us both since the end of the trial.

Tony was still an Inspector and I'd been promoted to Detective Superintendent at long last. Although he'd heard about my fall from grace, I didn't feel like telling him that promotion had marked the beginning of the worst period of my career and my life. That would have to wait for another time. Now was the time to celebrate with a few pints before taking the train back to Hull. It also gave me the opportunity to thank Tony properly for his unstinting friendship and support from the very beginning, when I hadn't a clue how to lead such a complex investigation. The fact that we got the result we wanted and deserved was because Tony and me had insisted from day one in, as Mr Bernard put it, transparency in everything we did — nothing hidden, no corners cut, no rewards offered, no inducements, no ends justify the means tactics. And, of course, we were blessed with some of the most outstanding detectives I'd ever had the privilege of working with.

We didn't speak much on the way back. All I could think of right now was Natalie and it was some comfort to know that I couldn't have done any more for her. From the very beginning, we hadn't judged her as a prostitute, or drug addict, but as a victim who'd been bullied into a life of misery and despair. We'd achieved more than I could ever have imagined when I'd received the call from the ACC back in July 1998. The whole experience proved to be the most difficult challenge I'd faced in my career and its complexity had taken me by surprise. Springsteen's song, 'Walk Like a Man', captured perfectly how I was feeling: I hadn't known how many bloody difficult steps in life I'd have to take on my own, either. And I wondered if other people felt the same, and wished that somebody had told them when they were young, just how hard life was going to be. Then again, perhaps you were better off not knowing.

Tired and hungry, I looked out of the window as the train cut through the darkness outside and my thoughts turned to my Dad, and the night before he died. For some reason, we'd argued over how he was disillusioned with modern life. I was to blame, and I never got the chance to say I was sorry because he'd suffered a heart attack the next morning. Knowing my Dad though, he'd have forgiven me as if it'd never happened. It was my biggest regret in life, one that still haunted my every waking moment. To make me feel better, I imagined that he was sat opposite me instead of Tony, telling me how proud he was of me. I'd tell him that I was sorry for the argument, and ask him why he hadn't taken better care of his health so that he could have lived longer and given us more time together. I'd have given anything for that to have really happened.

Pulling into Hull station signaled the end of a unique chapter in my career, one that would be unlikely to be repeated. Tony had proved to be the perfect deputy and a diamond of a human being. We shook hands and promised to keep in touch but we both knew it was unlikely. Tomorrow would be another day, another investigation, with different detectives.

What happened to me not long after promotion to Superintendent was never far from my thoughts. I'd become even more aloof, more distant, and more of an outsider looking in than ever. But, although the future seemed about as bright as the cold and gloomy station platforms, at least I had unforgettable memories to look back on, other cases to look forward to, and a loving family waiting for me back home.

Epilogue

Darren Adams died in HMP Lindholme on 12 November 2017, after serving 18 years for the murder of Natalie Clubb. The cause of his death is not known.

Michael Larvin served his sentence for assisting Adams to dispose of Natalie Clubb's body. He died from a drug overdose shortly after his release from prison.

The following is a poem written by Neil Pattison from his prison cell, just before he took his own life:

I look out of the window and see the trees lay bare
Not like the summer, with all the blossom there
The branches are all empty, not a leaf in sight
But soon I know the buds will grow,
It will be such a delight
To see the buds all open, they may be pink or white
Like a bride in her gown, for all the world to see
The tree is like an Angel bride, put there for you and me.

About the Author

Paul was born and raised on a council estate in Hull. He initially studied to become a chemical engineer and was awarded a PhD degree before working as a post-doctoral fellow at the University of Toronto, Canada.

He joined the police service in 1982, and served for thirty years reaching the rank of Chief Superintendent. Most of his career was spent in the CID and he led many high-profile murder investigations both as a Detective Chief Inspector and Detective Superintendent.

Paul is retired and lives in East Yorkshire. This is his first book. His second book, RACHEL, is a true account of the police investigation Paul led into the disappearance of Rachel Moran in the early hours of New Year's Day, 2003, in Hull.

Copyright

This book is copyright material and must not be copied, reproduced, transferred, distributed, leased, licensed or publicly performed or used in any way except as specifically permitted in writing by the author. Any unauthorised distribution or use of this text may be a direct infringement of the author's rights and those responsible may be liable in law accordingly.

Copyright Paul Davison 2020

Paul Davison has asserted his rights to be identified as the author of this Work in accordance with the Copyright, Designs and Patents Act 1988.

Although this book is based on real people and real events, some names, places, and identifying features have been changed in order to preserve their privacy. Judge Klevan's summing up of the evidence, is a faithful representation of what was said in court. It was taken from court transcripts. All other words spoken by individuals, including the three barristers, are my interpretation of what was said at the time. I have tried to be as accurate as possible.

Printed in Great Britain
by Amazon